OPTIMISTIC
L I F E

Memoir

Lessons in Love, Loss, and Loyalty

TRACIE ROSSER-GREEN

KP PUBLISHING COMPANY

ISBN: 978-1-960001-39-9 (Hardcover)
ISBN: 978-1-960001-41-2 (Paperback)
ISBN: 978-1-960001-40-5 (eBook)

Library of Congress Control Number: 2024924735

Editor/Proofreader: Renee Aldrich/KP Publishing Editing Services
Cover Design: Juan Roberts, Creative Lunacy
Literary Director: Sandra Slayton James

Scriptures marked NIV are taken from the NEW INTERNATIONAL VERSION (NIV): Scripture taken from THE HOLY BIBLE, NEW INTERNATIONAL VERSION ®. Copyright© 1973, 1978, 1984, 2011 by Biblica, Inc.™. Used by permission of Zondervan

American Airlines™ is a trademark of American Airlines, Inc. The use of the American Airlines name and trademark in this book is for descriptive purposes only and does not imply affiliation with, endorsement, or sponsorship by American Airlines, Inc. All references to American Airlines™ (or AA) are made in the context of the author's personal experiences and are not intended to infringe upon the trademark.

"Continental Airlines was a former airline that merged with United Airlines in 2010. The references to Continental Airlines in this book are for descriptive and historical purposes only."

Published by:

KP Publishing Company
Publisher of Fiction, Nonfiction & Children's Books
Las Vegas, NV 89117
www.kp-pub.com

Printed in the United States of America

My Beloved Mother (Barbara Ruth—Tiny)

From the moment God planted me in the beautiful garden of your heart, your tender, loving care blossomed around me. Your dedication to motherhood consistently focused on nurturing and nudging me in the most significant ways. Thank you for giving me life and teaching me how to live it!

As the wind beneath my wings, our connection is like a compass, with you as my guide. My heart is bursting with immense gratitude that God blessed me to be "your baby girl." As the most powerful, consistent encourager in my life, you are the forever influence on my very existence. With limitless love and admiration, I pray that my life will echo yours. My greatest desire is that people will see a little of you in me!

When I decided to write this memoir, I never imagined the roller coaster of emotions that I would experience while reliving our family memories. Combined with the unforeseen fretful calls of life, this journey took much longer to complete than I initially anticipated. At no point did I consider aborting this treasured vision of our family. Despite the delays, my determination kept me on course, knowing I would eventually cross the finish line.

I love you always and forever!

Baby Girl

> *"Honor her for all that her hands have done, and let her works bring her praise at the city gate."*
>
> Proverbs 31:31

"Do unto others as you would have them do unto you."

Luke 6:31

CONTENTS

Name Reference - Maternal Relatives

Real Name	Nick Name/Name Called	Related To
Barbara Anderson Rosser	Tiny (Author's Mother)	
Minnie Pate Sims	Momma Minnie	Tiny (Grandma)
Florence Pate Anderson	Mother/Flo/Virginia	Tiny (Mother)
William Rayburn Anderson	W.R. / Uncle Dub	Tiny (Brother)
Charles William Sims	Billy	Tiny (Uncle)
William Anderson	Grandpa Bill	Tiny (Granddad)
Boone Anderson	Boone	Tiny (Father)
Jessie Pate Warren	Aunt Jessie	Tiny (Aunt)
Edward Clay	Cousin Ed	Tiny (Cousin)
Alan Clay	Cousin Alan	Tiny (Cousin)
Benita Council	Bunny / Cousin	Tiny (Cousin)
Steven Anderson	Steve / Cousin	Tiny (Nephew)

Paternal Relatives

Real Name	Nick Name/Name Called	Related To
Elbert William Rosser	Al (Author's Father)	
William Elbert Rosser	Grandpa	Al(Father)
Amelia Wilson- Rosser	Grandma	Al (Mother)
Ivy Rosser (Wright)	Auntie Ivy	Al (Sister)
Marilyn Rosser (Davis)	Auntie Marilyn	Al (Sister)
Harold Rosser	Uncle Harold	Al (Brother)
Robert Wilson	Uncle Rail	Al (Uncle)
Joseph Wilson	Uncle Joe	Al (Uncle)

1

WE ARE ONE

My life is like an abstract quilt woven from the struggles and triumphs of my ancestors. The hardships my family faced propelled me forward, while their victories fueled my belief in a hopeful future. Knowing even a glimpse of one's heritage is priceless. For instance, my grandmother, Florence Virginia Pate, whom we all affectionately call "Mother," embodies that legacy.

As a teenager, Mother left home to pursue a college education. She enrolled at the University of Missouri-Kansas City to become a teacher. On this campus, she met a medical student named William Boone Anderson. They felt an immediate connection after their very first conversation. Ironically, they were both from Montgomery City, Missouri. They agreed that even growing up in such a small country town, it was possible not to know everyone. As the two of them became better acquainted, there was one other thing these two college friends found interesting. In their families, they were both primarily addressed by their middle names. From that day forward, they fondly referred to each other as Virginia and Boone.

As the days went by, their friendly conversations continued. Soon, they realized that they were from different family backgrounds. Boone was the eldest of two brothers. Wallace was his only sibling. These brothers were raised in the city, living a much more prosperous life than Mother's family. Boone had grown up fellowshipping with his family in the local Baptist church. His father, William Shakespeare Anderson (Bill), was an educated man who worked as an elementary school principal. His mother, Stella Mae Thomas-Anderson, was a homemaker of bi-racial descent. After being afflicted by severely crippling Rheumatoid arthritis for many years, Stella lived her days filled with excruciating pain. As a result of her illness, she passed away in 1932.

Mother had grown up in a completely different atmosphere. Her parents, Nathaniel Pate (Nat), who was also of biracial descent, and Minnie Rae Stevenson-Pate (Momma Minnie), were livestock and produce farmers. Mother was the youngest of four siblings, consisting of one brother (John Wesley) and two sisters (Jessie Gertrude and Helen Ruth). A third sister (Ara Elizabeth) passed away from an unknown birth disorder before her second birthday. Shortly after their meeting, Nat passed away in 1937. Despite their vastly diverse backgrounds, the relationship between Boone and Mother blossomed swiftly into a love that resulted in marriage.

The young couple soon had their first child, a son William Rayburn Anderson (W.R.) After his birth, Boone decided to put his college aspirations on hold. His top priority was finding a suitable job for his growing family. He applied with the Wabash Railroad to seek what he considered a decent job. Boone was successful in gaining employment by laying train tracks. He continued to work in this position for the next four years.

There were few employment opportunities in Montgomery City for women to work outside the home. Thus, Mother had become a stay-at-home mom. In the coming years, she spent many of her days helping her mother, Minnie, with the duties at the family farm. The family raised chickens and harvested vegetables that were sold daily. Many revered her as an excellent cook, baker, quilter, and seamstress.

While all these changes happened, her mother, Minnie, also found love again. It was a well-received union, to the delight of everyone in the family. Her new husband was Reverend Charles William Sims. The two of them were already very well acquainted. Reverend Sims led the Harpers Chapel Methodist Church ministry, where Minnie was the Sunday school teacher and choir director for many years. It was also the church where Mother and her siblings were raised.

By this time, all Minnie's children were adults. Reverend Sims was 28 years older than Minnie and had no children. That missing piece of his life was short-lived. Everyone in the family was surprised when Minnie became pregnant. Her youngest child, Mother, was twenty-one years old at that time. In January 1939, Minnie gave birth to Charles William Sims Jr. (Billy). The entire family was thrilled as they welcomed a new member. All his adult siblings had the house buzzing with joy and commotion as they doted on "their" new baby brother.

During that time, Mother became pregnant again. Coming from a large family, she welcomed the thought of W.R. having a sibling. Her heart desired that this child would be a girl. On February 24, 1940, Barbara Ruth Anderson (Tiny), my mom, was the second child born to Boone and Mother. It is said that her earthly arrival was a memorable surprise to the entire family. Mother's water broke unexpectedly, and Barbara was born prematurely. The family midwives gathered for the delivery, with her grandmother, Momma Minnie, leading the charge. For all initial appearance's sake, the ladies agreed that Barbara was completely healthy. There was, however, one issue.

3

It was that Barbara was tiny! During the after-birth cleanup process, the room began to echo with the voices of everyone present. The one thing they continued repeating was, "She is Tiny." That is when the nickname Tiny was officially established. From that day, Boone and Mother's young family continued progressing well.

Tiny and every other member of her family were born at home. The births occurred outside of St. Louis, Missouri, in the rural town of Montgomery City. My great-grandmother Minnie and her sisters were midwives for the family's baby deliveries. Montgomery City had a local doctor who was notified after each birth for a house call. The purpose of his house call was to examine the baby, verify the weight, and make a note of the time of birth and the child's given name. These standard details were the necessary steps for official preparation and recording of a birth certificate. Of course, hearing all the details of Tiny's family history, especially the story of her birth, intrigued me.

One morning in August, Boone left home and headed to work. No one knew this would be his final day. That afternoon, there was an unimaginable accident at the railroad job site. On August 5, 1942, the New York Times newspaper published an article about an out-of-control speeding train jumping a track. In an instant, 25-year-old Boone, along with nine of his coworkers, lost their lives! Suddenly, my 24-year-old grandmother, Mother, was a widow with two young children, ages two and five. This horrific tragedy immediately shattered the future for her and her children.

Heartbroken and overcome with grief, Mother found the coming days and weeks to be extremely challenging. Of course, her concerned family members rallied around her in compassionate support. While she was not left physically alone in this struggle, her emotions took a horrible beating.

The ongoing stress left Mother feeling helpless and alone! As time moved on, a shocking reality began to creep in. It was when Mother faced the fact that she did not know how she and her children would survive financially. Her primary source of comfort was to do the only thing she knew how to do: pray. She prayed that God would give her the guidance, wisdom, and strength to move forward.

In 1945, our country was in the depths of World War Two. Mother's brother, John Wesley, was serving in the military. His tour of duty ended with an honorable discharge. The family in Missouri knew that the end of his tour of duty was approaching, but they did not have an exact date. Rather than inform the family, John decided to come home and surprise everyone. One evening, the family heard a knock at the door by the local police. John's slain body had been found a few blocks from home. Still in uniform, he had been robbed and stabbed to death. John's death sent Mother and the entire into a tailspin of unimaginable sorrow!

After things calmed down, Mother bravely and optimistically decided to leave Missouri. However, Mother was reasonably well educated and intelligent but had never worked. It was a fact by which she refused to be discouraged. Mother was fearlessly determined that no matter how difficult things became, she would do whatever was necessary to provide for her family. While this was the only life Mother had ever known, this city had become filled with heartaches. In her hopes for a better future, the prospects were too small for her vision. At that time, Montgomery City presented no opportunity for her advancement.

Later that year, Mother moved away. With her two young children, Tiny and W.R., in tow, she packed their belongings and boarded the train to Portland, Oregon. She followed the steps her older sister, Jessie, her husband, James, and daughter, Joyce, had taken a few years earlier.

Jessie had already found some success in Portland. She and James were both gainfully employed by the railroad. They had purchased a multi-unit property in the city, promising to provide a unit as a home for her sister. Several other extended family members had left Missouri and were also living in Portland. This sense of joining a community was also reassuring for assistance with childcare. Some family members had migrated to California and various other West Coast cities. None of them had ever expressed regrets about their decision to leave Missouri. No matter how minimal the progress was, each had found some form of success in their transitions by acquiring stable employment.

Immediately after the three arrived in this strange, new city, the first order of business was to enroll W.R. and Tiny in school. We all know that children are very flexible. In no time, the two of them adapted to their new surroundings. They quickly made friends with classmates and the other children in their neighborhood. Once her children settled in school, Mother eagerly searched for employment. Mother had one aspect of her life that she considered an asset in her job search. She aspired to become a teacher during her college enrollment at the University of Missouri. Mother majored in a series of classes primarily focused on English literature. As a result, she was exceptionally well-spoken. Her sister and brother-in-law both held maintenance jobs with the railroad. It was Mother's first job application. While waiting for a response, she did not remain idle. Mother knew that time was of the essence and that her promptly finding a job was crucial.

Portland was vastly larger than any place she had ever lived. The primary mode of public transportation was to ride a cable car. What a fascinating new adventure this was! As she boarded the cable car for the first time in her life, Mother was on her way to venture through the hustle and bustle of the city. With her mind set on placing her best foot forward in her job search, she continued knocking on every door with potential for employment. Mother was not intimidated by the unknown or doubted her ability. Putting her trust in God, she moved like she had something to work with, honestly believing that something good would happen to her.

Though Mother was a very petite woman, slightly over one hundred pounds and standing barely five feet tall, she eventually gained her very first job. The Oregon Shipbuilding Corporation hired Mother. It was a World War II emergency shipyard along the Willamette River in Portland. Despite this being a physically demanding job, she did not shy away. Instead, she allowed herself to be stretched, refusing to do anything other than remain confident. Given all her job training, Mother proudly mastered the duties of her position as Rosie the Riveter. God's power was greater than her weakness. It quickly became evident that moving her family to Portland was the wisest decision. Her faith in God, along with her determination, had proven to be advantageous for the three of them. They were finally self-sufficient and living on God's promise that says,

"Blessed is she who believed that the Lord would fulfill His promises to her!"

Luke 1:45

Even with Mother's busy new life, she remained homesick. She was also genuinely concerned about the welfare of her aging mother. With her family now scattered across the country, my great-grandmother lived with her aging husband and young son, Billy, in the family's Missouri home. Mother and her children frequently traveled by train for the next four years to visit their Missouri hometown.

In 1950, this routine trip resulted in very unexpected life-changing events. The highlight was that Mother met and fell in love with Creston Delmar Camp. Ironically, he was another Montgomery City resident with whom she had never crossed paths. Of African and Indian descent, Creston was tall, dark, and handsome. Indeed, she would have remembered him. He had recently returned to the city after being honorably discharged from the military. History repeated itself! The love bug bit them, and they grew close rapidly, sharing a whirlwind romance. By the end of the family vacation, Creston (Daddy) and Mother were married. That year, four people boarded the train for the return trip to Portland.

During those days, Portland was a predominantly Caucasian city. Most of the neighborhoods were sparsely integrated. North Portland was then and remains today as the city's primarily African American residential area. Mother shared with me that there was a level of blatant discrimination displayed by some.

In later years, the Washington Post published an eye-opening article by DeNeen L. Brown titled "When Portland Banned Blacks; Oregon's Shameful History as an 'All-White' State." This outpouring of racism was confirmed by the horrific, revealing pictures included in the article. Reading this article revealed a part of history that brought me to tears.

Mother's paternal grandfather was Caucasian. Her biracial heritage resulted in her fair complexion. The creamy, warm vanilla pigmentation of her skin and her silky hair proved to be a social advantage for her. While navigating her life in Portland, Mother could move cautiously throughout the city without hesitation or the fear of racial questions. She believed in advance that the Lord was ordering her steps. Having been raised in a Godly home where she and her siblings spent most of their free time at church, the Christian lifestyle inspired her to raise her children in a similar Godly manner. It included instilling the value of diversity in them. Mother's motto was that no matter what a person's race, everyone should be able to live in love and harmony with one another.

Except for periodic trips to visit relatives in Missouri, Chicago, and California, Tiny primarily lived in Portland for most of her childhood. Mother continued to seek the finest possible education for her children avidly. Some schools had pretesting requirements for incoming high school students. Tiny's entrance exam scores deemed her academically qualified for acceptance into the prestigious, predominantly white Girls Polytechnic High School. There, she enjoyed healthy friendships with girls of many different races. This culturally diverse daily environment contributed to Tiny's lack of understanding of racial bias and discrimination. Uncle W.R. was enrolled at the all-boys Benson Polytechnic High School.

Being African American and living in Oregon had pros and cons for our family. Along with the ability to obtain a margin of financial security, the educational opportunities were greater than they would have been in Montgomery City. By now, Mother's baby brother Billy was also a teen. Minnie and Reverend Sims had grown too old to give him the attention he needed. Knowing Billy would have more excellent opportunities for his future living outside Montgomery City, Mother convinced her parents to allow him to move to Oregon, and Billy lived in Oregon for several years before joining the military.

In a pattern similar to Mother's marital history, with Tiny spending summers in Chicago, with family, she had the pleasure of meeting Elbert William Rosser (Al) at her cousin's home, and the summer love affair began.

Al, my father, went on to complete his military assignment in Ft. Louis, Washington and Germany while Tiny continued to live in Portland with her parents.

I was the second member of Mother's family to be born in a hospital. Tiny's brother W.R. and his wife, Evelyn, had welcomed their son Steven thirteen days before my birth while living on a military base in Portland, Maine. Just as hospital births were something unusual for my family, my birth was a noted change for the staff at Portland, Oregon's Emanuel Hospital. On more than one occasion, Tiny shared with me the detailed story of my birth. The highlight of the conversation was her recollection of the events that took place during the ensuing period of hospitalization the two of us had.

During the labor process, Tiny had internal complications that caused severe hemorrhaging during my delivery. Unfortunately, "our" birthing experience left Tiny's body with extensive damage to her female organs. It caused her to have a series of ongoing complications and infertility issues that would last forever. To add to her physical drama, I was born with a heart murmur, referred to as a "hole in my heart." Tiny said hearing those words was an alarming blow to a joyful event. To say she was frightened is an understatement, which made our hospital stay longer than average.

Fortunately, the doctors were very reassuring. As the days went on, she became more relaxed. Tiny said she could not have been more confident with the special medical treatment I received. In addition, she was grateful for how physically comfortable the hospital staff made her, adding that everyone treated her with the utmost respect. The bigger part of the story was regarding how curiously members of the staff received me. Even though they were extremely kind and supportive, it was obvious that our race, and particularly my dark chocolate complexion, made us somewhat of a novelty to them.

Tiny told me that her doctor displayed no qualms when telling her specific hospital statistical facts. These were topics that would generally be insignificant to a patient. During a routine daily exam, he stated that I was the first African American baby to be born in that hospital. Tiny said she really did not know how to respond, so she smiled and remained silent. After there was no reaction on her part, he added that I was the only girl born that day. Tiny said that for the remainder of our stay, all the doctors and nurses from various departments would constantly come in and out of her room. With smiling faces, they would start by asking my mother how she was feeling. After the basic pleasantries, it became apparent to Tiny that these staff visits weren't geared toward medical needs. Instead, it was about them wanting to see the "baby." These medical professionals did not try to hide their curiosity.

With total humility, Tiny added that every time this happened, she was overcome with a defenseless wave of emotions. Her feelings included being vulnerable, nervous, and very alone. She anxiously lay in bed, carefully watching as each person lifted me from the crib to hold me. Tiny said no one tried to speak softly. She was able to hear every word of their conversations. Without hesitation, they repeatedly said, "she has a lot of hair; feel it." Other comments were, "She was born with a veil over her eyes," and "Look, her eyes are already open. She is already alert, and her eyes are following us." While all these comments were true, my mother felt none seemed worthy of so much attention.

Although Tiny was stunned by the ongoing blatant display of white curiosity that she consistently witnessed during the time that we spent in the hospital, she never verbally protested. After our release, Tiny thanked God that she did not speak out against their actions. She knew that we needed them to care for us, and she was humbly grateful for that. In addition, more than one ongoing issue required the two of us to become regular patients at this hospital. Our continued medical care by these doctors would be necessary because my mother needed follow-up gynecological treatment, and yes, I did have a heart murmur.

After my birth, Tiny's future aspirations leaned toward perfecting and advancing her clerical studies. Mother and Daddy always believed in Tiny's abilities. Her parents were very supportive when she enrolled in classes at Multnomah Business College. Tiny would have to work a little harder to balance her time between studying and parenting. Mother and Daddy made themselves available in any way possible to assist with my care taking. Tiny knew that, at some point, she wanted to become gainfully employed. Within no time, the clerical skills she acquired in high school were enhanced. This training led Tiny to acquire excellent secretarial skills as a speed typist. In addition, she became proficient in shorthand and data-key punch operations.

Upon Al's honorable discharge from the U.S. Army military, he joined Tiny and I in Portland—by this time, I was starting to talk. As happy as he was to be permanently together with us finally, there was one thing that he found surprising! Just like everyone else in our house, I addressed my grandparents as Mother and Daddy (though some called Daddy, Creston), and I called my mother Tiny. Of course, that meant my father was Al. Try as he may to change my vocabulary, it proved to be a futile losing battle. I would not budge on the names.

Eventually, Tiny convinced Al to accept my choice of words. The two of them finally agreed that I did know who my parents were. When I address them, they are Al and Tiny, but with discussions or introductions, I refer to them as my parents. While some people would consider my choice of words as being disrespectful, that did not matter to Al and Tiny. I displayed proper parental respect, so they conceded to live with my use of their names. Everyone else would have to accept this oddity as well. After all, Al already had his nicknames for the two of us, saying that it was then and remains amazing today how much alike we are. Not only in looks and stature but in how we speak, think, and carry ourselves. He said we are genuinely like fruit and tree. Tiny is a tough act to follow, so I take his observation as a genuine compliment. From that day on, Al often refers to Tiny as "Hun, babe, or precious." I know he addresses me when he says, "Suga or little precious."

The time had come for Al and Tiny to face the reality of their unknown future. They had to focus on the things that they were able to control. The primary goal was for Al to find a job. It proved to be easier said than done. At that time, the job market in Portland was extremely limited. Race and education were key deciding factors in hiring practices for prime jobs. Jobs such as porters, bellhops, cooks, waiters, and janitorial work were the standard positions for young African American men. Although Al had not attended college, none of these available job options appealed to him.

It proved to be a crucial time in Al and Tiny's lives. They would have to make a major life-changing decision—would our family continue to live in Portland or relocate to Al's native hometown of Chicago, Illinois? When they were talking it out, they tried hard not to make a hasty decision or one based on emotions. The primary goal was to gain stable employment. After evaluating the different options, Al and Tiny decided that relocating the family to Chicago would be the most promising opportunity for them to achieve their goals.

A few positive facts helped in making the decision. Having been born in Chicago, Al knew the city well. All his immediate family still lived there. Tiny also had a few Missouri relatives and friends who had migrated to Chicago. In addition, the Midwest location was only a short driving distance from Tiny's birthplace in Missouri. Being near family members was always important to Al and Tiny. Add to that the fact that Chicago was a much larger Metropolitan city.

Although Al and Tiny were incredibly young, they were also highly mature, bold, and self-confident when making plans for their future. The two of them were full of optimism, energy, and excitement. While Al and Tiny had many big dreams, they had not mapped out a blueprint that revealed how to make them happen. They made their plans based on one specific word of God. Because they had prayed for God to guide them, the decision to relocate came from Him. Their shared optimistic belief was that a positive future would be possible if they were together! The rest of the family prayed on the decision, clinging to God's word that reads,

"Therefore, I tell you, do not worry about your life."

Matthew 6:25

Al left Portland alone, driving to Chicago in his Red 1957 Chevy convertible. Immediately upon his arrival, he hit the pavement running. There was no time to waste in his relentless search for employment. His diligent efforts paid off in just a few short days. Al stopped by the home of a friend named Charlie Dixon. Al had a certain group of men that he trusted for both wisdom and guidance. Being several years older than Al, Charlie was placed in that group. Once my father told him he was looking for a job, Charlie said his company was hiring. He shared all the detailed information with Al.

Al acquired skills as a teenager and with a self-taught love for cars, and his mechanical military training proved valuable. These qualities made him marketable, enabling him to gain employment immediately with International Harvester Tractor Works. At the time, that company was willing to offer young men stable employment opportunities with decent pay. From Al's very first day on the job, it was an easy transition for him. In addition to Charlie, Al realized he already knew a few other men employed there. It helped make him immediately comfortable. Shane was a childhood friend who had gone through the military with Al. He also gained employment there. It quickly became quite clear that leaving Portland was the best economic decision for our family. From the beginning, Charlie and his wife, Eula, welcomed us into their family as one of their own. Charlie fondly nicknamed the three of us AT&T, and I called him Uncle Charlie.

The next order of business was for Al to find a suitable apartment for the three of us to live. He had no idea where he would begin to start looking. Sitting in his car, visualizing the city, he asked God for guidance. By this time, Al had lived away from Chicago for several years, and his time in the military had allowed him to live in other cities in America and abroad. The bulk of his Army days were spent in Germany. The time away was enough to see and experience different levels of a higher-quality lifestyle. In looking for our first home, Al was committed to providing us with a home in a neighborhood that was a level up from his humble beginnings.

Al is the second of four children. Before starting their family, my Grandparents' Willam (Grandpa) and Amelia (Grandma) migrated to Chicago from Macon and Columbus, Georgia. Grandpa had found employment as a school janitor, and Grandma was a housekeeper. Despite Al's description of growing up in abject poverty, he never minimizes the level of love and comfort that his parents always gave. Grandma and Grandpa moved into the newly constructed Ida B. Wells housing project as their family grew. While living there, Al received his early elementary education at Holy Angels Catholic School and James P. Dolittle Public School.

In later years, Grandma and Grandpa learned of a brand-new housing development in the far south suburban area of the city. They made the decision to relocate the family to the Chicago Housing Authority Altgeld Gardens Homes. Al furthered his education in the Chicago Public School system and graduated from George W. Carver High School. To this day, Al is the type of person that meets no strangers. He immediately made friends with several children in this new neighborhood. When some of the guys graduated high school, they all entered the military together. This group of men continued to share highly close bonds with one another. Ernest and Shane are still Al's closest friends, referring to each other as brothers. Their relationships have all the traits of brotherly love for one another.

That afternoon, while scouting neighborhoods, Al visited his Uncle Robert (Rail). He was one of my Grandma's two brothers. When Rail was not performing as a professional backup musician with some big-name musicians, Uncle Rail was a salesman. From when Al was a young boy, Uncle Rail was a man he really admired. He was an unspoken mentor in my dad's eyes. Uncle Rail and his family had lived in this same two-bedroom garden walk-up apartment for several years. During his youth, Al visited their apartment on many occasions. The corner apartment building was located on the south side of the city in the African American, middle-class West Chatham district.

Before arriving at Uncle Rail's house, Al had no idea that he and his family were in the process of moving. This news came as quite a shock. When Al arrived, they greeted him with their bustling excitement. Uncle Rail, his wife, Alice, and their son, Bobby, had just purchased their first home. As they discussed the upcoming move, the apartment was full of laughter and rekindling love. They were relocating to a brand-new development in the south Chicago suburbs.

Things began to speed up when Al told Uncle Rail he was looking for an apartment. Uncle Rail wasted no time arranging a meeting and conversation between Al and the property owner, Mr. Joyner. The two of them had a face-to-face meeting that same day. Once Al and Mr. Joyner were introduced, they had an immediate connection. Within minutes, the apartment rental agreement was made, and upon Uncle Rail's family officially vacating the apartment, this garden-level unit at 33 West 81st Street would belong to our family!

Mr. Joyner was an older gentleman who did not live on the premises. Uncle Rail and Al suggested to him that rather than hiring an outside maintenance company, they could do all the cleanup and painting themselves. Without hesitation, Mr. Joyner agreed to this. He became so impressed with Al's work skills and sense of responsibility that he offered Al the position of an on site maintenance person. The primary duty would be to ensure the building's furnace was always working and filled with coal. In exchange for accepting this responsibility, Mr. Joyner would reduce the rent. Of course, Al gratefully accepted this position.

God's favor did not stop there. Later that afternoon, Uncle Rail drove Al to a gas station a few blocks away owned by a friend of his. When they arrived, Uncle Rail introduced Al to Mr. Woods, and as they continued talking, Mr. Woods learned of Al's mechanical skills. He hired Al on the spot to work weekends at the gas station. His duties included doing minor auto repairs such as oil changes and tune-ups, repairing flats and tire rotations, and taking control of the tow truck for road service. These favorable events were surely nothing but the Grace of our merciful God. The Bible says,

"So do not fear, for I am with you; do not be dismayed, for I am your God. I will strengthen you and help you; I will uphold you with my righteous right hand."

Isaiah 41:10

As you can see, when it came to providing for our family, Al had a spirit of determination bolstered by extremely broad shoulders. With a mindset that was both purposeful and intentional, there was no chance my father would turn down any opportunity to increase his income. Al says he felt extremely positive about how things were falling into place. Humbly, Al stated he knew he had done nothing special to warrant such favor. His thoughts were that where God guides, He really does provide! In what seemed like just a matter of a few days, not only did Al find us a place to live, but he was successful in finding not one job but two jobs. He had achieved the goals he established for himself when he got to Chicago. Now that Al had accomplished these two objectives, it was time for the family to reunite. He did not have a telephone, so he gathered his dimes for a lengthy pay-phone conversation with Tiny. They were both so excited! A few days later, Tiny and I boarded the train. We were leaving Portland to start our new life in Chicago officially.

When Uncle Rail moved, his family planned to furnish their new home with everything brand new. As a result, they gifted Al and Tiny by leaving the entire apartment fully furnished. Remembering their own struggle as newlyweds, Uncle Rail and Aunt Alice made every effort to help fulfill Al and Tiny's needs. This gesture, indeed, was a surprise! Immediately after our arrival, Al told Tiny there were a few home improvement projects that would need attending as soon as possible. He added that she would need to decorate the apartment to better suit her taste. As older apartments went, all the rooms were substantial. Al and Tiny agreed that this apartment was more than adequate in size, comfort, and location as a first home for us. Of course, they wanted to add some of their personal touches. Given their economic status at this time, Al and Tiny did not make hasty decisions. Considering each room, they planned the details of how they would proceed. The most crucial consideration in making wise financial choices was the fact that they needed everything! Even though these improvements were at their own expense, they took no liberties. They had the utmost respect for Mr. Joyner and wanted to address every change with him in advance. When they met with Mr. Joyner, he saw how meticulous they were; he freely approved of them making any changes.

As Al and Tiny examined each room, no furniture pieces were missing. While the hand-me-down furniture was incredibly decent quality, the years of use had caused it to be worn, old, and scuffed. After careful examination, Al and Tiny agreed. Although this furniture did not reflect their youthful personalities, it would temporarily serve the purpose. They continued going room by room, slowly deciding how to spruce things up. I would say this was when Tiny became an innovator in contemporary decorating. Throughout the years, Tiny had developed excellent cooking skills from the women in her family. Home economics was one of the required courses at her high school. She decided that the kitchen would be the first room they would complete. With sunny yellow walls and white appliances, it quickly became a cheerful dining spot. After thorough painting and cleaning, Tiny could put everything in order.

Once the two of them had completed the kitchen work, Al set a date for some friends to join him for a painting party. Tiny prepared a pot of spaghetti, slaw, fried chicken, garlic bread, iced tea, and a few beers, and everyone was ready to go. That weekend, this group of men quickly brightened every wall, washing all the windows and waxing the hardwood floor. Their efforts made the apartment start to sparkle like a new penny. After the walls in every room were freshly painted, Tiny's tasteful, shabby chic decorative creativity set in.

The next step was to tackle the bedrooms. They refinished all the master bedroom furniture pieces with high-gloss black paint. Al's crew painted the master bedroom walls soft lavender and accented them with matching window dressings and bedding of various shades of a lively purple print. They chose to update my bedroom furniture with a glossy white paint color. The highlights for my room were pink walls with a glittery white ceiling, and the doll-patterned linen and accessories were the final change. The sofa and chair in the living room were very formal, with old and dingy cushions, different from Al and Tiny's style. Camouflaging the worn furniture cushions with bed sheets was certainly unappealing to them. As they continued to evaluate room by room, they counted every penny. The goal was to stretch their resources as far as possible.

They purchased a new bamboo couch, chairs, and a glass-top coffee table for the living room. Added to that were comfortable, bright orange-colored seat cushions, a small bamboo bar with stools in the corner, and a bright orange area rug under the table. Of course, they removed the heavy brocade drapes in exchange for airy bamboo shades. As with any young person's home, there was the splurge for a stereo and television. Tiny and Al filled the living room with plants, photos, and miscellaneous accessories; it took on an island-like atmosphere. Al and Tiny's home improvement handiwork made every room uniquely one of a kind. The environment was clean, comfortable, and very inviting. Anyone crossing our open door's threshold was sure to be pleasantly surprised. As you moved about, you realized that every inch of the apartment was a place of comfort and peace. It was a finished product that truly displayed Al and Tiny's personality. The atmosphere had all the welcoming energy necessary to make it a happy house! They could not stop thanking God as they walked from room to room, admiring their finished product.

Just a few weeks earlier, Al had stepped out on faith. With his mind set on success, he arrived in Chicago unemployed and homeless. His resume consisted of courage, determination, and prayer. Suddenly, Al and Tiny successfully completed some of the things they once considered an out-of-reach dream. It was evident that their lives finally reflected their independent characters. They had taken the first step toward being responsible, mature adults. Al and Tiny considered his employment success and having a decent place to call home answers to their prayers. With a spirit of grateful humility, they thanked God for his provision. They followed with petitioning the Lord to continue to be their guide and foundation. Al and Tiny knew that this apartment was only the beginning. The reality was that they still had a long way to go toward building stability.

"For this reason, a man will leave his mother and father and be united to his wife, and the two shall become one flesh."

Matthew 19:5

2

STRADDLING
THE FENCE

From the outside, looking in, it seemed that everything was in perfect order for Al and Tiny. Still, they both knew one shadow was hanging over them that needed to be rectified. It was their first time living together under one roof, and they were not married! God was showing them that His hand was over their lives. His grace had already showered them with an abundance of unearned favor. Moving forward, all they wanted was to stay on the right path. Neither of them intended to become comfortable playing house without following the word of God. They would not allow the devil to take hold of their morals, thoughts, actions, or any other aspect of their lives.

That Saturday, they left the apartment for an early afternoon walk. It was the first opportunity to take a familiarizing close look around our new neighborhood. While walking, the conversation centered on the possibilities of when, where, and how they would get married. They knew there was not enough money to pay for a large, traditional wedding. As they slowly strolled, they came upon The Commonwealth Community Church. It was a quaint neighborhood corner church located three blocks from our apartment. They approached the church where two Caucasian men were working in the yard. My parents spoke, and a conversation ensued. Ironically, one of the men introduced himself as the church pastor. After a lengthy conversation explaining how they came upon his church, Al and Tiny shared a portion of their story with him. They asked this pastor if they could make an appointment to be married at his church. The pastor followed their request by asking how large the wedding would be. With no desire to boast about the events of one day with an elaborate ceremony, they replied that the ceremony would be small, with just a few family members and friends in attendance.

The pastor told them he lived in the house next to the church. He asked if they had a few more minutes, inviting them inside to meet his wife. When they entered, his wife was cooking in the kitchen. They sat and waited until she could join them. Once the pastor introduced Al and Tiny to his wife, he told her that this young couple would like to schedule their marriage for our next available date. They said this lady had a charming personality that ushered them in to discuss the personal details of their lives comfortably. They could release their past without feeling shame or judgment as they talked. After a heartfelt conversation in which Al and Tiny shared the details of their relationship, the pastor and his wife prayed over them.

The pastor's wife agreed to confirm their wedding arrangements after the prayer. Al and Tiny were both expecting her next move would be to look at a calendar. Instead, she looked at them with a big smile and said that, given the circumstances, she saw no reason to wait any longer. That was followed by her asking them, "How about getting married right now?' Al and Tiny were stunned! Without any hesitation, they looked at each other, and they both replied yes! They had already gotten their marriage license, knowing marriage was their next priority. The pastor's wife and the church gardener agreed to serve as their witnesses. Al and Tiny immediately left the church to change clothes and retrieve the license. It was confirmation that God's timing is always perfect!

That Saturday afternoon, Al and Tiny were officially married in the sight of God. Fully elated by the day's events, the newlyweds joined hands as they cheerfully strolled back home. They were nothing short of amazed! With a sigh of relief, they excitedly agreed that this day was truly cloaked in God's favor! Moving forward, the Commonwealth Community Church became our family church. Years later, the leadership of this church changed. The new female pastor was none other than the famous actress Della Reese.

After their wedding, Al and Tiny arrived home and turned on the stereo to play their favorite new record, "At Last" by Etta James. The newlyweds danced for a while before having another idea. This day, they should have a little extra! Knowing they had so many goals ahead of them, they decided on a way to celebrate without breaking their budget. It was something they agreed was perfectly in line with the day's events. The two changed their clothes to something casual, got in the car, and put the top down. As the sun settled, they drove to the Arlington Park Race Course. The newlyweds dined on Vienna hot dogs, French fries, and milkshakes for a toast that evening! They even splurged on two-dollar bets as they watched the horses speed around the track.

While Tiny longed to enter the workforce, she found the absence of childcare a massive barrier to her working. Childcare was not something they had prepared for because they had not factored in that there would be a need. Before she could take any further steps toward her career goals, she prioritized securing a proper babysitter. Grandma, Grandpa, and Al's younger brother Harold were longtime residents of the Altgeld Gardens housing projects. Al and Tiny knew I was safe whenever I spent time with them. I looked forward to weekend sleepovers. Most of the time, my cousins, Sharon, Bev, and Stacie would be there too. My grandparents would make sure we had a wonderful time, often including an outing to a park or the Zoo.

Still, except for an occasional weekend, my parents wanted to avoid the Project atmosphere becoming a consistent part of my daily upbringing. As with our extended family, Al's two sisters, Ivy and Marilyn, lived in various neighborhoods throughout the city. Each of them had jobs, husbands, and children of their own. Childcare was not a concern for them as Ivy had three daughters, Sharon, Beverly, and Stacie, and Marilyn had two sons, John and Willie, and two daughters, Debra and Rosemary. There were no potential circumstances for my cousins to be home alone. Rapidly, Al and Tiny came to a starkly negative realization regarding their lack of everyday childcare options for me. In all their future planning, they neglected to consider that they did not have what is referred to as a "village" in Chicago!

Al and Tiny would need time to make the necessary childcare adjustments. When Mother and Daddy scheduled their annual vacation to Montgomery City to assist with this dilemma, they included a two-week detour in Chicago. The two of them were more than happy to schedule this stopover for multiple reasons. After all, this would be their first opportunity to visit the three of us in our new home. Al and Tiny were equally excited about the routing of their trip, so they began using their efforts to spruce up the apartment in preparation for their arrival. It would be the first of many such family gatherings. When Mother and Daddy's one-week Chicago visit ended, we all left together to vacation in Missouri. I cannot tell you how much Tiny loved this family time! When we entered the Montgomery City limits, people would start waving. As we drove through the streets of this small town, the Illinois license plate was a dead giveaway as to who we were.

Once we arrived, Tiny could visit her maternal grandmother, Momma Minnie, her paternal grandfather, Grandpa Bill, and all the rest of her extended family members. Our vacation timing was geared so that we could attend the annual Montgomery City July 4th homecoming gathering. This yearly event is a big weekend-long celebration for this small town's past and present African American residents. It is when relatives and friends from all over the country return to Missouri. Daddy is from a huge family. Members include a variety of generations, including adults and children of all age groups. Vacationing in Missouri was always a fun-filled experience for me. The weekend had nonstop food, music, dancing, games, hugs, smiles, and lots of love. Of course, there was a flurry of picture-taking. Whether a person knew you or not, no one was a stranger. This small-town atmosphere contained all the ingredients for a huge family reunion.

Due to the unresolved childcare business waiting for them in Chicago, Al and Tiny stayed only a few days. They were anxious to get back to find a suitable sitter for me. Two weeks later, Mother, Daddy, and I returned to Chicago. While Tiny and Al had been diligent in their efforts, they had not found suitable childcare. It was indeed a dilemma! When we left Portland, the doctors at Emanuel Hospital gave Tiny a copy of my medical records. I was now under the cardiac care of La Rabida Children's Hospital in Chicago. The heart murmur that I had at birth was still an active health issue. One part of my recommended treatment and recovery plan was that I have adult supervision to ensure proper rest. There was a special emphasis on no excessive playing or excitement. Al had the same heart condition at birth. He was the living proof for our family that with time, limited stress, and proper care, children can outgrow this disorder. While my prognosis was good, the issue continued concerning Al and Tiny. It was the primary reason they were never interested in entrusting my daily care to a stranger.

When it came to helping family members, Mother and Daddy were immensely self-sacrificing. They extended their stay in Chicago for as long as they could. The time came for them to return to Portland. They were only in their forties, and both had jobs in Portland. The four of them agreed that the best solution at the time would be for me to continue the trip back to Portland with Mother and Daddy. So many major life decisions had to be made on an impromptu basis! Fortunately, there were no concerns about my having any separation anxiety issues. I loved Mother and Daddy enormously and was not the type of child to cry or cling to Al and Tiny. My ability to adapt allowed everyone to be at ease with this resolution. The option of having me spend this time with Mother and Daddy was twofold with Tiny. Yes, she and Al needed the time to find a proper babysitter. But the motive went beyond that for Tiny. She always wanted me to maintain the same closeness with Mother and Daddy that she shared with all her relatives in Missouri and throughout the country.

As always, I excitedly looked forward to the days we spent riding the train. Immediately after we boarded, the fun began. On previous trips, Daddy told me the "story" of a mountain goat named Rocky. He was supposedly the legendary mascot who looked out for the trains. While riding, I sat patiently staring out the window as we rode through the Rocky Mountains. If I happened to see a goat, I would get so excited, screaming, "There he is!" Mother and Daddy would chuckle and agree. The two were eager to take advantage of every moment they considered positive exposure. Even at an early age, they would point out every landmark to me along the way, emphasizing what it meant to leave one state and cross over into another suddenly. Most of the train staff enjoyed having a talkative child as a passenger. I relished the special attention I received when I met the porters. Meals in the dining car were another special treat, especially dinner, because it always included ice cream sundaes. As this trip ended, it would be months before Al, Tiny, and I would be together again.

My absence allowed Tiny an opportunity to look for a job. While Al served in the military, Tiny completed several clerical courses at Portland's Multnomah Business College. Tiny thought she could surely use these office skills to gain her very first job. After putting in several applications, weeks went by, and Tiny still had not secured employment. She felt that valuable time was being wasted because there were many days that she spent hours sitting alone at home. By now, Tiny was becoming very anxious about the future. She was eager to start earning money and accepted a position at a nearby Plaid Stamp Store. These were stamps earned through grocery store and gas station purchases. Once you collect enough stamps, you can exchange them for various household items at any of their locations. Tiny saw this job as temporary. It did not pay much but provided something for her to do while Al was working.

Tiny's next venture was to apply for a temporary holiday position with the United States Postal Service. Due to the amount of mail generated during the Christmas season creating the need for more workers. Tiny was assigned a position as a mail sorter. While this job offered a greater pay scale than the Plaid Stamps store, the Post Office presented much harder work than Tiny had ever experienced. Sorting mail, lifting, and bending in a warehouse environment was far from the clerical office vision Tiny had for a career. The reward was that the money she made during that holiday season was incredibly profitable!

Tiny and Al decided that the funds would be used for the first major furniture purchase in the home. They agreed that their top priority was to make sure that whenever I returned from Portland, I would be pleasantly surprised and amazingly comfortable. With their usual excitement, they purchased a brand-new white French Provincial bedroom set. The room was complete with every imaginable additional piece of décor any young girl could want. The result was a fantasy bedroom that was fit for a princess! As an adult, I realized there were many other things that their money could have been used for. As always, their main focus was me first!

While Tiny struggled to establish her place in her administrative work world, God's favor was on Al at his job. International Harvester had a policy of closing for three paid weeks during the Christmas Holidays and through New Year's. This time off was a God-sent blessing! Following Tiny's seasonal stint with the post office, they got in their car and drove to Portland to celebrate the holidays with me and the family. Al, Tiny, and I had not seen each other in four months. This brief time together was a wonderful treat!

When the time came for the two of them to return to Chicago, I was left to continue living with Mother and Daddy for the next six months. Life in my grandparents' house was always enjoyable. By this time, Tiny's brother W.R. (Dub) was discharged from the military. He and his family had moved back to Portland to establish permanent residence. For some reason, as a baby, I never pronounced his name correctly. To me, he has always been Uncle Dub. Like myself, their son Steven was an only child. While W.R. and Evelyn worked, we spent many days together at Mother and Daddy's house. Steven is thirteen days older than me, which made our relationship incredibly special! We were not only playmates but as close as I imagined having a brother would be.

In addition, two families on my grandparents' block had children of my age group. Greg, Margo, Fred, and Cathy were the Taylors. Because my grandparents were close friends with their parents, my relationship with them was like having another pair of cousins. In addition to being playmates, our families worshiped at the same church. There was also the Warren family of boys. While some brothers were older, Marlon was the closest to my age. The two of us also shared a lot of time together. Even after my grandparents moved to another neighborhood, these childhood friendships remained.

In 1960, Chicago began the two-year construction project of the fourteen-lane Dan Ryan freeway. In doing so, it was necessary to tear out several residential blocks of homes. Al and Tiny watched for months as our neighborhood was transformed. Our building was on the corner of Eighty-First and Lafayette Streets. Once the freeway construction work was completed, our street became a one-way southbound street. There was no longer a neighbor across the street from our building. We could look directly across the freeway at State Street, now a one-way northbound street. At that time, we were a one-car family. Al's job was in the northwest suburban village community of Melrose Park. It would have taken him an unreasonable amount of time and several bus transfers to commute using public transportation.

Shortly after Al and Tiny's arrival back in Chicago, Tiny enrolled in a beauty college. However, it was short-lived when she secured a clerical position at The University of Chicago John Crerar Library. She was so relieved that her skills and educational preparation would be used. The route Tiny took from our house would conveniently take her to work. Everything was finally falling into place. As a result of Tiny's outgoing personality and enthusiasm, it was not long before she began to make new friends at the job. One person was a young female from Alabama named Geri Griffin. The two of them hit it off immediately. Geri did not have a car either. Things worked out perfectly. The two of them shared a portion of the bus ride together. As time went on, their relationship grew into a friendship that would last a lifetime.

The future was starting to look brighter for our family. Al decided that what was valuable outside was less important than inside our home. Through obstacles or hardships, my dad never wavered. Instead, he remained confident and prudent in the management of our household. With the development of the Dan Ryan freeway in our neighborhood, the public transportation for Al was greatly improved. That is when Al decided to sell his red 1957 Chevy. Al and Tiny used the profit from the sale to completely refurnish our apartment with brand-new, modern furniture. In keeping their future guests in mind, they insisted on purchasing a roll-away bed.

It would be several months before our family would have a car again. Al dug his heels in full force, working as much overtime as possible. He even became a member of his company's credit union. For many years, they talked about how excited he was when the account reached one thousand dollars. Al told Tiny they were on their way, saying that no matter what happened, the credit union account would never be less than one thousand dollars. That is when their household finances got better. After several months of diligently saving, purchasing a red convertible Pontiac Bonneville was our family's new mode of transportation. Shane bought the same red car. It reminded them of the car club days of their youth.

Later that summer, things really started to change. Mother's brother Billy and his fiancée Rosemary left Montgomery City. They came to Chicago to evaluate the big city life for themselves. When the two arrived, Al wasted no time helping Billy secure employment. While the two Missouri transplants spent their days venturing to learn the city, our apartment was their transitional place to live.

The timing of their move to Chicago could not have been better. Tiny and Al followed the usual end-of-summer routine to Portland. The difference was that the three of us would be returning to Chicago together this time. Having Uncle Billy and Rosemary with us was a blessing in disguise. Al and Tiny could comfortably go to work knowing that Rosemary was home with me. I had my very first experience with a live-in sitter! I really loved the two of them as I know they did me. Rosemary and Billy eventually went their separate ways, but our bond was solid with both of them. Thus began a constant flurry of people who temporarily lived with our family. This pattern of family and friends in our home has continued for as long as I can remember, even today. After all these years, through social media, Rosemary and I continue to share the greatest love and respect for one another.

Although our life included a revolving door of people at any given time, Tiny never lost focus of what she called her "divine God-given assignment as my mother." Most days, no other children were in our house when there was a party, special event, or visitor. Yet, I never felt alone or lonely. Tiny made it her priority to be not only my mother but my very first friend. As an only child, I never felt slighted for companionship. Tiny was always there for me. When Tiny was not working, we spent most of our days doing everything my heart desired.

Both Al and Tiny took their parenting responsibilities very seriously. Their love for me was with intent and purpose. During our downtime, Al and Tiny provided a lifestyle specifically designed for me. They wanted me to enjoy all the pleasures a child could desire. Together, we jumped rope, rode bikes, played jacks, board games, and every other kid-friendly activity. We filled our summer weekends with picnics and days on the beach. There were also lots of trips to Brookfield Zoo and Riverview Amusement Park. Chicago also has plenty of indoor venues that are excellent for winter activities. My favorite places include the Shed Aquarium, Adler Planetarium, and various museums. Bowling and roller skating are also very popular indoor activities. Al and Tiny wanted to expose me to places and adventures within their financial reach. Indeed, they were ambassadors for giving all they had to create a happy childhood for me successfully.

I do not want to imply that every moment of my childhood was filled with fun and games. Al and Tiny knew that being my parents had to come with some basic guidelines. As I got older, there was additional emphasis on my academic growth. Both of them closely scrutinized all my school assignments. There was no point in my rush to get finished. The two of them had very set standards. Al and Tiny were both sticklers when it came to organization and structure. Sloppy work was unacceptable. I would have to do it over if my penmanship was not neat. Tiny told me that turning in an assignment or application was like painting a picture. She added that presentation is the first impression or image that someone has of you. It represents the type of work you will do for them. Telling me these things made a lasting impact on me.

Regarding penmanship, I was blessed to have three shining examples. Mother and Tiny have the most admirable handwriting you can imagine. In addition, my Godmother Sherl not only had impeccable penmanship but was a remarkably gifted calligrapher. I always admired both of her handwriting styles. Sherl explained to me that the definition of the word calligraphy is "beautiful writing." At that point, I began to focus on and practice calligraphy and being neat when writing.

Another thing high on the list of priorities was my spiritual growth. For as long as I can remember, one of their top priorities was for me to have knowledge of God and develop a personal relationship with him. Decent values, prayer life, and a connection to God were constant topics. From the beginning of my reading days, I had my children's Bible and an expansive library that included various Bible storybooks. As a result of this exposure,

I am still an avid reader. Al and Tiny continuously taught me to thank God daily because He provides everything we have.

Although my prayers have grown and changed through the years, I still remember my first prayers. These words left powerful imprints on my mind. As a young child, blessing our food while sitting at the dinner table or kneeling side by side with Al and Tiny for my bedtime prayers was something that I looked forward to. Among my early childhood memories, I count these specific family prayers as some of my favorites. Through the years, I realized that Al and Tiny's intentions were always to help me become all I could be. I now know they had a vision for possibilities that I was too young to see in myself. Al and Tiny were determined that I would be a faithful servant of the Lord and a good student. Together, we evolved through what they referred to as the necessities of life for productive growth. As I look back, I appreciate their efforts.

1962 was an eventful year for our family. That September, I would start kindergarten at Amelia Dunne Hookway Elementary School. The name was later changed to Lenart Regional Gifted Center. The school was one block west of our apartment and one block east of our church. Surprisingly, my first day of school is one that I still vividly remember. The teacher asked each student to meet a new friend during the four-hour class. Our teacher instructed us to exit the classroom holding our new friend's hands until we introduced them to our waiting parents on the playground. My friend Stephanie and I followed the teacher's instructions, and our mothers met one another.

That day, Tiny and Stephanie's mother, Mattie, also grew to become lifetime friends. In the coming days, we met another girl on the school playground. Jovanka (Jo) was one year older and in first grade. Unfortunately, Jo's mother had already gone to be with the Lord. As the three of us talked and played together daily, it was as if we had known each other forever. For over sixty years, whether near or far, the three of us continue to be the best of friends, having shared every imaginable life experience. Surely, this had to be a part of God's plan.

As we got older, Stephanie and I attended Sunday school together. Even if Al and Tiny had a late Saturday night with their friends and were not going to church, it was mandatory that I went to Sunday school. During those years, my closet was divided into three wardrobes: church, school, and play clothes. Tiny selected my outfits the day before. Tiny took pride in making sure that everything was neat and perfectly coordinated from head to toe. Afterward, Al would whisk me out of the house and drive me to the children's Sunday school. It was an outing that I looked forward to. Tiny and Al knew our church was a safe, supervised opportunity for me to learn God's word, sing, and socialize with children my age. Besides attending school, it was my first taste of independence from Al and Tiny's watchful eyes. Between the devotion of our parents and these youth classes, Stephanie and I learned to love God genuinely. Praising God together is a bond that we continue to share.

From the very beginning of their marriage, Tiny and Al shared a healthy, active young adult life. Tiny has always loved to cook and entertain. Because our apartment was larger than most of their friends, everyone cheerfully gathered there on the weekends. Al and Tiny would come home from work on Friday and start getting things prepared. One of the first things was to make sure every inch of the apartment was spotless. We had hardwood floors throughout the entire apartment. I can remember Al meticulously waxing them until they shined like glass. The whole weekend would be filled with people and laughter. There was an aroma of food, drinks, and cigarettes. A few folding card tables were scattered for cards and board games. The stereo was loud, and music, singing, and dancing continued nonstop. Even the walls vibrated to the beat.

Those with children would bring them, too. We kids would be right there, safe and secure with our parents. While the adults were having their brand of fun, we would have our simultaneous party in my bedroom. Go Fish and War were our preferred card games. We were not hot dogs or cold-cut children. There was never a separate kid's dinner menu except for adding chips, dip, popcorn, or nuts. We ate whatever the adults ate. The one exception is that Kool-Aid™ was our choice of drink. As a result of the frequent gala weekend festivities in our home, I learned to enjoy socializing and entertaining at an incredibly early age.

Occasionally, these weekend gatherings would include an impromptu concert performance. The show stars were Tiny, Nancy, Terry, Lurl, and several other lady friends. Our living room became a mock stage where they would take their places as they sang. Everyone agreed they were exceptionally good as they imitated all the popular soul groups of that era. The adults and children would gather to clap and cheer them on. As their faithful audience, we enjoyed every moment of these concerts. Eventually, some girlfriends tried to take their singing more seriously. They formed a singing group called The Stingers. Although their attempt at singing never took them to big-time stardom, they enjoyed many irreplaceable days together and had lots of fun trying! Tiny rarely missed a concert because of her love of music and dance. And yes, she took me too! My going out with Tiny and her friends never seemed strange to me. I always thought I was supposed to go everywhere Tiny went. Many of her friends who had children my age felt the same way. If there was an outing without other children in attendance, Tiny was open for me to invite a friend, always ensuring I had the proper balance of interactions with adults and children.

Slowly, during the early Sunday morning hours, the party would end. Sunday was our family day reserved for just the three of us. After church, it was time to put the house back in order. Less than thirty-six hours earlier, Al had waxed the floors throughout the entire apartment. From all the dancing, the floor was now like sawdust! Al doing another waxing of the floors was included in the cleanup to take us through the week. Clothes had to be cleaned and ironed for the week, which meant a trip to the laundromat. While the washers were going, we would go next door to the grocery store. Al's favorite Sunday dinner was steak, baked potatoes, corn on the cob, and salad. Desert followed with either a peach, cherry, or blackberry cobbler topped with French vanilla ice cream.

Our family has always been that of a modest, hardworking, blue-collar lifestyle. While we were not wealthy and never lived in a sprawling home, there has always been an overwhelming degree of welcoming comfort in the atmosphere. Like an unseen force that drew people in, our home was an open-door environment full of life and love. Often, that apartment housed many more residents than just the three of us. One thing we always had was a roll-away bed. As an adult, the square footage had no influence during the years we lived in that two-bedroom apartment. More people than I can remember, or you can imagine, either visited, passed through, and even moved in through the open door of our home. I do not know how we accommodated so many people. What I do know is that Al and Tiny have never been self-serving. Early on, they realized that anything God had blessed them with was to be a blessing to others. My parents had a mindset that there was always room for more. Ultimately, our apartment became a frequented, safe refuge for anyone in need. It was a foundational place of restoration for all.

Clyde Allen (Al) and Nancy Harden were among the closest couples that my parents had socialized with. The two of them had grown up with Al in the Altgeld Gardens. By now, they were married with three children: Dorothy (Dot), Gwen, and Clyde Jr. (Butch). Ironically, they lived in an apartment just a few blocks west of our church. Their family was at our house, or we were at theirs almost every weekend. Nancy was the one person that Tiny would swap childcare days with. Their house was another trusted place for my care and health issues, so I was allowed to spend lots of time at their home. Through the years, Nancy and Mother became very fond of one another. If anything came up to prevent Al from making the drive to Portland, Nancy would gladly ride the train with Tiny. Gwen would spend some summers in Portland with me as we grew older.

The relationship of the guests in our home and the nature of their visits varied. People came from all over the country and from all walks of life. God knew in advance the needs of everyone who came to live with us. One thing is for sure: our family is proof that God always provides! I have very fond memories of my next temporary live-in sitter. Ruthie had grown up in the same housing project as Al. She was a single parent with a daughter named Kita, who was slightly younger than me. The two of them lived with us for an extended period when Ruthie was unemployed. Once again, Al and Tiny gained live-in childcare, and I gained a playmate. Eventually, times got better for Ruthie, and the two of them moved on.

Following Ruthie was the arrival of Anna, Tiny's younger cousin from San Francisco. Before coming to Chicago, Ana was no stranger to us. While Al was in the military, Tiny and I left Portland and spent an entire summer with our California relatives. Since Tiny had relatives living there, from her paternal and maternal parents, this was a time for everyone to catch up. When it came to people living with us, Cousin Anna was a favorite of mine. Of course, this being her first time living away from home, she was happy with the safety of being with familiar family members.

It was like having a big sister in the house when Anna came to live with us. She shared my room, so we would stay up late at night reading, snacking, watching television, and talking. Once again, I was blessed with a live-in sitter I admired and loved! When Anna was not involved with her school studies, she allowed me to tag along everywhere with her. We would ride our bikes, shop, or go to a movie. I saw the city of Chicago through younger eyes than my parents. It was during the 1960s when Afro-hairstyles initially became popular. At that time, Ana wore her hair in an Afro. We both had a lot of hair; occasionally, I was allowed to shed my ponytails and wear an Afro. I even tried to have my fingernails polished and dress like Ana, the much older girl. I remember feeling sad when her time with us ended, sending her back to California. Because of our heartfelt ties with these family members, our yearly cross-country drives always included a stop in California for a few days.

The flurry of guests continued with short visits. There were even occasions when a family friend's wife kicked him out of their home for a few days. Our cozy apartment was the next best place for him to land. Tiny always went out of her way to ensure everyone felt comfortable and at home. I am telling you, the door was always open for any reason you can imagine. It did not matter what brought people to our home. Our house provided an inviting atmosphere that everybody wanted to come to. It was always available, and everyone was treated equally by Tiny and Al. Their hearts are big enough to help anyone in need.

"Is it not to share your food with the hungry and to provide the poor wanderer with shelter."

Isaiah 58:7

Tiny and Al have always been devoted family members and friends to all. I have realized that Al and Tiny did not need to be great for God to use them. Their generous giving is an unspoken, anointing ministry from God. In my opinion, it has always been their call. These years were filled with an abundance of one-of-a-kind things and experiences. The highlight was the mass of spiritual brothers and sisters that came into our lives. It never mattered to them if someone was on the giving or receiving side of the relationship.

Sherl was our most frequent out-of-town visitor. She and Tiny had been friends since Tiny moved to Portland. They attended elementary and high school together, and, like Stephanie and I, their mothers were friends as well. Through the years, their relationship grew as close as sisters. As a child, Sherl had a longing for big city life! She was a naturally gifted artist and tailor, which led her to leave Portland immediately after high school. Her next stop was Manhattan, New York, where she attended Parsons School of Design. Sherl's dedicated studies, hard work, and diligence paid off for her in a big way. As the years went on, her career reached its pinnacle. She became affluent and well-renowned in the design field. Having been briefly married and divorced, Sherl was a single woman on the move.

Much of Sherl's career involved both domestic and international travel. Africa was a frequent destination for her, and her home was a true reflection of these visits. Seeing the world was something that she truly enjoyed. Out of her love and generosity, Sherl wanted to share some of her travel experiences with me and Tiny. Our first trips to Washington, DC, Philadelphia, and New Orleans were with Sherl. She went out of her way to ensure that any travel time the three of us shared was amazing! As with so many women, Sherl had been unsuccessful in having her own children. Because of the family-like love the three shared, Al and Tiny had selected her to be my loving godmother. Sherl made an extra effort never to treat me anything less than extraordinary. I always felt privileged to be her "one." Even if Tiny could not make the trip to Manhattan, Sherl's penthouse was one of the few trusted places that Tiny and Al would, without hesitation, allow me to visit unaccompanied for weeks.

During my youth, many of the years that Sherl did not come to Chicago, Tiny and I would go to New York. Before our arrival, Sherl would have an extensive itinerary planned for every day of our stay. She ensured we saw Broadway Plays, toured all the New York tourist attractions, and ate at the finest restaurants. We would spend hours shopping at every nook and cranny in the city, from the garment district to Fifth Avenue. Both Sherl and Tiny were ladies who liked to dress very classy. Even though they were from families of humble beginnings, they were raised to have high-end desires. They never wavered in wanting only the finest things in life! As I grew up, the two of them and Mother instilled those same desires in me. They told me it was better to have one "good" pair of shoes than ten inexpensive pairs. That was the same consensus they fostered with everything else in my wardrobe.

One of our New York garment district trips left a lasting impression on my memory—Sherl designed and tailored a one-of-a-kind trench coat for Tiny. The style was a single-breasted A-line, made of heavy-duty khaki-colored cotton gabardine and chocolate brown leather. The materials were patterned in ten inches of alternating horizontal stripes. Everyone who saw the finished product agreed that it was gorgeous! Anytime Tiny wore this unique coat, it garnered many compliments as it was truly outstanding and unforgettable.

As most young girls do, I always watched my mother closely, hoping to be like her someday. Tiny is a pretty woman with an amazing eye for style and fashion. On occasion, Tiny would buy something for herself and a similar outfit or color for me. What a thrill! I thought we were twins. On the weekends, I loved playing with her jewelry, putting on her high heels, and dressing up in her clothes. After baths, Tiny would give me splashes of her perfumes and allow me to rub my body with sweet-smelling lotions. Though I was far too young to wear makeup, there were times when I was allowed a little hint of lipstick or nail polish. You know, this made me feel too cute and oh, so grown up!

"Train a child in the way he should go, and when he is old, he will not turn from it."

Proverbs 22:6

3

WHAT THE HECK?

Tiny was always a firm believer in equality. Even growing up in Portland, she had not experienced the level of discrimination she encountered in some Chicago neighborhoods. Tiny was appalled by the amount of hungry people living in substandard housing and the inequality in the public school system. It was the catalyst that led her to become interested in civil rights. In 1966, she and her friend Nancy decided to participate in the infamous Chicago Freedom Rally. Led by Dr. Martin Luther King Jr. and the Reverend Jessie Jackson Jr., 35,000 people convened at Chicago's Soldier Field. In the crowd's excitement of pushing and shoving, Tiny fell. Though not significantly injured, she was left with a scar. It did not bother her at all. Instead, she celebrated it as a reminder of her day in history. From that day forward, our home library grew with the addition of African American authors. Tiny was inspired to fight for dignity and justice and determined that we learn more about our ancestry. She constantly told me to be comfortable in my skin and to always conduct myself with class and integrity.

In December 1966, we followed our usual holiday tradition. I went to Portland when school was out, and Al and Tiny joined us in time for Christmas. Just before coming to Portland, Tiny resigned from her position at The University of Chicago John Crerar Library. Upon her return, she would have a new job waiting for her. In January 1967, Tiny started working as a teller at American National Bank. It was another public contact position where my mother was sure to meet many people. As always, it was only briefly before Tiny met and befriended a co-worker. Single and with no children of her own, Liz and Tiny became quick friends. It was the beginning of a beautiful forever relationship.

On January 26, 1967, Chicago was hit by a quiet storm. It was the biggest "unexpected" blizzard in the city's history. In less than 24 hours, Chicago was covered with approximately twenty-three inches of snow. It was the most significant snowfall recorded in Chicago's history. Everything came to a screeching halt. As with any other winter morning, Tiny had traveled by bus to her new job at American National Bank in the Loop. By mid-morning, the news began to report the severity of the snowstorm. There was a weather alert that directed businesses and schools to close immediately. People all over the city were frantic. There was a mad scramble to get home.

The densely snow-covered streets caused Tiny's bus ride home to be exceptionally slow that day. Tiny has always been a friendly person and a real talker. These characteristics carried over from her everyday home life to her public contact work life. Without hesitation, as the bus slowly crept along, Tiny started a conversation with the other ladies on the bus. Each one shared how far away they lived. Understandably, everyone on the bus had anxieties about how they would make their way home to their families. After a few minutes of talking with these ladies, my mom realized that, just like her, they all had one common goal. Getting home!

As the bus suddenly came to a stop, the driver advised everyone that the road ahead was closed, and he could not take the risk of driving any further! Sitting on the bus in the bitter, freezing cold was not the best choice. Our home was several blocks away. During normal weather conditions, it was within walking distance. Tiny decided to exit the bus and bravely started walking before it got dark. The wind was blowing so fiercely that she had to walk backward, and that is when she saw one lone car slowly coming down the street.

Tiny stepped into the street when the car approached the bus, waving her arms to flag the driver down. Once the car reached her, the driver stopped. Tiny told this stranger that she only lived a few blocks away. She asked him to please give her a ride as far as possible. The man kindly told her to get in. When Tiny opened the car door, everyone rushed off the bus. They all started frantically pushing each other as they struggled to jump into this strange man's car. The bus was full, so there were more passengers than this car could hold. The man stepped out of the car and looked over at the crowd of people on the passenger side. He firmly announced that he would give a ride to as many as the car could hold. The only stipulation was that the lady who stopped him had a seat in the car before anyone else! Tiny said, he also added that he was not going any further than our house, so everyone would have to get out there. Finally, Tiny and as many other people as possible settled in the car.

Tiny has always lived her life like a welcoming open door. She always greeted people with her infectious smile. It is a radiant beam that invites everyone she meets. When graced by her presence, they are guaranteed to be surrounded by the warmth of her love, the dignity of her character, the power of her being, and an overflowing wealth of wisdom. All of that is combined with so many other positive attributes. Tiny always had an unbelievably soft, kindhearted nature. Whether a person is in need or not, Tiny always has a giving, serving spirit. Al and Tiny had a framed scripture on their kitchen wall that read,

"So, in everything do to others what you would have them do to you."

Matthew 7:12

As the gentleman continued to drive, Tiny mentally made one of her intentional Good Samaritan decisions. She decided that once they got to our house, she would extend a trusting invitation to these unknown individuals to come inside. Tiny wanted to allow them to gather their thoughts for making their way home. Without hesitation, most of them gratefully accepted. After all the day's events, imagine my dad's surprise to find himself hosting a house full of strangers! While at our house, they could warm themselves, use our phone to contact their families, and have something warm to eat or drink. This generous humanitarian outreach continued when Al and Tiny allowed each of them to remain in the safety of our house until they could make arrangements to get to their homes. Again, there was that open door. As the day went on, everyone slowly decided to be picked up or start walking from the shelter in our home. They all seemed very thankful, and a few stopped to exchange phone numbers with Tiny. You would think that someone from this group would surely reach out. Surprisingly, the promise to stay in touch was not genuine—no lasting relationships developed from the events of that snowy day.

Records show that while it snowed for twenty-nine hours straight, high winds created massive snow drifts. The entrance to our building was at ground level, and by the time it stopped, the snow had our apartment doors barricaded. The only way we could exit was for Al to climb out of a window and shovel us out. This phenomenon paralyzed the city for days to come. Schools and businesses were closed while waiting for the snow to thaw or shovel out. I will never forget that winter. On our block, everyone walked from one house to another. Neighborhood parents were making hot chocolate and apple cider. All the kids were playing in the streets, having snowball fights, and making snow angels. For the children, it had created a winter wonderland. At the same time, our parents had some major adult concerns. People all over Chicago were caught off guard. Several people throughout the city were reported dead. Businesses remained closed, preventing people from purchasing primary necessities, including groceries. It caused the city to be plagued with uncontrolled looting. There were even news stories reporting that several grocery stores were vandalized. In a panic, illegal acts were taking place in otherwise respectable neighborhoods. These events of this massive storm made history.

Spring came, leaving the rest of the year uneventful. Mother and Daddy did not make their usual summer journey to the Midwest this year. When school was out, I flew alone to spend the summer with them in Portland. These weeks were something I always enjoyed. Mother and Daddy never let me get bored. Instead, they always made sure I enjoyed their favorite drive-in movies. Traveling carnivals, rodeos, and the circus were annual summer events on Portland's waterfront. Added to that, I always loved to be a tag along with the guys. Many onlookers would have deemed me to be an adventurous little girl. Others might have called me a tomboy. Even when Daddy, Uncle Dub, and Steven went fishing or to the archery range, I convinced them to let me go, too. The Portland summer fun always ended with the family spending at least one day at Jantzen Beach Amusement Park.

Once again, Al and Tiny made the summer cross-country drive to pick me up. There is one thing that I grew up hearing Tiny say, "Out of fifty-two weeks in a year, at least two of those she dedicated to time spent with her mother." You could say that Tiny has always been a momma's girl! Al and Tiny wanted me to see as much of this country as possible. While driving, we would spend the night and one full day in every major city. Our trips were afforded as much flexibility as time permitted. Sometimes, we went out sightseeing, which caused us to get behind schedule. Al and Tiny are both excellent drivers. They would take turns driving twenty-four hours daily to make up for lost time. The goal was to arrive in Chicago in just enough time to attend a Labor Day bar-b-que with family and friends. The next order of business was that the first day of school was that week. Fortunately, Mother always sent me home with more than enough school supplies to start the year.

Keeping with tradition, in December 1967, as soon as the winter school break started, I left Chicago alone on a flight to Portland. Tiny and Al would join us a few weeks later to celebrate Christmas together. They were busy finalizing things at home and purchasing gifts for the family. A week before their scheduled departure, they were victims of a crime. Al kept his car parked on the Lafayette side of the building in view of the windows. Unbelievably, someone had broken into our family car and stole the battery. Nothing like this had ever happened. That was a shocking surprise to Al. Fortunately, he had full access to the gas station where he worked. He walked to the station, got a new battery, and installed it.

That weekend, Al and Tiny were in the house getting dressed for a holiday party. Al went outside ahead of my mom to warm the car. Suddenly, he stormed back into the house, saying, "It happened again." To their dismay, in the brief time they were in the house, the car battery was stolen a second time. What a way to start the holiday! Not only was this annoying, but it was an unexpected, costly expense. The police stated that car battery thefts seemed to be widespread practice during the winter months. After all this repeated, staggering drama with the car, Al and Tiny could not wait to get to Portland. Spending time with family seemed the best way to unwind and calm their frazzled nerves.

Before they could get out of town, all hell broke loose! A terrifying dark encounter delayed their travel plans even further. One week before Christmas, someone broke into our home! The adversary came like a roaring lion looking for someone to devour. What proved to be the most frightening part of this burglary was that the culprit entered boldly during the middle of the night. It happened while Tiny and Al were at home, asleep in their bedroom. Can you imagine waking up to a cold house and finding your daughter's bedroom window had been pried open? It was especially startling because we had never opened that window. The window was not only locked but had inadvertently been painted shut. For anyone outside to gain entry through this window would have required time and determination. Al found the torn screen in the flower bed right outside of the window, along with damaged plants and muddy footprints.

As Al and Tiny continued walking through the house, they noticed snowy, dirty footprints in every room. Silent footprints made in the dark led directly to the area rug along the side of their bed! Yes, this undetected perpetrator had boldly walked right into Tiny and Al's bedroom, where he stood staring at them while they slept! Tiny said the shocking location of these footprints brought a wave of chills over her. Once they confirmed that the house was empty, she and my dad grabbed one another as she burst into tears. As Al and Tiny gasped in disbelief, their first reaction was to thank God for their lives. He had placed his hedge of protection around them. Then, there was a second, equally important prayer. They were overwhelmed with thankfulness that I was in Portland. If this had not been during the Christmas school vacation, I would have been asleep in my bedroom, the point of entry.

When the police arrived, they walked the entire perimeter of the building. After examining the crime scene, they shared their suspicion with Al and Tiny. Previous experience and expertise with crimes such as this led the police to believe this home invasion may have been committed in various ways. The first possibility was that due to the quiet, undetected nature of the break-in, the perpetrator seemed to be experienced because the way he conducted the crime had all the characteristics of a cat burglar.

Another officer added that due to our apartment's location, anyone could lurk on the freeway's opposite side. There, they could clearly observe our comings and goings, including when our lights came on and off. The final theory was that the perpetrator was someone closer to home than my parents knew or someone who had been inside our house before. The fact that they chose my bedroom window led the police to believe the intruder knew this room was unoccupied. Admittedly, the most logical answer was the latter. Tiny and Al saw the truth in the statement, "If walls could talk."

This last possibility was a sickening thought that seemed unimaginable! To hear these words coming from the police, Al and Tiny were totally enraged. Feelings of suspicion and confusion quickly crept in. When the police left, they sat together to review these unbelievable theories. As far as they knew, they had no enemies. Their first thought was that it could be connected to the strangers on the bus. After struggling with that idea, the next question reared its ugly head. Was it possible that behind the smiling face of a trusted acquaintance, there was someone who could commit such a devious act of betrayal? That caused them to take a detailed inventory of their social circle. Suddenly, they faced the reality that although they had lots of acquaintances, these people may not all be loyal friends. For a moment, some of them even became possible suspects.

Even today, at the thought of this nightmare, I am enraged. I realize this emotion can be alleviated if a better reaction follows. I Praise the Lord for placing a hedge of protection around Al and Tiny that night! But for the Grace of God, they could have been killed as they slept. Or perhaps they could have been awakened to be involved in a face-to-face confrontation with this monstrous intruder. God tells us in his word that,

"The thief comes only to steal and kill and destroy; I have come that they may have life and have it to the full."
John 10:10

The events of this horrific evening are a testament to the power of God and his Holy Word. Apparently, the degree of trust and generosity Al and Tiny showed to others was with the right motives. It is possible that their acts of kindness were being distributed to the wrong people or in the wrong environment. By the end of the day, Al and Tiny were both driven to carry negative feelings of uncertainty and loneliness. Understandably, the events of that night left my parents totally engulfed in a wave of fear and insecurity. Vulnerability gripped their entire being. That afternoon, my dad nailed the window shut and boarded it up.

Al is an avid game hunter, so there were guns in our home. The next day, he insisted on training Tiny to use a handgun. For the following nights, neither of them was able to sleep. Instead, they stayed on guard, sleeping in shifts. In the coming days, Al canvassed the people he was acquainted with in our neighborhood. It included the second and third-floor elderly residents of our building. He told everyone about this brazen intrusion. Of course, no one said that they saw anything. Al and Tiny agreed that they could not continue living in a constant state of fear and stress. Within days, they decided our family would move as soon as possible. Al and Tiny made the plans and put them into motion immediately. This series of terrifying, unplanned events all happened so suddenly. No one in Chicago decides to move during the dead of winter. It was now just one week before Christmas! At this point, they could see no other option. They were already off work for the usual holiday trip to Portland. Those vacation plans came to a screeching halt. Tiny and Al had to do whatever was necessary to find a safe, new home for our family as soon as possible.

When they composed themselves enough to share the events with all their family and friends, everyone was baffled! Who would do such a thing? At that time, I was in the fifth grade. With the upheaval and chaos in Chicago, Tiny, and Al would not be coming to get me. While they re-grouped, I would need to stay in Portland with Mother and Daddy. I finished the last half of the fifth-grade school year at Highland Elementary School in North Portland. That school has since been renamed Martin Luther King Elementary School.

Daily, Tiny, and Al started venturing around the city to look at rentals. They found the available apartments to be substandard and discouraging. The Lord did not forsake them. It did not take long before the blessing of a safe, new home presented itself. Long-time friends Clyde (Al) and Nancy offered their assistance. These two had recently moved from their apartment in our neighborhood. They had been successful in the purchase of their very first property. It was a duplex roughly fifteen minutes away in the South Chicago district. Clyde's younger sister was about to be married. After the wedding, she and her husband were supposed to move into the upstairs unit. Somehow, they abruptly aborted the plan for his sister. These wonderful friends explained the urgency of our situation to their family members. Without question, they gave my parents the first choice for the apartment. Praise God! When you trust and believe, He will not leave you alone. A beautiful scripture says,

"Carry each other's burdens and in this way, you shall fulfill the law of Christ."

Galatians 6:28

Nancy and Al demonstrated this most lovingly, proving that loving kindness and support are what friends are for. Nancy hugged Tiny and whispered, "You are my sister." Suddenly, God was using these two dear friends as the vessel to supply our family's need for a new home!

Within a week, the current apartment was dismantled and ready to go. Al and Tiny worked tirelessly to ensure all boxes were labeled and packed. A group of friends would assist them in the Saturday afternoon move. There were still some things to do on moving day. Al and Tiny each had different finishing touches to take care of. Al left home early that morning to run errands and rent a moving van. Shortly afterward, Tiny left on the bus to go to the bank. They had timed the day so Al would pick her up for the drive home together.

What a sense of relief in knowing that the nightmare was almost over. When Al and Tiny arrived at the apartment, they happily got out of the car. An unfathomable, appalling blow met them as they approached the back door. They found our kitchen was wide open with the door off the hinges, lying in the middle of the kitchen floor! As they stepped inside, they realized our apartment was completely empty. Can you imagine their shock? Every box packed for the move, and every piece of furniture was gone. Within a few hours, someone had annihilated my parents' entire life. As if to further humiliate them, the lowly pack of thieves had left a card table and two chairs in the middle of the kitchen. Al and Tiny were speechless with shock and rage. I cannot begin to imagine their adrenaline rush. Even after all they had been through, this was unimaginable. They agreed that they could not envision anyone who would target them in such a ruthless way or why. Suddenly, it was as if our lives had pivoted on a dime, leaving us in the depths of unbelievable despair.

While Tiny contacted the police, Al immediately went to the elderly upstairs occupants of our building to ask if they had seen anything. When questioned, these neighbors said yes, they did. They knew we were moving that day. Unsuspecting, they saw a truck pull up and load the contents of our apartment. Our neighbors had watched everything we owned being removed out the back door. The lady was nervous and very apologetic. She honestly thought it was the moving company. They were too old to give an accurate description of the perpetrators. Al was stunned by the details of this calculated attack. In broad daylight, our neighbors had witnessed our life being loaded into a stranger's truck and driven away.

When the police arrived, they investigated the surroundings. They suspected that due to the location of our apartment, someone could easily have been parked directly across the freeway. They would have been undetected as they sat and watched my parent's every move. The trained eyes of the officers went on to make an additional observation. Tiny had packed a suitcase with enough clothes and lingerie to last until they moved and were able to finish unpacking the boxes. The suitcase was gone, but some female items had been left behind, tossed on the floor like rags. It was as if someone had taken the time to be selective.

For this reason, the police believed a woman was present during the move. Unfortunately, no one was ever apprehended for these grossly evil crimes. Al and Tiny were in the darkest, stormy season of their lives.

This event happened on an unseasonably warm December day. Al and Tiny were both wearing thin, waist-length leather jackets. They were left with nothing of our family's life except the clothes on their backs. They moved that day from one empty house to another. All their friends rallied around them, giving my parents money, clothes, and anything else they could spare. Since Terry and Tiny were the same size, she did not hesitate to make sure my mother had the necessary amount of winter clothes. Mr. Joyner had been so kind to my parents. Al wanted to stick with his original thank-you plan. He planned to prepare the apartment for the next tenant by cleaning and painting it. My dad contacted his friend Phillip (Peewee) in the coming days. He picked Peewee up, and the two of them worked all day. It was also a way for him to relieve some of his anger. While they were working inside the apartment, you would not believe what had happened. To add insult to injury, someone stole Al's car battery for the third time!

With their nerves completely rattled, Al and Tiny had to get as far away from home as possible immediately. The next day, they took a flight to Portland. What a Christmas! When they arrived in Portland, the atmosphere was full of tears and sullenness. The dark cloud of these events continued to hover over each day. Every material thing Al and Tiny owned was gone. They were understandably hurting, and their spirits were broken. I had never seen Al and Tiny so sad. The two of them felt as though they had been tried in the fire.

While Mother was supportive, she was the strong backbone that they needed. Not the type of woman to beat around the bush, she told them that they were acting like someone died, adding that these were just things. To lighten the atmosphere, Mother reminded them that they did not even own a toothpick when they moved to Chicago. Adding to that, she bluntly threw in the fact that their life had been built on a collection of plaid stamp dishes and someone else's throwaway furniture. Finally, Mother said more positive results will come from prayer than emotions and self-pity. Her firm advice to them was always to believe that all you have, you can get again, and this time, even better!

That day, Al and Tiny began to pull themselves together. They started to focus on how they would use their resources and energy to move forward. God was with them even in the depths of this very dark valley, leading them to stand firm. The first thing Tiny and Mother did was go shopping at the department stores. The timing was perfect to catch all the After-Christmas sales. By the time Al and Tiny left Portland, they had foot lockers full of new clothes and accessories for the current Chicago winter weather. Our family members put together a sufficient donation to cover the cost of acquiring a few modern furniture necessities.

Before returning to Chicago, with tears in her eyes, Tiny shared with me what she deemed her biggest loss. Surprisingly, it was not the jewelry, clothes, jazz album collection, or furnishings. Tiny's greatest pain stemmed from her heartbreak because they had taken one "special" box. This box contained certain things that belonged to me. For years, she had placed my baby pictures, shoes, dresses, and several other memorabilia items from the first years of my life inside this box. By the end of our talk, Tiny pulled me close to her. As she hugged and kissed me, she whispered softly, "I have you, babe. Mother is right. Everything else I can get again." At this young age, Tiny made me realize that it is not what you have but who you have. She continued by telling me that starting today, we will put this sadness behind us and Embrace Life! By the grace of God, our family did just that. I have never forgotten her tearful words, "Embrace Life!" Many years later, these are the words I chose to use as my mantra on letters or cards. I now use this quotation when sending e-mails and text messages as times have changed.

The time came for Al and Tiny to ease down the road. Our God is a miracle worker who will supply all our needs. For the second time in their young lives, Al and Tiny were starting to rebuild our family life in a new home made entirely from scratch. No matter how painful the path ahead was, Al and Tiny had to encourage themselves to move forward. They knew that to overcome this mountain, they had to pull themselves together. That meant doing their part by getting up and working hard. It was the only road to climbing out of what seemed like a famine.

Getting settled into the new apartment was like Deja vu. All their friends rallied around to help them get settled. With the support of friends and family, it became apparent that God's promises and mercies are new every day. Al and Tiny said that they suddenly realized it was not what they had that was important, but who they had! A sense of ease came over them for the first time in weeks. The love and support of loyal friends were all that was necessary to lighten their hearts. After they completed cleaning and painting, their brand-new furniture was delivered. Although a degree of struggle was involved, God met our family's every need. Eventually, our lives returned "somewhat" to a normal routine. What was meant for evil turned out to be good. This entire life-changing experience was a catalyst that started our family on a closer walk with God.

A harsh, unexpected reminder of the unsolved burglary happened when I returned to Chicago for the Easter spring break. Tiny and I were shopping in Sears with Nancy and her daughter Gwen. While our parents were in line to pay, Gwen and I noticed a lady wearing one of Tiny's coats. We knew it was her coat because it was the unique, one-of-a-kind trench coat that had been designed and tailored for Tiny by my godmother Sherl. Gwen and I ran to the register to report what we had seen to our mothers. When Nancy and Tiny turned to look, they were stunned to see we were correct. What a shock! The two of them made eye contact with the lady. Immediately, it is evident that she recognized them. Without hesitation, the woman dropped everything she held and ran toward the store exit. Tiny and Nancy put down their purchases, and the four of us followed the woman in hot pursuit. Unfortunately, this woman escaped our chase by jumping on board a passing bus. We all stood on the curb in disbelief at what had happened.

This afternoon's events were the topic of conversation among my parents and their friends for many days to come. This encounter reignited all the heartbreaking, negative emotions Al and Tiny had diligently tried to overcome. Though Tiny said she did not recognize this lady, her dramatic fleeing escape made it obvious that this woman recognized Tiny. If from nowhere else, the assumption was that she had probably seen Tiny's picture in the stolen box containing our family photo albums!

Within days of this startling incident, my spring school break was over. With just three months left in the school year, I boarded a flight to Portland, where I would complete the fifth grade. When the school year was over, that summer was the first time Al and Tiny did not make their annual drive to Portland. After all the financial losses they had gone through, the expenses of a cross-country vacation were not feasible in their budget. Mother and Daddy also decided to divert their vacation funds, knowing their money would be better used to assist my parents further. Without hesitation, Mother and Daddy forfeited their frequent trip to the Midwest. When school was out in June, I packed my things and flew home alone to Chicago.

This summer of 1968 marked the official beginning of my life in our new neighborhood. I still had my two special friends, Stephanie and Jo, in our old neighborhood. Due to the frequency of my travels, I had become accustomed to not seeing them for months. Still, while I was in Portland, we always maintained communication. We wrote plenty of letters, postcards, and an occasional splurge for a ten-cent-a-minute phone call. With this move, even being back in Chicago made these two friends seem so far away. Al and Tiny had been genuinely concerned about how this change of neighborhoods and new friends would affect me. With Al as our designated driver, he and Tiny communicated with the parents of these two friends. They all agreed to allow us to gather occasionally for weekend visits. Tiny and Al felt a degree of importance in my not feeling uprooted completely.

Despite my back-and-forth living, my parents always wanted me to have a balanced childhood. Without a doubt, I know that Al and Tiny never wanted me to feel lonely or alone. Surprisingly, I was not as concerned about the move to a new neighborhood and school change as they were. I was an only child with a lifestyle that made me well accustomed to solitude and change. It would not have been devastating if I did not immediately make new friends. I already shared a loving, established family type of relationship with Al and Nancy's three children. Dorothy (Dot), Gwen, and Clyde Jr. (Butch). As my father did with Clyde (Al) and his brothers, we always referred to one another as cousins. The other plus was that the four children would live in the same duplex, walking to and from school together. For the first time, Al and Tiny could execute their work schedules freely, without the fear of my being at home alone. In those days, coming in and out of the home alone was called a latchkey child. Despite the bleak circumstances that forced this move, there seemed to be a glimmer of hope for a better life.

Although there had been constant change in where I attended school, I remained academically successful. Still, Tiny and Al were concerned that the repeated change of schools was creating an unstable foundation for me. Ultimately, they had no other choice. My original school, Amelia Dunne Hookway Elementary, was fifteen minutes away by car. Due to Al and Tiny's work schedules, I could not commute and continue attending classes there.

Though the new neighborhood would mean my attending a third elementary school, the years spent between Chicago and Portland had already proven my adaptability. Once the summer was over. I enrolled in the sixth grade at Edward Coles Elementary School. Any anxiety that my parents had proved to be unwarranted. It was three blocks from our home in a safe environment. It was not long before I started making new friends at school. The teachers were hands-on and very well-qualified. I completed the sixth through eighth grades at this school without any adversity.

As big as the city of Chicago is, our new neighborhood was surrounded by pleasant, unexpected familiarity. Three sisters, Renee, Carol, and Vera, lived in the building directly across the street from us. Ironically, their family was also from the Altgeld Gardens, where my father had grown up. Renee had been classmates with Al, Nancy, and Al. What a small world!

Additionally, the youngest sister, Vera, was one year older than me. Yes, this family became our immediate connection in our new neighborhood. Every day, Carol and Tiny shared the same bus route to work, forming a forever friendship. Due to the age difference between Vera and her older sisters, she, too, was living life like an only child. We became fast friends, enjoying a loving relationship that continues today.

Vera began with a trip down memory lane during a recent telephone conversation. She started reminiscing about our "good old childhood days" on Crandon Street. The conversation delighted my heart when she spoke about Al. He was always so lighthearted and kind to any of my friends. Vera shared with me that one of her fondest memories was Al fixing breakfast for us on Saturday mornings. She recalled every detail of the menu, which included him making biscuits from scratch. Once complete, he would set the table and call our names. When we arrived, Al would smile and say, "Ladies, please be seated. Your breakfast is served." Al would treat us as if we were adults in a fancy restaurant and he was our waiter. It was one of the many ways that Al went overboard to make me, and my childhood friends, feel extra special! Like Vera, I, too, have fond memories of this time in my early teenage years.

In addition to these sisters, every other house on our block had children my age. Next door was Carol and her three daughters, DeeDee, Cheryl, and Lulu. Carol shared my parent's passion for weekend Bid Whist parties. Shortly after we moved in, another family came to our block. Laura McKenzie-Watts and her family arrived from Mississippi, moving directly across the street. It was a natural growth for our neighborhood as she had ten children. Laura's personality was a fit for the other ladies. After meeting my grandparents, Laura fell so in love with them that she named her next baby Creston. Al and Tiny became friends with almost everyone on the block. It was a united neighborhood where every household looked out for one another.

During the evenings and on the weekends, the adults would go in and out of one another's houses for coffee, gather for card games, and plan block club barbeques. After school and on the weekends, the street would be full of kids playing. There would be a variety of activities simultaneously going on. Our block was covered by bike riding, jumping rope, skating, ball playing, and anything else you can imagine. The winter months were filled with snowball fights, building snowmen, making snow angels, and ice skating. Our new neighborhood proved to be one toward healthy family living. It was filled with people who shared a common goal of togetherness, which included an evident balance of camaraderie and respect for one another. Al and Tiny were once again living their dream. This neighborhood change restored peace and happiness to our family.

———

I have a treasured lifetime memory of a hot July 1968. Chicago is known for its unforgettable summer heat. It was a time when Tiny and Nancy were always looking for a way to entertain their children. This summer, they planned a special surprise outing for their girls. We had no idea where we were going, but we could bring a few friends. After piling up the cars with as many girls as they could, we drove to the famous Regal Theatre. Through the years, we had all accompanied our parents to attend many adult concerts there. As we listened to the music of many of the Motown groups that our parents enjoyed, we joined in with the dancing and singing.

That day, Tiny and Nancy never told us who we would see. Once we arrived, we all realized that this concert was different. We looked at the marquee, and everyone started to squeal. We learned that we were attending our first youth concert. Imagine the excitement and hysteria that followed. Total exhilaration! The concert was titled "The Battle of the Groups," featuring The Jackson Five! Tiny and Nancy could not stop smiling. These were two mothers who never stopped pouring into their children. I can still see the joy on both of their faces!

Another highlight was my Uncle Harold's high school graduation. Neither of my parents had attended a prom, so they decided that Harold's prom would be their treat. I remember my father's excitement as he took the big brother's lead. They needed to rent a tuxedo and even a car. On prom night, Harold and his date gathered in our living room for pictures. They looked quite handsome together, making this a proud night for my parents.

Throughout the years our visits to Montgomery City would also include spending time with Tiny and Uncle Dubs paternal grandfather, William

Shakespeare Anderson (Grandpa Bill). Having lost his wife Stella followed by sons Boone and Wallace in earlier years, Grandpa Bill was the only remaining Anderson family member living in Montgomery City. In his youth, Grandpa Bill had been a local high school principal. He was quite a popular man, well known through the city by all. Sadly, the years of living alone in a large house combined with growing old had caused him to become a miserly, reclusive man.

In 1969, our entire family gathered in Montgomery City for the annual summer picnic. To their surprise, Tiny and Uncle Dub discovered Grandpa Bill's health was rapidly declining. After multiple back-and-forth trips, they convinced their grandfather to leave Montgomery City. Agreeing to take his first trip to Portland, Grandpa Bill relocated to live with Uncle Dub, his wife Evelyn, and their son Steven. Being surrounded by family while receiving quality health care was the intended course of action. In March 1971, our family once again traveled to Montgomery City. At eighty-one years old, we were returning Grandpa Bill to his hometown, where he would be committed to his final resting place.

For the next few years, our lives were pleasantly uneventful. The degree of normalcy was a welcome relief. I had become well-adjusted to the school stability in the new neighborhood. More importantly, Al and Tiny were both working jobs that they deemed economically suitable at the time. I watched the two of them happily go to work every day. There was a constant conversation in the house with an emphasis on their focus on saving money. Their goal was to get themselves into a financial position where they could afford to purchase property of their own. It was a positive time for our family.

Grandma always prepared the holiday dinners. Everyone in the family would gather, filling the house with laughter and love. She was an excellent cook who sought to please everyone's taste buds. Amazingly, she would find the time to prepare everyone's favorite dessert in addition to the meal. Imagine seeing a piano draped with a tablecloth and topped with various sweets. You could find German Chocolate cake, sweet potato pies, banana pudding, lemon, chocolate and cherry tarts, bread pudding, and other mouthwatering treats. We never could figure out how she was able to prepare so much.

"She gets up while it is still night; she prepares food for her family,"
Proverbs 31:15

With my grandmother's guidance, Tiny was able to elevate her cooking skills. Grandma's mouthwatering dressing and gravy were a Thanksgiving highlight. After all these years, I continue to use the same dressing recipe, and it continues to receive compliments.

No matter how smoothly your life appears to be going, things can abruptly change from one day to the next. 1971 brought another devastating blow to our family. Late one evening, Grandma called my father. She advised him that she was waiting for an ambulance to arrive because Grandpa had suffered a heart attack. I remember my dad throwing on his clothes and frantically rushing out the door. Al discovered he had to stop at the gas station first! Even though our house was at least thirty minutes from my grandparents, he still arrived before the ambulance. Apparently, a late-night call to the projects was not alarming! Al immediately proceeded to perform CPR on Grandpa, but it was to no avail. That night, Grandpa made his transition to be with the Lord.

"For you know very well that the day of the Lord will come like a thief in the night."
1 Thessalonians 5:2

Grandpa had never been a drinker, smoker, or party goer. For all appearances, he was a healthy man for his senior age. He had not been ill, so of course, this unexpected loss sent Al and his siblings into a tailspin. Everyone agreed that we did not see this coming. Since this was the first death in the Rosser family, losing Grandpa was extremely hurtful. Ready or not, after over forty years of marriage, Grandma was suddenly a widow. Her comfort became a top priority for her children. In the coming days, weeks, and months, everyone in our family rallied around to help Grandma adapt to this drastic lifestyle change. Fortunately, Grandma was a very strong woman, and Uncle Harold was still living at home. Displaying the grace God would want each of us to have when death crosses our paths, she slowly adjusted.

> *"He will wipe every tear from their eyes. There will be no more death' or mourning or crying or pain, for the old order of things has passed away."*
>
> Revelation 21:4

4

WHAT YOU WON'T DO FOR LOVE

In June 1971, I graduated from the eighth grade. By this time, the environment of gangs and violence on the Chicago streets was becoming concerning. The atmosphere was what my parents considered to be a threat. Al and Tiny were wise enough to know I was naive and vulnerable. Both my safety and my education were of high priority. We sat together for one of our "family table discussions." In the end, we all agreed that, once again, I would spend the bulk of the summer in Portland for Al and Tiny's peace of mind. As the start of my freshman year neared, the three of us had to make an even bigger decision. The question was where I would go to school in September. Like most households, Al and Tiny's work schedules would cause me to go to and from school without either being home. I would be living the life of a latch-key child. This reality was both uncomfortable and unavoidable for Al and Tiny. Ultimately, we all agreed that I would stay in Portland for my first year of high school. This move had both pros and cons. There was a high school within walking distance of my grandparents' home. I already knew some students there, so my years in Portland helped me smoothly transition.

While living in Portland, our family fellowshipped at Bethel AME Church. Family prayer time together was still a big part of our lives. At fourteen, I felt a tug in my heart to get closer to God. I wanted to be more like Jesus the more I went to church. That is when I independently made the meaningful decision to be baptized. Tiny was truly elated! She told me that years before, God had made her realize that planting the seed of his Word in me would not be in vain. I am so glad that Tiny guided me to love the Lord. It was the first time I can remember wanting to be sold out to Christ.

It was not long before we all mutually realized that a year of only seeing each other for holidays and school breaks no longer satisfied our emotional needs. Not being close to one another was becoming increasingly hard on each of us. The three of us realized that I would be out of high school in a few short years. It is our last opportunity to share quality years. As we talked about our future together, we agreed we needed to make a choice. That was if I would continue to stay in Portland or return to Chicago.

Al and Tiny have always placed tremendous value on my life and an immeasurable desire for my success. I was attending Portland's Thomas Jefferson High School. It was the closest school to my grandparents' house in North Portland. I liked the school atmosphere, and I was doing well academically. One of the required subjects was keyboarding. It was an introductory to typing class. Al and Tiny had purchased an electric typewriter for me in the sixth grade. With Tiny as my teacher, I was already an accomplished typist. Instead of taking the class, I was offered a position in the school newspaper with extra-curricular after-school typing assignments in the Guidance Counselor's Office. It was one of my favorite assignments!

Within weeks, Tiny and Al made one of their most sacrificial decisions. Rather than have me return to the uncertainty of teen life in Chicago, they decided to leave their jobs and move temporarily to Portland. Of course, I did not fully comprehend the depth of their decision. At the time, I did not realize I was literally cloaked in their sacrificial love. Every meaningful decision Tiny and Al made was motivated and driven by their love for me. In the coming months, Al and Tiny liquidated all their belongings in preparation to leave Chicago. Much of our furniture was still relatively new, so they decided to upgrade Grandma's house with it. They knew that with hard work, they could purchase something new once we were settled. The experience of all the losses they'd been through had taught them to expect God's best.

Since they each had excellent work backgrounds, it took only a short time after arriving in Portland before they both found suitable employment in their respective fields. Al was a trade mechanic. He took a job in his field at Howard-Cooper Corporation. Tiny had left a banking job with American National Bank in Chicago. Her experience secured her a position with Far West Federal Savings.

Before starting the school year, Tiny and Al met with the guidance counselor about my performance. He quickly said he felt I was enrolled at the wrong school. He suggested that the student environment at Jefferson High School was not the best and that I was not being academically challenged enough. That was all Tiny needed to hear. Jefferson was the only predominantly African American school in Portland. Unfortunately, it was not among the highest academically rated. Within days, I was transferred immediately to Ulysses S. Grant High School. This campus was thirty minutes away by public bus. It didn't take long before I started meeting a few people at this school. Even though I was new to the environment, I was a typical teen lured by everyday teen temptations.

After school and on weekends, I continued socializing with most of my friends from Jefferson High. For some reason, I could not see the importance of being in a school so far away from my neighborhood friends. That is when things started to get dangerous for me. I strayed off course and began making a series of unwise choices. These choices were entirely out of character, and they could potentially become detrimental to my future. Yes, I cut some of my school classes. Because of the fun I thought I was missing, I still felt the lure of being with my former Jefferson High crowd. Yes, I went to parties and movies, which sometimes led me to break my curfew. Yes, yes, yes! I was moving in the wrong direction. Thanks to my own immature decisions at that time, my teen years were not always the best. I had lost my perspective, often operating in a manner that was uncharacteristic of me.

Some young people think their parents are too hard on them. The experiences of my teen years tell me that the presence of a loving, caring parent is irreplaceable. When I look in the rear-view mirror of my life, I can only thank God that I had parents who were committed to no nonsense about my upbringing. For some reason, I thought Al and Tiny would look at my report card grades rather than focusing on my attendance. After all, I was on the honor roll! Oh, how wrong I was. When Tiny became aware of my antics, she was outraged to the degree that I had never seen her! It did not matter to her that my schoolwork remained above average. Cutting school classes for any reason was not acceptable.

"Folly is bound up in the heart of a child, but the rod of discipline will drive it far away."

Proverbs 22:15

When it came to pride, dignity, and doing things decently and in order, Al and Tiny were sticklers. They were not willing to compromise. Tiny told me that I was still her child and that I would have to do things her way.

Immediately, Tiny suggested ways to correct my behavior, which I considered highly drastic measures. She was making plans to take control in what I considered to be an unrealistic initiative-taking manner. She first told me that if I cut one more class, she would have to intervene. Her solution was to quit her job and personally escort me to school every day. Once there, she planned to walk me to each classroom and sit in the hallway during class. As insanely radical as this seemed, I had no doubt she would fulfill her threat. Al was equally disappointed. His job was close to Grant High School. He calmly said that if I did not get it together alone, he would drive me daily to and from school. Even if our schedules conflicted, I would have to go to school early or stay late based on his work schedule. Once again, Al and Tiny were willing to sacrifice their all to stop me from going down the wrong path. They finally settled on having a daily calendar that required each teacher's initials to confirm that I was in class! It was the best thing that could have happened to me. My skipping class days ended abruptly.

While Al and Tiny did not condemn me for my actions, they felt that their full, hands-on action steps would be required to reign me back in! As bad as things were, I still did not realize I was playing with fire. It is a period in my life that I will never forget. It was the first time I could remember Al, Tiny, and I being at odds with one another. While Al is the quieter, calmer disciplinarian, Tiny is highly outspoken. I saw not only my mother's disappointment in my actions but that this situation seemed to cause her some degree of pain. Immediately, I started to re-evaluate my priorities. Taking full responsibility for my actions, I realized nothing was important enough to warrant this type of upset in our family. Fortunately, we have always kept things from festering or carrying over, not even into the next day, since no one is guaranteed another day.

As the evening went on, Tiny and I finally agreed that we had settled our differences. That night, she made a heartfelt declaration to me. No matter what the circumstances, Tiny was always transparent with me. She spoke to me with nothing less than honesty and truth. Because of her struggles, she never tried to sugar coat her past. Tiny reminded me that she had once been a frivolous teenager, adding that some decisions could impact your whole life! She followed that declaration by stating that I was living proof of her young, wayward actions. It was the first time my mother had spoken to me in such a blatant manner.

Tiny said all of this very calmly without raising her voice. She looked at me with her beautiful smile, but her words were overflowing with strength and determination. I sat silently, pondering every Word with focused, undivided attention. The conversation ended with Tiny saying she was my mother, giving her specific responsibilities, rights, and authority. She added that until I became an adult, she would never give up, turn her back, or take her hands off, guiding my potential. By the time the conversation ended, Tiny had made herself crystal clear. I cannot remember when she did not live up to this promise.

Thankfully, my teenage stint of frolicking on the wild side was brief. Through all the rebellion, my schoolwork was never in jeopardy. God had gifted me with the ability to remember most things—especially if it interested me. I have always liked learning, and I studied extremely hard. Even when I cut school, I was competitive enough to keep up with my classmates. I would always have someone tell me what went on in class. If there were a homework assignment, I would complete it. Whether in the evening or on the weekend, I always went above and beyond to ensure I finished my assignments on time. I would voluntarily register for a Saturday or summer school class if the school offered something interesting. Despite my teen antics, I continued to excel academically. Still, I missed many amazing opportunities. My God-given talents were almost forsaken because of my lack of drive and desire.

Before I knew it, I hit another bump in my teen road. Except for Mother, everyone in our family was a cigarette smoker. One day, I was sitting alone in the house and decided to try one. I took a Virginia Slim from Tiny's pack and was sitting in my room, practicing. Tiny came home from work, smelled the smoke, and witnessed my coughing first attempt. Her reaction was something that I did not expect. She asked how long this had been going on. When I told her it was my first attempt, she started to cry. She hugged me and said, "Tracie, please do not smoke." Tiny went on to say that this was one time that she was asking me to do as she said and not as she did, adding that just because she does something does not make it right. With tears in her eyes, Tiny told me that no matter what, she did not want me to be a smoker. Tiny said she felt smoking was unhealthy, unnecessary, and unladylike. I was totally shocked by her comments and puzzled by her reaction. After all, she was a smoker! Still, I did not want to be the cause of another upsetting situation in the family. Instead, I decided to honor her request. To this day, I have never been a smoker. Shortly after this incident, both of my parents stopped smoking.

In June of 1973, I celebrated my sixteenth birthday. To my surprise, Al and Tiny's birthday gift to me was a lime green Ford Pinto. Al had taught me how to drive early, using the empty, open highway roads of our cross-country trips as my driver's training course. At the time, we were still a one-car family. I never dreamed of getting my car before Tiny got hers. Once again, my mother had placed me ahead of herself. Al and Tiny said they did not want me on public transportation anymore. I was so excited! As always, Al filled my car with gas. I realized that without asking, he could always verify how many miles I had driven. In addition, the lime green color stood out. I cannot tell you how often family friends would innocently say, "I saw your car at the mall today, or I passed you at the hamburger stand." Portland is a small city where both Al and Tiny know several people. That lime green car was a definite eye-catcher. They now had a way of subtly verifying many of my comings and goings. I was so glad that I was no longer living frivolously.

That summer, I had my first job experience. Charles Leech, the guidance counselor from Jefferson High School, offered me a paid summer school tutoring position. The position was at a continuation school for high school students who were struggling in the areas of reading, spelling, and math. I jumped at the opportunity to be back among my neighborhood cronies. My first day on the job was a truly memorable event that would last a lifetime. The guidance counselor introduced me to another tutor my age. LaTanya lived in Pasco, Washington, but spent the summer in Portland in his home! He said he felt the two of us had many similarities and many things in common. By the time the summer ended, our friendship was solidified!

LaTanya and I both agree that our meeting was truly meant to be. We made plans to stay connected through a long-distance friendship. For the next few years, we would continue to meet during our summers in Portland or whenever she drove in from Washington. We would write letters or share an occasional long-distance phone call between meetings. As far as I was concerned, this was my most rewarding high school summer! My personality was more positive than it had ever been on the campus of previous high schools. My God-sent sister friend LaTanya and I have spent over fifty years sharing experiences, talking, visiting, supporting, and loving each other. Although most of our lives have been separated by miles in our hearts, we have never been apart!

While I had managed to clean my act up and make it through one year, I was not thrilled about returning to Grant High School in the coming fall semester. I am so glad my story did not end here. After much investigation by Al and Tiny and recommendations from my counselors, I transferred to John Adams High School for my junior year. It was the newest high school in Portland. In addition to general education, Adams offered a curriculum geared toward current events, debates, and humanities. Multiple opportunities for direct experiences outside of the classroom revolutionized my way of thinking. This environment was transformational for me. Attending John Adams High School is where I finally discovered how to pour my extra energy into myself. This school proved to be a perfect fit for me.

As the school year went on, I became a model student. After Christmas vacation, my principal and guidance counselors requested a meeting with Al and Tiny. I could not imagine why because I had been doing everything to the best of my abilities. To our surprise, the meeting had nothing to do with a negative report. Instead, the discussion was that there was a recommendation by teachers and counselors to elevate me to the senior class. The consensus was that I had completed all the courses required for graduation.

They added that keeping me another year would not only be unnecessary but could be unproductive and possibly result in a repeat of my previous behavior. Ultimately, Al and Tiny agreed to the unexpected advancement. I returned to school in January as a senior. We had already taken our school pictures, so they told me to go to the photographer immediately to have a senior picture taken. When they printed the yearbook, my picture was in both the junior and senior class sections. I considered all of this a living testament that God truly is the God of another chance.

> *"For I know the plans I have for you," declares the Lord, "plans to prosper you and not to harm you, plans to give you hope and a future."*
>
> Jeremiah 29:11

He not only redeemed me but advanced me as if the previous tumultuous season of my life had never happened.

As the last six months of the school year continued, there was one surprise after another. Portland is known as the City of Roses. The Rose Festival is one of the biggest annual events in Portland. Each year in June, the city has three weeks of parades, food, and festivities throughout the city and along the Willamette River waterfront. It was the sixty-sixth year of the city's celebration. A larger part of this event involves the student body of each high school nominating several academically qualified candidates to compete for the title of Rose Festival Princess of their school. I had several reasons for never dreaming of being a viable contender for this honor. The primary reason was that I had not grown up as a Portland "hometown girl." After having attended three different high schools, I felt anonymous. I was not known well enough among my peers to become a contender.

To my surprise, I was nominated by my school's student body. It was another unexpected turnaround. Once the school faculty approves a nomination, candidates must draft an essay about themselves. Thanks to my counselors, teachers, and family's encouragement, I mustered the courage to author my essay for entrance into the competition. My essay was accepted, making me the only African American contestant of the five Princess of John Adams High School candidates. The selection was finalized by winning another closed-vote election by the students.

On the beautiful spring coronation afternoon, I stood on the stage before a standing-room-only auditorium. It was unimaginable! To calm myself, I clenched the hand of my escort, classmate, and neighborhood friend Marlon. I looked at the audience in total awe, honored that I was nominated. My heart knew that God had me during my storm. I have always enjoyed reading the Biblical stories of miracles performed by Jesus. Without a doubt, I knew that only He could have made such a miracle out of my mess.

"The Lord does whatever pleases him, in the heavens and on the earth, in the seas and all their depth."

Psalm 135:6

At this point in my life, I began to really understand that merely having a position on this stage was the unearned Favor of God on my life.

Of course, my entire family had taken the day off from work. They were all seated in the auditorium, ready to cheer me on. That day, God gave me the favor of standing before them without the smell of smoke or any traces of soot from the past three years. Being crowned the winner was quite a shock to me but not to Al and Tiny. Talk about two proud parents! They were both over the moon! In all my learning, growing, and rebellion during those high school years, one thing always remained steadfast with me. I knew that Al and Tiny always wanted the best for me. The two of them saw my potential and abilities that I never saw in myself. Because of their unwavering dedication, I have never wanted to disappoint them.

The next few weeks were a fascinating whirlwind of activities. It included after-school and weekend training sessions in public speaking, networking, and more. Once the training was complete, the next two months required daily community service visits to hospitals, senior centers, youth organizations, businesses, and other civic organizations. What a transformational opportunity this was for me. The court consisted of fifteen high school princesses. We were given pageant wardrobes and spent most nights in hotels with chaperons. It was a time of becoming acquainted with one another. They treated us like royalty, dining at the finest restaurants, traveling the city in limousines, and riding on floats in three parades. As we made our way throughout the city, we saw photos of ourselves everywhere we went. The organization proudly displayed our faces at banks, shopping malls, billboards, and posters at businesses. Articles and pictures of our daily events were repeatedly on the front page of the local newspapers. Not a day went by that I did not receive phone calls and congratulations cards from family, friends, neighbors, and every imaginable direction. As I graciously smiled, thanking everyone, I must admit that I was uncomfortable at times.

After the community leaders and members of the Rose Festival judged the entire iconic court, the day came for the Queen's coronation award ceremony. This event was held days after my seventeenth birthday, during the first week of June. As I stood on the stage of Portland's twelve thousand-seat Memorial Coliseum, my participation confirmed that anything is possible with God. Despite my poor choices and self-inflicted mishaps, God was the fixer and the forgiver. While I was unaware, He continued to shower me with benefits that would make me complete in every good thing. I am so grateful that God changed my behaviors and restored my true values. He brought to fruition what He had already designed for this time in my life.

Seeing my achievements delight in Al and Tiny was my biggest victory. Behind the camouflage of my smiles, I sincerely regretted the time I had wasted acting out in school. Undeniably, some of my high school actions had to be a huge disappointment to my parents. On this day, I felt Al and Tiny had a reason to think that what they sacrificed for my high school education—relocating to Portland had not been in vain. While some parents would have reacted to my actions in a much different way, Al and Tiny loved me enough that they never condemned me for any of my shortcomings. Instead, Al lovingly said, "Everyone makes mistakes. We are all human." Hearing Al's words felt like a rainbow after a storm. Tiny was more of an iron fist in a golden glove. She never tried to make a wrong seem right. Her words were, "Once is a mistake, and twice is a habit." When we talked about the pitfalls of life, Al and Tiny never hesitated to say that they wanted my future to be better than theirs. In my immaturity, I never felt that our life was anything less than perfect. As I listened to their comments, I realized that my future would be much different if they had anything to do with it. Al and Tiny were on a mission to ensure their struggles would not repeat themselves.

I returned to my high school campus for the official graduation ceremony in the coming days. My diploma was the final confirmation that I had completed high school in only three years, graduating with honors. It was an accomplishment that still made no sense to me. I realized that God was always for me, even when I was not for myself. He had used my rights and my wrongs in His matchless way. During the months before graduation, my parents and I were caught up in the daily festivities of the Rose Festival. None of us stopped to realize that by skipping my senior year of high school, I had missed some crucial steps toward college preparation. One of the rewards of being crowned a princess was a fully paid one-year scholarship to the school of your choice. When the Rose Festival scholarship committee asked me what school I would be attending, I literally had no idea.

Al, Tiny, and I realized that I had yet to take any college tours, fill out applications, or complete the basic steps for advanced preparation. Suddenly, selecting a college was a significant decision for us. As was our family ritual, a "sit at the table," was when the three of us gathered for a serious conversation. Our first thought was to consider Oregon State and The University of Oregon. They were quickly ruled out because they were both located in cities that were miles away. Attending either of these colleges would require living on campus, which the scholarship did not cover financially. We looked at several community colleges throughout the metropolitan Portland area. While they were a last-minute possibility, we did not stop searching.

After much conversation and prayer, we agreed on what everyone considered to be the safest decision. The campus of Portland State University is located in downtown Portland, twenty minutes from my parent's home. My application was accepted for first-year classes starting in the fall. At that time, I aspired to major in journalism. Since I loved to talk and investigate the details of events, I hoped to become a television news reporter someday. Thanks to this fully paid academic opportunity, our family agreed that I would continue living in Portland for at least one additional year.

"Being confident of this, that he who began a good work in you will carry it on to completion until the day of Christ Jesus."

Philippians 1:6

5

BOOMERANG! JOY AND PAIN

As it turned out, there was another major benefit to Al, Tiny, and me being in Portland. Although many years had passed since Al's first attempt at becoming employed in Portland following his discharge from the military, the degree of racial segregation in the workplace had not changed much. When Al went to the interview, he presented his letter of recommendation from his Chicago employer, International Harvester. One of the questions the interviewer asked was what brought him to Portland. Al explained that he had a daughter in high school and wanted to give her a better educational opportunity. The conversation continued for a while in a friendly and positive manner. When they finished becoming acquainted, the new employer hired Al.

On the first day, Al reported to the workplace, he was the only African American employee in his department. Each day, he would come home and share the events of his day. He said the other workers were not very friendly, greeting him with silent nods and stares. Al is a very pleasant, talkative man. Anyone who knows him would say that he meets no strangers. Of course, this atmosphere made him feel extremely out of place. Al soon realized he was working in a very imperfect company filled with segregation.

Daily, Al sat in isolation while having lunch in the workplace. It was something he had to become accustomed to. Having people watch him as he worked while never helping, repeated scrutiny of his work, questions about where he learned his skills and the ongoing question of why he moved to Portland were frequent confrontations. As a result of this blatant prejudicial environment, Al found himself uncomfortable at work for the next two years. These negative surroundings were an unimaginable cultural difference from his Chicago work environment.

Nevertheless, he did not let these obstacles deter him. Al has never been a quitter. Instead of allowing himself to show any signs of bitterness or intimidation, he held his head high and pushed through. Because of what was personally at stake, Al controlled his emotions. Al was motivated by the fact that he had a family to support.

Despite the obstacles, Al remained true to form as a very diligent worker. As his character had always been, he always accepted growth opportunities. He learned that his employer, Howard Cooper Corporation, offered advanced training in his mechanical field. These classes included taking evening and weekend courses at a trade school. Without hesitation, my father signed up to take every class offered. These courses were scheduled after work and on weekends. The additional hours did not matter to Al. He was open to furthering his knowledge as much as possible. As a result of completing these courses, Al's qualifications advanced, and he became a certified journeyman mechanic. Additionally, expanding his credentials qualified him for a higher pay scale. Besides Al's negative workplace environment, my parents lived an enjoyable life in Portland.

In early January 1973, Al and Tiny attended a friend's housewarming party. By the following day, Tiny started suffering severe abdominal pains. No one could imagine what caused this sudden attack. The day went on, but Tiny had no relief. Finally, it was clear that she needed medical care, and Al took her, and she was admitted. After hours of tests and examinations, the doctors came to speak with us in the waiting room; they had diagnosed her condition as Pancreatitis. To further emphasize the severity of this attack, they added that she was in critical condition! Immediately, her treatment included the insertion of tubes down her nose for days and having her stomach pumped.

Tiny remained hospitalized for the next two weeks, where she spent most of her days in the intensive care unit! Our entire family was shaken. At least one of us was always there, spending night and day at her bedside— family and friends from near and far united in constant prayer. The doctors advised us that her condition was due to the alcoholic drink she had at the party. They went on to ask if Tiny was a heavy drinker, stating that this condition was common among alcoholics. This line of negative assumptive questioning was highly shocking. Tiny was far from being an alcoholic. She did not drink liquor that was deemed hard alcohol, and she only drank socially or on special occasions.

Al said that they had joined in a toast at the party. Tiny's glass contained a sparkling white wine called Asti Spumante. Nevertheless, the doctors added that she should never drink any alcoholic beverage again. Her system could no longer tolerate or digest alcohol. Her doctors bluntly told us that one drink could kill her. As I previously said, Tiny had never been a heavy drinker. After hearing all the potential risks from the doctors, Tiny said, "No problem!" By the time Tiny was released from the hospital, she had lost a lot of weight. Her body was fragile and frail. That life-threatening episode was the last time my mother ever consumed an alcoholic beverage.

As I moved into adulthood, this horrific event was the life lesson that deterred me from having a desire to drink. I did try a few fruity mixed drinks in my early twenties. The results of alcohol consumption proved to be something that I did not really like. My body had a different intolerance in that I would immediately become sleepy. After several random attempts to drink with my friends at social events, I decided that having a drink was not worth missing the party fun. Both the side effects and the taste of alcohol were disagreeable to me. Al and Tiny always told me that it is easier to fit in with the crowd than to stand out. They said I should think for myself and have the courage to be different. When I shared with Tiny that I couldn't handle alcohol, she sealed the deal by reminding me of how sick she had been. She told me always to count the cost of things, adding, "Nobody is going to die for you, so don't let anyone live for you." Once my friends saw that I was not going to drink, I earned the title of being the designated driver.

In less than a year, Tiny suffered another major medical event. She and my grandmother were having a casual conversation when Mother noticed what appeared to be a swelling in Tiny's neck. It was a subtle change, but a mother always knows what her child looks like. Tiny's immediate reaction was to touch her neck. To her surprise, there was a hardness that she had not noticed before. That day, she scheduled an appointment with an Ear, Nose, and Throat doctor. After being examined, the doctor determined that the swelling was an irregular growth referred to as a "goiter" in her thyroid gland. We learned that there are several types of thyroid disease. Tiny had developed the auto-immune Graves Thyroid disease accompanied by

Hyperthyroidism. In addition to the goiter, this condition was causing her to continually lose weight without trying.

In her case, the recommended medical treatment plan was to avoid surgery. Instead, the alternate way of goiter removal was to dissolve it. This method would require having Tiny drink radioactive iodine. Everyone in our family was puzzled and overwhelmed by both the diagnosis and treatment plan. Just hearing the words radioactive iodine sounded so harsh! None of us had ever heard of such a thing. Of course, Tiny was hesitant to submit to this treatment. Before agreeing to undergo what sounded like a highly drastic treatment plan, she went to more than one additional doctor for a second opinion. Unfortunately, the diagnosis and prognosis given by each second opinion doctor were repeatedly the same. Our family was still extremely skeptical regarding this procedure.

A few weeks later, Tiny agreed to go through with the procedure of drinking the radioactive iodine. This potent drink did not take long to dissolve her thyroid gland. After she healed, Tiny would have to take a synthetic thyroid pill for the rest of her life. As her treatment continued, we learned that Thyroid Graves' disease comes with the possible side effect of causing your eyes to protrude. When this change in Tiny's eyes started to take place, my mother's eyes became extremely sensitive to wind. Even during the slightest breeze, such as when seated near a fan, her eyes constantly water and tear up. Although her vision remained perfectly intact, Tiny started wearing "Attitudes," nonprescription clear eyeglasses, and these glasses protected her from the wind and a subtle camouflage of her bulging eyes. This medical event and the irreversible side effects were frightening for our entire family.

Talk about two years of one medical roller-coaster after another! Once again, we really had to lean on prayer. The blessing in all of this was knowing that God always knows what will happen before it happens.

"Dear friend, I pray that you may enjoy good health and that all may go well with you, even as your soul is getting along well."

3 John 1:2

In this move, God had brought Tiny "home" to Portland—surrounded by family before the manifestation of this health crisis. Had she been living in Chicago when these medical issues occurred, things would have been vastly different. Primarily, Tiny would not have received the irreplaceable first-hand healthcare her mother gave her. No matter how horrible a circumstance is, God is always in control! These illnesses caused Tiny to be under the constant care of doctors for the following year.

Shortly after my high school graduation, Al came home from work and angrily shared the details of his conversation with his manager. After working for over two years, the hiring manager unexpectedly approached my father. He said, "Congratulations; I saw your daughter's picture in the newspaper. It looks like you succeeded in doing what you came to Portland to do. Now that she has graduated, I guess there is no longer a reason for you to stay here. Have you decided when you will be leaving Portland?" My father said. He was so stunned by the conversation that he hesitated before simply responding, "Yes, she made her mother and me very proud."

Even after all his accomplishments with this company, Al realized that he was working in a daunting situation. It remained apparent that there was a significant element of racism, and as a result, he was unwanted.

"If it is possible, as far as it depends on you, live at peace with everyone."

Romans 12:18

This damaging form of questioning was the icing on the cake for Al. He knew there would never be a welcoming atmosphere of integration, promotion, or future financial gain for him at that company. Al had had enough of the burden of racism he endured at the hands of his employer. He plainly stated that he would not stay in an unstable environment with no room for growth.

Because moving back to Portland was temporary, we lived in the house with Mother and Daddy. The years had been financially advantageous, but Al was ready to return to a more pleasant lifestyle. It was not long before Al declared that the time had come for our family to stick seriously with the original plan, which was to move back to Chicago eventually. After all our family had been through, I knew Al and Tiny's hearts were still in Chicago. They had given up their entire lives for two years, but it remained evident that Portland was not going to be their home forever. Chicago was the city where the two of them had lived and grown together their entire adult lives.

As the weeks passed, Al became increasingly restless about continuing to work at Howard Cooper. When his boss brought the subject back up, the negative atmosphere continued to cause a great deal of stress for Al. It wasn't long before he started to put plans in motion for him and Tiny to return to Chicago. We celebrated the Fourth of July in Portland. That week, Al made a shocking announcement to Tiny and me, firmly stating that he would call his former employer in Chicago. If there were a vacancy available for him, he would accept it.

Tiny didn't share the same eagerness to return to Chicago. The illnesses she had recently suffered had caused her body to become both physically and emotionally drained. At just thirty-four years old, Tiny's health had become frighteningly unstable. From one illness to another, she was under the constant care of several doctors. It was obvious that continuing to live in Portland with her parents to care for her offered Tiny a sense of security. Tiny reminded Al that she had been blessed to be under the care of an excellent group of doctors. At the very least, she wanted to finish the summer without changing cities and having to find doctors who were unfamiliar with her condition. In addition, she wanted to be in Portland when I started my first days of college.

As the days passed, I witnessed increasing division and animosity between Al and Tiny. The controversy had risen to a level that I had never seen before. Suddenly, our family was in a total state of chaos. It was the first time I could remember my parents not being in one accord. The communication level between Al and Tiny was at an all-time low. Al was determined to return to Chicago as soon as possible. As always, his decisions were fueled by ambition and opportunity. Al felt that since a job opportunity was available now, he had to take advantage of it. Tiny told Al that things were moving too fast for her comfort. They were accustomed to making annual cross-country drives in August. Tiny felt waiting until fall would be a better time to make another major move. Eventually, Tiny poured her heart out to Mother. While there was an apparent lack of compromise between them, Mother stated that she could see both sides. She did not try to influence Tiny's decision in any way. I distinctly remember her saying, "To thine own self be true."

Within days, Al contacted his sister Marilyn in Chicago. He told her he would be moving back to Chicago alone and needed a temporary place to stay. That was something no one in our family ever expected to hear. Marilyn had four children but still had enough room. Of course, she told him he could have a bedroom in her house for as long as he needed it. That is when reality set in with me. Al was going to make this bold move back to Chicago alone. I remember feeling speechless as I watched him load the trunk of his car with his suitcases. It was a tempestuous time in our family.

Early the next morning, Al drove off alone. For the next three days, the phone did not stop ringing. He called long distance from every rest stop. He was enraged that Tiny was not with him. On the other hand, Tiny was incensed that he had been so impatient. The frequency of their phone calls made it evident that this separation had nothing to do with a loss of love. It was fueled by a strong disagreement that led to an emotional battle. Once Al made it to Chicago, he immediately returned to work at International Harvester Tractor Works. At the same time, Tiny was still processing the fact that they were separated for the first time in their marriage because of a disagreement. They continued to talk on the phone every day. It was apparent that neither of them was at ease with this situation. The future stability of their marriage was shaken beyond belief, and Tiny's health was still a significant concern. Daily, Mother tended to her every need, nurturing her as only a mother could. As close as a sister, Nancy flew in from Chicago for a few weeks to help with Tiny's recovery and moral support. As the weeks went on, her health slowly continued to improve.

The fall of 1974 was the start of growth and change for me. In my mind, I constantly reflected on the sometimes harsh reality of the events that had happened to our family during the past three years. While good was abundant during those years, there was also considerable negativity. I could not deny the times that my actions were not pleasing to Al and Tiny. Inevitably,

I became increasingly more aware of the ultimate sacrifices and unselfish decisions they have always made. In moving to Portland, they had literally altered their lives for me. Al and Tiny had given up their home, friends, and, most importantly, their careers. As parents, the two of them had gone far above and beyond what most working-class people would do. They did this to provide what they considered the best educational opportunity for me. Without a doubt, they have both always had my best interest at heart, with a willingness to do anything to help me succeed. To this day, there are no words that can describe my gratitude. Tiny and Al are my personal living examples of unconditional love!

Once Tiny felt stronger, my father suggested Tiny join him in Chicago. He felt they could look for a new place to live and start fresh. Initially, Tiny was still resistant to making this move. I overheard her say that she felt like they were going in circles. It was Christmas before Tiny agreed to return to Chicago. She had final medical exams with all her doctors and obtained referrals for specialists in Chicago. When Tiny left Portland, she stated that she was open to restoration. She felt it was time to move forward, reuniting their marriage. The goal for them both was permanent reconciliation. Anyone could clearly see that their love for one another was still the strongest driving force.

Spending the holidays together in Chicago proved to be beneficial for their relationship. They were able to repair the damage of the past five months. After all the emotional upheaval, this reunion had a favorable outcome. Through the heartache and bitterness, their relationship seemed to have gotten better. It appeared that their old wounds strengthened their marriage. The two of them finally agreed that this breakup had to come to an end. It was time to take back their blessings.

"Therefore what God has joined together, let no one separate."
Mark 10:9

The temporary breakup of their marriage revealed so many things. Now, it was time for the hurt to heal. Through the years, they saw several young couples have stormy relationships that failed. I thank God that my parents' marriage had beaten these odds. Finally, Al and Tiny were together again in what seemed to be one accord.

They were committing to rebuilding their relationship, which required strength on both sides. There was so much involved in starting all over again. They had to focus on the big picture of finding a place to live. Like a Boomerang effect, they remembered all the stumbling blocks that they had overcome in the past. At the time, they were both living with my aunt Marilyn. She told them to take their time and find a neighborhood that they would both be comfortable in. It was not the first time that they had been living in imperfect circumstances. When they started the home search, they faced again deciding what neighborhood they would like to live in.

Al and Tiny decided the time had come for them to purchase a permanent residence. One of the first things they did was to start buying furniture. They wanted to take their time so they would not take the chance to move into an empty house. Suddenly, there was another stumbling block. Al had his mind set on a multi-unit property, but Tiny was totally against the idea. Having lived in apartments for their entire marriage, Tiny said she had experienced enough years of sharing walls and yard space with another family. Her heart longed for their next residence to be a single-family home. My dad saw owning property with multiple units as potential income. The two of them were once again at odds.

Agreeing on the property purchase evolved into a direction without compromise in sight. Instead of coming to a mutual agreement, this resulted in another standoff. When the ups and downs of life present themselves, my parents have always been realists. In most cases, they could talk things out even when they agreed to disagree. Their pattern was to remain flexible as they looked at both the positive and negative possibilities. Facing the decision to purchase a forever home was a significant, high-stakes investment. Fortunately, they were under no time limit to move. Al was still employed with International Harvester, and Tiny was unemployed. They remained in Chicago, living in the house with my aunt Marilyn and her children. While this controversy between Al and Tiny continued, I was still attending school in Portland.

> *"Trust in the LORD with all your heart and lean not on your own understanding. In all your ways submit to him, and he will make your paths straight."*
>
> Proverbs 3:5-6

6

BABY IT'S COLD OUTSIDE

Chicago is known for its extremely wintry weather. Many call it the windy city. January 1975 brought with it another challenge. Tiny started experiencing severe pain in her joints. Once again, she had been blessed to have the right doctors. They proved themselves to be true advocates for her health. After extensive testing, doctors advised Tiny that she was developing a chronic case of what could someday be crippling Arthritis. The doctors suggested that the Chicago winters were too harsh for her to live in. Their shocking medical recommendation was that Tiny should consider moving to a warmer climate.

Instead of being discouraged or complaining, Tiny is always optimistic. She does her best to remain positive about every blow bestowed on her. Tiny has a way of continuing to look forward in expectation of the good things life offers. Instead of allowing her medical status to bring her down, she decided to focus on the things that she could control. I remember Tiny telling me that when the thought "why me" crept into her mind, she pondered the situation for a while. Within minutes, she asked herself, "Why not me." Even faced with such horrific news, Tiny continued to have courage. She stood firm as a warrior and as a survivor.

This devastating diagnosis, along with the relocation advice from the doctors, was stunning, to say the least. At the time, Al and Tiny were still living with my aunt while looking for their own home. Suddenly, they were directed to make a dramatic change to their entire living arrangements. The Lord Almighty has sworn,

> *"Surely as I have planned so it will be, and as I have purposed, so it will happen."*
>
> Isaiah 14:24

The possibility of leaving Chicago was never on Al and Tiny's agenda. The mere thought of making another out-of-state move initially seemed unimaginable. In the following days, they realized that this was something that had to be given the utmost thought and consideration.

Since the diagnosis leaned toward an aversion to cold weather, Tiny took a mental inventory of her lifestyle as well as her family medical history. Tiny quickly concluded that there were a few factors that may have been the cause of her intolerance to the harsh Chicago winter. First and foremost, we had always been a one-car family. Through the years, Tiny had been employed at companies in the city's downtown area. Public transportation was convenient for her to travel to and from work. Wherever we lived, there was always a bus stop located in proximity. Tiny could catch a bus by walking a few blocks from our house. This daily commute caused Tiny to spend many years outside, standing on unsheltered corners. Winter can be unreasonably cold, wet, and windy, even with the warmest clothing.

Al worked as a heavy-duty mechanic for International Harvester while living in our first apartment. The company was so far from our house that public transportation was not a reasonable option. For Al to ride the bus to work would have taken him several additional hours daily. Hence, Al drove to and from work daily in our family car.

Though this was one theory behind the cause of these adverse health issues, it was not etched in stone. An inherited genetic condition was a second possibility for my mother's debilitating health condition. You see, Tiny's paternal grandmother, Stella Anderson, lived in Montgomery City. The winter climate in that city is much like the weather in Chicago. As a result of this illness, Stella passed away at the early age of forty.

No matter what the cause, Tiny now had an incurable medical condition. Day after day, her symptoms were becoming increasingly painful. Even as she battled her pain, Tiny remained as optimistic as possible. After weeks of constant testing, the specialists added Lupus and Fibromyalgia to her list of afflictions. These strange-sounding diseases were foreign to us. After obtaining second opinions, it became apparent that these doctors were accurate in their diagnoses. Anyone could plainly see that Tiny's body could not continue to undergo Chicago's extreme winter climate. It was an unforeseen dilemma that brought much uncertainty to our future.

Suddenly, after spending the bulk of their adult lives in Chicago, this city was no longer their comfort zone. Instead, Al and Tiny had to, once again, make one of the most challenging decisions of their lives. Although they loved living in Chicago, Tiny's health was far more important. It is true that our plans are not God's plans. After having experienced the devastating physical effects of the recent winter on Tiny's body, they decided. It was time for our family to make another move. Al took full responsibility for telling us we were moving forward, so everyone must stay positive. He has always been a man who would honor his vows in sickness and in health. Hence, the big question! Where do we go from here? Of course, prayer was the best thing that they knew how to do. The Bible says,

"Be strong and of good courage; do not be afraid, nor be dismayed, for the Lord your God is with you wherever you go."

John 1:9

That day, Al and Tiny became intentional with making plans for another gigantic move. Tiny had a distant older relative from Missouri, living in Los Angeles for many years. His name was Sylvester. Fondly, we all called him Uncle Syl. Through the years, whenever we drove across the country, we always stopped in California to spend a few days with Uncle Syl, his wife, and his daughter. As encouragement to my parents, he offered us a temporary place to stay. Uncle Syl really wanted our family to make Los Angeles our choice for a new home. Al's maternal Aunt Mary and her family were also long-time southern California residents. Should Los Angeles be the city of choice, we already had a family support group to assist us. It was not exceptionally long before a second relocation option presented itself. Al's lifelong childhood friend Ernest was living in Oakland with his wife and two sons. Ernest immediately joined in the conversation, agreeing that California had many good employment opportunities. He, too, offered our family temporary lodging in his home.

Just like our summer visits to Los Angeles, the Bay Area had always been one of our stopping points on our cross-country drives. During the same time that Mother moved to Portland some of her cousins had migrated to San Francisco and Oakland. In addition, Tiny's paternal great aunt Mary

Jane and her daughter Bunny had been living there for many years. Ironically, at the time of our relocation we realized that Cousin Bunny was living on the same street as Ernest. Al and Tiny spent weeks praying as they continued making careful evaluations of cities throughout the country with warmer climates. By June it was decided that the three of us would move to California since this was a state with which we were already somewhat familiar. The exact city that would be our next home was still yet to be determined.

After finishing my first college year in Portland, I flew immediately to Chicago to assist Al and Tiny with the move. The month of June was busy. Al and Tiny lived at my aunt's house, and I was with Al and Nancy in our old neighborhood. My parents had decided that most of the furnishings they left in storage would not go with us. This move was to be a completely fresh start. Day in and day out, friends and neighbors gathered to say goodbye. Many of them were there to help Tiny as she sorted through the pieces of our life. My mother was utterly composed as she faced deciding what to give away, what to toss out, and what to keep. Within three weeks, Tiny and Al made the final preparations. All the boxes were packed and ready for pick up by the movers. It was the final countdown of family life in Chicago.

On a hot Saturday evening in July 1975, family, friends, neighbors, and co-workers gave my parents a fabulous farewell party. Nancy hosted this special event at her home. For the final time, everyone gathered at our old Crandon Street address. The youth gathered in the backyard while the adults took over the house. I remember it like yesterday. We watched as people arrived dressed in their finest party attire. Tiny wore a beautiful white silk halter-back jumpsuit. She looked stunning! Al was very dapper and handsome in his black and white attire. As always, the two of them looked so undeniably good together! The music was playing, and cameras were flashing throughout the rooms. This party proved to be a bitter-sweet night. Eating, drinking, dancing, laughing, smiling, hugs, and tears filled the atmosphere. No one wanted to say goodbye. The party lasted into the early morning hours. As the guests finally started to leave, I heard Tiny and Al repeatedly saying their infamous welcoming words; "Come visit us anytime; we would love for you to come and visit; you know you are always welcome, and the Door is always Open."

The next day, the moving van arrived to take our belongings to Portland, where they will stay until we have a permanent location. Even at this late moment, Al and Tiny were still undecided as to whether Los Angeles or Oakland would be our new home. At that point, we were once again homeless. As usual, Al and Tiny had an overwhelming degree of confidence. Securing employment was the least of their worries. The only remaining unanswered question was where we were going. Our destination was still a coin toss, to be determined after spending a few weeks in each of these California cities.

During these last weeks, Nancy had been right by Tiny's side day and night. Nancy's middle daughter, Gwen, is one year older than me. Having known each other our entire lives, she and I were also very close. As we prepared to leave, everyone stood outside in the front yard, saying our final goodbyes. When we were about to get in the car, Gwen and I hugged each other. Without saying a word, we both started to cry. Gwen turned to Tiny with tears and said, "I want to go too." Due to our family's many years of a remarkably close relationship, Gwen felt comfortable making this statement. Like a member of our family, Gwen had vacationed with us many times and even spent summers with me at my grandparents' house in

Portland. People who met us assumed we were cousins, and we never told them differently.

Neither Tiny nor Nancy was expecting such an emotional goodbye. The two of them smiled and looked at each other. The decision was a simple conversation. Without hesitation, Nancy knew the door was open for Gwen to go with us. Gwen would spend the remaining summer months with us in California. Everyone continued visiting with the neighbors in front of the house while Gwen rushed inside and packed her suitcase.

Our first stop on this moving trip was in Montgomery City, Missouri. Tiny's grandmother, Momma Minnie, was now a widow for the third time. She was growing older, not in the best of health, and living alone for the first time in her life. Although she had never been to Portland, Tiny and my grandmother convinced her that moving to Portland would be best for all concerned. The benefit of her moving became even more apparent with the realization that Tiny and Al would no longer be a few hours' drive away. Agreeing to move to Portland would mean that Momma Minne would be closer to all of us. It would also put her in the house with my grandparents, where they could easily care for her.

We gathered Momma-Minnie into our car, and the five of us, plus my white toy poodle (Sugar), started our drive to California. Since Momma Minnie had never been on a cross-country drive, my parents planned for several cities along the way. They wanted to make the drive as memorable for her as possible. We drove across the country as if we did not have a care in the world. Al and Tiny did not sense an urgency. Instead, the trip had all the characteristics of being on an adventure. As we headed to our destination, we visited as many of the country's historical landmarks as possible. They wanted Momma-Minnie to see things that she had only heard about.

As usual, Al and Tiny's plans included having their girls in mind. They had prepared a special surprise stop intended just for Gwen and me. We found ourselves spending two days in Las Vegas! Over the years, my parents had been to Las Vegas before, but this was a first for me, Gwen, and, of course, Momma-Minnie. Seeing the crowds of people and the big city lights was amazing! Al and Tiny had made reservations for us to stay at Caesars Palace. At that time, minors were not allowed in the casinos. While Tiny and Al enjoyed the thrill of the city, Gwen and I stayed at the hotel, spending much of our time poolside, with Momma Minnie as our chaperon. Unbeknownst to us, this was not the extent of our surprise. Al and Tiny had pre-purchased tickets for us to see the Jackson 5 at The MGM Grand Hotel. We could not believe it! From our hotel room we could see the MGM across the street. It appeared close, but Vegas blocks are extremely long and deceiving in distance. That evening, the weather was scorching. Rather than have us walk across the street, Al and Tiny put us in a taxi. Gwen and I were two wide-eyed, mesmerized teens. That night, we indeed had the time of our lives!

The next day, we left Las Vegas and headed for Los Angeles. Momma Minnie only knew about California from pictures and postcards. It had been many years since she had seen many of her Missouri relatives and friends who had migrated to the west coast. Being able to rekindle relationships that were only maintained by mail for many years was a delight to her heart. Once the four of us arrived in California, we had no decision about where to live. We spent our first few days in Los Angeles and then on to Oakland.

Both cities were appealing in their own unique ways. The downside of moving to Northern California was the climate. We quickly realized that the temperature could drastically change with the seasons. The whole purpose of this move was to get to a warmer climate because of Tiny's health. Al and Tiny immediately applied for jobs in both cities without limiting themselves. Al had all the confidence, drive, and desire that a man needed to take care of his family. He said the first reasonable employment opportunity that presented itself to him would be the decision maker as to where our new home would be.

When I think back to this time in our lives, it is apparent that every action that summer was faith-based. This move was dependent on Al and Tiny's trust in God. When we left Chicago, the biggest risk was that they did not even have the prospect of jobs! In addition, we had no clear destination or address. Much of the uncertainty that we were facing was reminiscent of their initial move to Chicago so many years before. It was as if history was repeating itself in our lives.

Nevertheless, this move's catalyst centered on sustaining a better future for Tiny's health. Al and Tiny had a clear goal when making this cross-country move.

> *"Truly I tell you, if you have faith as small as a mustard seed, you can say to this mountain, 'Move from here to there,' and it will move. Nothing will be impossible for you."*
>
> Matthew 17:20

Here we were, two adults, two teenagers, an old lady, and my white French poodle, casually driving across the country. We were cruising the highways in my parents' new Cadillac, singing all the latest Motown hits on Al's eight-track car stereo, stopping to see the sights, and taking pictures as if this was a vacation. From the outside looking in, no one would have imagined the reality of our economic status. We headed for an unknown city where jobs, finances, and a permanent residence remained unconfirmed. Still, there was no visible evidence of anxiety or insecurity from Al and Tiny. Once again, they were making a fearless, faith-based move. As we drove from one city to another, we did not doubt that we were heading for a brighter future. The combination of Tiny's opposing health challenges and the unfulfilled Chicago home purchase plans led us to God's greater plan for our lives. Surely, God had his hand on us!

When we left Chicago, my grandparents had been excitedly anticipating our arrival. Al and Tiny advised them of our itinerary details in advance. Mother and Daddy knew all the surprise plans. Since this trip was during the era of pay phones, Tiny was considerate in calling them every night. She wanted to assure them that she was safe and where we were and to share each day's events. After being on the road for an entire month, we finally arrived in Portland. Uncle Dub and his family were all waiting at my grandparent's house, as were Mother's sister, Aunt Jessie, and her grandsons. From the moment we walked in the door, the house was alive with smiles, laughter, and love. That day, Al and Tiny delivered the most touching special gift to Mother. She could not have been more excited than when she embraced the precious cargo we all fondly called Momma-Minnie. After losing her husband, Momma Minnie was delighted to be surrounded by the secure comfort of her daughters, Jessie and Virginia (Mother). Momma Minne lived happily with my grandparents for the next nine years. It was then that her health began to fail. At the age of eighty-six, she peacefully transitioned into Heaven. All of our family journeyed to Montgomery City, where she was laid to rest.

We stayed in Portland for the next two weeks when our cross-country trip ended. It gave all of us a chance to rest and visit with family and friends. The daily events did not differ from our previous summer vacations. Al and Tiny were patiently waiting in hopes of gaining employment in California.

By the end of the second week, Al and Tiny started receiving phone calls from potential employers. These were companies requesting their presence for job interviews in California. Within days, the four of us packed our bags and got back on the road.

Al's first interview was in Los Angeles at Southern Pacific Railroad. He was hired successfully for a mechanical position in the downtown Los Angeles train station. Tiny's first interview was in the northern California Bay San Francisco Bay Area- for a customer service job opening with Continental Airlines. Tiny decided to go to the interview. She wanted the experience of knowing what type of questions they would ask. Her clerical and banking skills were just what they were looking for. Yes, she was hired! Since Al had already secured employment in the Los Angeles Area, Tiny had to decline the position. She explained her moving status to the interviewer, adding that my father had just accepted a position in Los Angeles. The interviewer was very impressed with Tiny's candor. He told her he would transfer her information to Los Angeles, adding that they had no openings then. That day, Continental Airlines added Barbara (Tiny) Rosser's name to the waiting list for a position in Los Angeles.

Al and Tiny accepted the invitation for our family to move in with Uncle Syl' and his wife temporarily. Their house was three blocks east of La Brea Avenue on the west side of Los Angeles. LaBrea Ave. is a major thoroughfare running north and south throughout the city. Using this street as our landmark, it only took a few days to get our bearings to and from his house. Once comfortable, we immediately started driving daily to scour the various neighborhoods. Our goal was to learn our way around as we looked at the different areas for potential homes. If we saw a rental sign in a building of interest, we would make a second drive by at night. Al and Tiny wanted to get a feel for the safety of the areas.

When we arrived in Los Angeles, this strange new city was a blank slate for all of us. We lived the first few weeks with Uncle Syl and his family while we set out to find our new home. The plan was that once we got our place to live, Al would fly back to Portland. Everything we left at my grandparents' house was ready to go. Al and Uncle Dub would rent a U-Haul to drive our furniture and my Pinto to California.

"The path of the righteous is like the morning sun, shining ever brighter till the full light of day."

Proverbs 4:18

7

SUNSHINE BLUE SKIES

As a starting point, Al was comfortable with his railroad position. While working at the railroad, he discovered classes offered at Trade-Technical College. The campus was not exceptionally far from the railroad, so Al enrolled in some evening courses. If my father could find anything to enhance his skills, he was always ready and willing to try. Al was always a hardworking man who never let anything stop him from his "hustle" full of drive and determination. He would even work weekend odd jobs by putting the skills he had acquired as a mechanic, house painter, electrician, air conditioning and refrigeration repairer, and so much more to use.

Tiny and Al told Gwen and me to start driving around looking for apartment vacancies. A two-bedroom, two-bath apartment was what we were searching for. Uncle Syl directed us to several small, quaint family buildings in his west Los Angeles area. He lived in an older neighborhood filled with duplexes. They were all nice, but in our eyes, something was missing. Since Tiny found work near the Los Angeles International Airport, we narrowed our search to the South Bay area, where Al had a childhood friend named Bobby living. In recent years, he and his wife Ramona moved from Chicago along with their children, his sister Roslyn and mother Lorena.

Their daughter Toni and sister Roslyn were close in age to me and Gwen. They were living in Inglewood then, so Gwen and I were already somewhat familiar with that community. We decided to start our apartment search in that area.

As the day went on, we found a for rent sign in front of the Sun Garden apartment building in Inglewood. When we went inside, the manager was kind enough to allow us to tour the model apartment. It was beautiful! She then asked our ages. Gwen and I were eighteen and nineteen at the time. At that point, the manager told us that this building was for adults twenty-one and older. The two of us gasped in disbelief. Shocked by this age requirement, we exited the building having had our short-lived dream deflated. As we walked out of the building, to our surprise Al and Tiny got out of their car. It was amazing that we would find ourselves at the exact same location. This was not only a street, but an area of Inglewood that none of us had ever been to before.

Being the determined, smooth-talking type, Al convinced the property manager that his girls were very responsible and mature. He assured her that there would be no problem with her waiving the building's age requirement. Tiny and Al saw living in this building as a positive starting place for our family.

That day, God blessed us far beyond anything we had ever imagined. He opened the door, allowing Al and Tiny to plant our family in a two-bedroom, two-bathroom poolside unit in the Sun Garden Apartments. This newer building was a huge, three-story, ultra-modern complex complete with many amenities, including a jacuzzi, sauna, recreation room, and tennis court. There was security in the underground parking area, to top it off. Coming from life in the Chicago Inner City, we had never imagined ourselves living in an environment like this. We were accustomed to living in dark, brick buildings. The streets of Chicago were filled with cars showing signs of erosion from the harsh weather.

Contrary to this, no matter how old California cars were, most of them still looked as if they were fresh from the dealership floor. Without a doubt, Al and Tiny had made the right relocation decision. Moving to California was already proving to be a better life!

Immediately after we moved in, I realized they picked this apartment with "their girls" in mind. As always, Tiny wanted our home to be an inviting and comfortable place that I would always want to be. Once again, she was right! This new home was an excellent environment for our family. Within weeks of moving into our apartment, my Chicago childhood friends, Stephanie and Jo, came for a two-week visit. The four of us ventured all over this new city, its suburbs, and beyond. We spent every day driving around in my Ford Pinto, exploring the city's good and bad areas. Some days, we got lost, but we did not care. The goal was to learn our way around. Stephanie had already enrolled for the fall college semester in Chicago. Due to the upcoming start of school, she stuck to the two-week visitation plan.

Jo decided to stay in California longer. Her dad had two siblings living near us with their families. She also had cousins who were just a few years older than us. Jo's two-week visit lasted two years. Gwen, Jo, and I continued to scour the city. We added Roslyn as our fourth person. She had been in the city much longer than us and knew her way around. At one point, Roslyn invited us to a barbeque in her neighborhood. We met her friends, but no lasting relationships came of it. After two years, Jo moved back to Chicago after deciding to start a family with her high school sweetheart.

Our family was only in California for a little while before we all started to meet people. There were various friendly young adults to mingle with right in our building. These relationships instantly helped make our move to Los Angeles much more appealing. I accepted an invitation to a barbeque with two of our new building acquaintances. It was at the home of Gail and her mother, Marcella. Ironically, they lived just a few blocks away from Uncle Syl.' What a wonderful afternoon it was. At the time, I had no way of knowing that Gail and I were destined for a future of true sister-friendship.

Gwen and I were both fascinated by the California lifestyle. We noticed that most of the ladies wore sculptured acrylic nails. Since we were unemployed and not in school, we attended Marinello School of Beauty. Within a few months, the two of us were both licensed manicurists. That was a short-lived fantasy. Al was not about to let fun deter us from enrolling in college classes that he considered more relevant. Gwen's parents felt the same way. Once it was definite that Gwen was staying beyond the summer, her parents, Nancy and Al, flew out separately. They each wanted to see the circumstances for themselves. That 1975 summer vacation turned into Gwen living with us for over two years. Having Gwen with me to discover the unknown areas of Los Angeles gave me a sense of confidence that helped to make my move easier.

Within months of our arrival in California, more people than you can imagine started coming to visit. Of course, Gwen's mom, Nancy, and dad, Al, were among our first visitors. To this day, many of our Chicago friends say our home is their "Winter Retreat." At one point, I remember Tiny looking at the calendar to ensure no overlapping guests. Without a doubt, for the first two years of our life in California, there was an average of one or two guests every other month. Each guest has been unique in their own way. While most were vacationers, some had more specific reasons for coming. Many were even considering relocating to make California their home. One of the first to follow was a childhood friend of my father's named Ed and his wife, Delores. They also moved into the same building. It never really mattered what brought a person to our house. We joked, calling our home "The Rosser's Do Drop Inn." Al and Tiny kept their word to everyone that the door was always open!

By now, I am sure you know that Al and Tiny are both extremely outgoing people. Al has a heart of gold that always shows in his behavior. Tiny is always thinking of others, and she rarely meets strangers. During our first year in California, Tiny contacted another relative. Cousin Ed was her mother Virginia's cousin. While he was much older than Al and Tiny, age did not matter. Ed, his wife Pansy, and my parents formed an immediate bond. We would be at theirs almost every weekend if they were not at our house. Everyone loved to play cards and board games.

Another thing Ed and Al had in common was a love for fishing. Ed's adult sons, Alan and Charleton, still lived in St. Louis with their families. Whether in our city or theirs, our families continue to get together frequently.

It was through this cousin relationship that we gained a new family member. Ed's wife, Pansy, was from a small family. She had one older, widowed aunt named Connie, who had absolutely no other family. As time went on, with Tiny leading the way, we all developed a family-like relationship with Connie. She was the same age as Mother, so during her frequent visits to California, the two of them became great friends.

Everyone in our family has always been interested in high-quality clothing. We made wholesale purchases for years when visiting my godmother in New York. Now, the clothing venture has changed. In addition to their day jobs, Tiny and Al became licensed to make wholesale clothing purchases in the garment districts. With a clothing business idea in mind, they founded AT&T Design Works. Of course, the name was our three initials. Al and

Tiny began traveling to New York to make bulk purchases. Their merchandise consisted solely of silk, linens, wool, and cashmere for both men and women. Al and Tiny never wanted the company to become a brick-and-mortar location. For many years, they sold this merchandise at private homes and small business parties locally and across the country.

During the two years Tiny worked at the Continental Federal Credit Union, many employees from other departments crossed her path. Her outgoing personality caused some people to desire her as their teller of choice. One of these employees was a Ticket Agent named Joy. The two of them eventually met outside of the workplace for lunch. During their socializing, the subject of church came up. Tiny said we had been visiting churches but had not joined a specific congregation. Joy was a member of Crenshaw United Methodist Church. She invited us, and as days off permitted, we became frequent visitors.

There was a second employee who also frequented the credit union. Vernetta worked in the corporate office as an executive secretary. In the same way, Tiny and Vernetta became friends outside of the workplace. Shortly afterward, my mother transferred to the airport, where her new friend Joy was waiting in the wings to assist her with the transition. Not long after this, Continental Airlines' upper management office relocated. Vernetta had to decide whether to move to another city or join the team at LAX. By this time, Tiny had become proficient at her ticket counter position. She encouraged Vernetta to accept the local airport position and paid it forward by assisting her with on-the-job training.

In 1977, Tiny became a ticket agent at Los Angeles International Airport. Due to the varying shifts, she needed her own transportation. Up to this point, she and I were working things out by sharing the use of my Pinto. For the first time in her life, Tiny would have her own car. The credit union had a repossessed car auction, so Al and Tiny decided to see what they offered. They told me to come along to share my opinion. The parking lot was filled with a variety of cars to choose from. A metallic gold-colored Oldsmobile Cutlass on the lot caught our eye. It was spotless, had low mileage, and even had a sunroof top. Al and Tiny discovered that the price was right, and they purchased the car.

That afternoon, Al took the keys to my Pinto and Tiny's new car to check the oil and fill them up with gas. We got to the parking garage the following day, and everyone went their separate ways. That is when they told me that the new car was for me. They said Tiny was only driving to and from work so the car would be in the parking lot all day. On the other hand, I was buzzing around the city. The two of them confirmed that their plan had been for me to have the newer car from the beginning. That is why they had me go to the auction to select the car. I was at a loss for words. Once again, Al and Tiny displayed their selfless love for Tracie first!

We had come to a point where Gwen and I were both employed. She was attending a local Jr. College and working for Diners Card. I studied at the Fashion Institute of Design and Merchandising located in downtown Los Angeles while working as the LAX Marriott Hotel Gift Shop supervisor. That year, Gwen decided to strike out on her own. She moved into her own apartment, fell in love, and started a family. Several years later, the couple took their sons and moved to Chicago. The distance of her relocation was never a disconnect for us. We are in constant communication and visit each other as often as possible. Gwen will always be a part of our family.

Having mastered his trade to the highest level, Al was again looking for a better employment opportunity. Every employment application he submitted was accompanied by documented confirmation of his work ethic, experience, and skills. Within a few weeks of exploring new possibilities Al was successful in gaining a position with Flying Tiger Cargo Airline. This company was located near our home at Los Angeles International Airport. Working at this location provided Al the convenience of no longer having to make the daily commute to downtown Los Angeles.

Al's knowledge made him quite comfortable with his Flying Tiger position, which quickly moved him into the Lead position. He would literally push himself, doing whatever was necessary to make things happen, including working a lot of overtime. Whether it was a local job or flying to cities and even countries as far away as Barranquilla, Columbia, he was willing and ready to use his mechanical skills. Since his managers knew Al was incredibly good at his job, they had total confidence in his abilities.

By this time, Tiny and her friend Liz in Chicago had been friends for over a dozen years. Liz had also left her bank job for employment with the American Airlines™ Reservation Office. The airline benefits allowed the three of us to take many wonderful stateside and International vacations together. Aruba, Jamaica, and Nassau were our favorites. We took Mother and Liz's mother, Helen, one year with us. Neither had ever been outside the United States, making this an extraordinary vacation.

Naturally, Liz became a regular visitor from Chicago, occasionally bringing a friend or coworker. When Liz brought her coworker Carol to visit, she fell in love with California and our apartment building. During this time, AA closed its reservation offices in Chicago. When they returned to Chicago, Carol immediately submitted her job transfer to Los Angeles. Once a transfer position became available, Carol and her husband Billy moved to Los Angeles and into the same apartment building we lived in. The available unit that they rented was right next door to ours.

In the spring of 1978, Carol called me to say that AA was hiring. I cannot tell you how excited I was! My interest in applying for this job was a topic that put Al and Tiny at odds. The three of us gathered for our ritual-istic "family table discussion." It was a major decision that we all needed to agree on. Tiny started the conversation by pointing out that I was twenty years old, and it had become increasingly apparent that I was not serious about college. My mother continued by saying that she had watched me spend the last three years treating school like someone riding a bike: stop and go. Tiny and I had never discussed my school habits before, but as al-ways, she was overtly honest and undeniably correct. There was absolutely nothing I could say in my defense. While good at what I attempted, I had become a "Jill of all trades." In Tiny's opinion, I should go for it if I wanted to work.

Initially, Al was against my dropping out of school. He felt I was young and still had time to decide my future. In his opinion, there were better em-ployment choices. On the other hand, Tiny saw my genuine eagerness, which led her to encourage me to pursue my dreams. After much conversa-tion, Al finally conceded. He told me that taking this job meant making some profound lifestyle changes. I would be making a commitment that included agreeing to grow up and settle down. My parents had always taught me to be independent. Applying for this job would be a significant turning point in my life. That day, Al and Tiny gave me my wings. Now, it was up to me to learn how to fly.

Although I was enrolled at the Fashion Institute of Design and Merchandising, I still applied for the job. I intended to work part-time and continue taking classes. In April 1978, I went in for a group interview with AA. The interviewer was a very pleasant, classy African American lady named Audrey. After the interview and testing, she called the prospective employees into another room one at a time. In the end, there were two of us left sitting. Audrey returned to the room and announced we were the only successful candidates. That day, AA hired Anne and me. Audrey was not only instrumental in my hiring, but she became a mentor. Today she is my friend.

I left the interview to turn in my resignation at the Marriott. I had become close friends with a front desk employee named Elaine. When I went to tell her that I was quitting, she said so am I. Unbelievably, she had also had an interview with AA. We were both hired for the same position. They immediately sent us to Dallas for a month-long training class. While in Texas, Anne, Elaine, and I bonded together. We formed a lasting friendship that we still share today. When I returned from training, there was one slight problem. The personnel department notified me that the job would be full-time, which interfered with my school schedule. I accepted the full-time position in the Beverly Hills reservation office staffed by hundreds of people. The calls we received covered the entire western United States.

I was still friends with James, whom I had met in our apartment building. He and his friends had taken me to the barbeque at his sister Gail's house a few years earlier. When I mentioned my new job to him, he told me AA had hired Gail a few weeks earlier for the same position. The two of us had not seen each other in nearly a year. Within days of starting the job, there was a new hire orientation meeting in which Gail and I recognized one another. From that day forward, our relationship blossomed. Eventually, we arranged for our mothers to meet one another. Marcella and Tiny hit it off immediately. Of course, this led to Gail and her family becoming a forever part of our family. I am happy to say that she and I remain lifetime sister-friends.

Immediately after training, I started meeting many people I enjoyed being with. We would gather after work at our homes or go dancing at the local clubs. I was delighted to have this job filled with people my age and all the great benefits. It was not long before I made another workplace friendship. Sharon (Shay) was a part of the next new hire group. We had not talked inside work but worked the same swing shift. Night after night, we would walk to the parking lot together, finding ourselves driving the same route towards home. One day, we asked each other where we lived. As it turned out, we both lived in Inglewood, less than five minutes away from one another. For the next eleven years, we became carpool partners and confidants. Through the years, we have shared many good times and bad. Our families bonded, and today Shay and I are lifetime sister friends.

I soon realized I had a genuine passion for working at AA. Through this work environment, my social circle has enlarged positively. Even today, I continue to share friendships with the ladies mentioned and many more from my initial airline days, including Samantha, Diane, Teri, Hollis, Joyce, Pat, Kim, Lory, Joanne, Eddie, Patty, Marcita, Shaune, and Toni. Because of my background of being with adults, I did not limit my budding work relationships to my age group. Marian, Martha, and Geneva were all older ladies, and I enjoyed sitting near them at work. Due to their ages, I introduced every one of them to Tiny. As the relationships grew, we discovered that Marian was from the same Chicago neighborhood we once lived in. When Martha learned that Tiny was from Portland, she mentioned having cousins in Portland that she had not seen in years. As the conversation unfolded, they discovered Uncle Dubs's wife (Evelyn) and Martha were estranged first cousins! Another older lady was Veetrice; ironically, she and her husband Beason had attended high school in Chicago with Al. They lived just a few blocks from us in Inglewood. What a small world!

By now, you probably already know that I never returned to school as a full-time student. I would take an occasional class of interest through the years, but not with a serious career goal in mind. Instead, I climbed the customer service ladder, building a career with AA lasting over thirty-four years. I never had any regrets about my decision to leave school. After all, I now had an airline position that I enjoyed, just like my mother! I would say that our family was moving positively into the 1980's. Al was working in his mechanical field for Flying Tiger (which eventually became Federal Express), and Tiny was a ticket agent for Continental Airlines. Far more outgoing than Al or me, this public contact position suited Tiny's personality well.

Our visitors were not only coming for pleasure trips. While serving in the military, Uncle Harold was stationed in San Diego. At one point, he suffered a critical injury. Uncle Harold needed an off-base place to recover after being released from the hospital. Rather than return to Chicago, he came to stay with us in Inglewood. After a few weeks, Harold fully recovered, allowing him to resume his military duties. Harold returned to Chicago after he was discharged, where he started his own family. I gained another cousin when his son Harold was born. Through the years, Harold continues to schedule vacation trips to visit us in California.

Harold was not the only military family member stationed in California. After Harold was discharged, my cousins, John and Willie, joined the Marines and were stationed in San Diego. On any given weekend, one of my cousins would leave the base and drive to our house. Al's sister Marilyn traveled from Chicago to visit my parents and her sons often. In addition, Grandma, Aunt Ivy, and other cousins all made occasional visits from Chicago to sunny California.

Six years had come and gone since we arrived in California when Al and Tiny received a letter from the management company of our apartment building. It was a one-year notice advising the tenants that the property was being converted to condominiums. Before the conversion date, the tenants would need to make the necessary arrangements to purchase their unit, or we would have to move. This notice came as quite a surprise! We all enjoyed the extraordinary times living in the Sun Garden Apartments. Although our unit was quite comfortable, neither of my parents desired to purchase it as our final home. The two of them said that just like God had guided them to this apartment, He would take them to a better place. I can still hear my father saying, "Changing the name to condo will not convince me to buy this apartment."

While driving, a road construction detour in our neighborhood caused Gwen and I to drive roughly ten blocks from our apartment. We saw a house with a for sale sign, so I stopped to get one of the fliers from the sign. When we got out of the car, we noticed the house appeared to have an additional structure behind it. It prompted us to quickly walk to the back of the property, where we found three one-bedroom bungalow units. I heard a whisper in my heart, "This is it!" Gwen and I rushed home with the flier to relay our findings to Al and Tiny.

Our level of excitement caused them to take a drive to see the property immediately. After looking closely, Al and Tiny agreed that this property would work. My parents didn't waste time calling their real estate agent, Annette, who arranged an official property viewing the next day. We all agreed that the inside of the property was sufficient size. Immediately behind the house was the unexpected bonus of a private patio area. This separation between the house and the units was everything Tiny longed for. As we continued the tour, there was a separate second patio area for the tenants to share. All it took was one walk through the property for Al and Tiny to decide. After years of disagreement and strife, their property ownership visions were about to come true. It is true that,

"He has made everything beautiful in its time."

Ecclesiastes 3:11

Before Al and Tiny finalized the property purchase, they hit a stumbling block. Al was planning to finance by using his Veterans Home Loan GI Bill. When the loan officer submitted the paperwork, they were told the maximum loan amount was insufficient to meet the amount needed to qualify for the building purchase. In addition, the bank required six months of mortgage payments after all closing costs were paid in their bank account. Mother was in Portland waiting on pins and needles for the call to hear everything was finalized. When Tiny explained the extra money requirement, Mother did not hesitate to offer her assistance. She would send them some money the next day via the Western Union.

The next phone call Tiny made was to Sherl. She was also waiting to hear that they had closed the deal. When Tiny told her they had to have more money than the down payment, she jumped right in to assist. Since Tiny worked for the airline, Sherl told her to fly to New York the next day for additional funds. She met Tiny and Al at the airport to make the trip quick. Surprisingly, the envelope she gave them contained twice the amount they had discussed! It goes without saying that these two women sincerely wanted our family to have this building. Having never seen the property themselves, they simply loved Al and Tiny and trusted their choice.

That evening, Al and Tiny discussed their financing dilemma with Cousin Ed, Pansie, and her brother John. Without hesitation, both Ed and John spoke up. These men told my father that they had used their GI Bills to purchase their homes, adding that the Government would allow them to use their loans again. They went on to offer their loans to Al to elevate his loan qualification.

"A friend loves at all times, and a brother is born for a time of adversity."

Proverbs 17:17

This unexpected generosity resulted in them telling Al to advise the loan officer that he had two other veterans who were going to partner with him in purchasing the building.

Al and Tiny presented this partner loan idea to their real estate agent Annette. She fully agreed that this would work. Annette made the necessary adjustments to resubmit the paperwork to the lending office. Having John as the additional purchasing partner combined with the extra monies in the bank from Sherl and mother made it possible for the loan to be approved. One year later, Al and Tiny were able to obtain a property Quit Claim Deed. With their signatures this simple transaction permanently removed John's name from the property.

I soon learned Tiny's enthusiasm about this property purchase came with a hidden agenda. I was twenty-five years old and worked for AA for over four years. Tiny's motherly instincts told her it would not be long before I wanted to try living alone. She saw this property as a secure starting point for all of us. I could experience my first taste of independence by living in one of the units while she and Al lived close but separately. There was that open door for Tracie again. While Tiny and I were discussing plans for me to occupy one of the units in the building, we had a heart-to-heart conversation. The topic was reliving all the changes in our lives during the past seven years.

Tiny told me how glad she was that Gwen decided to relocate to California with us, admitting she had concerns about how I would manage the transition alone. She felt our family was headed for life in a strange new city. Tiny considered me extremely outgoing yet overly naive, which she described as vulnerable. Her main concern was that she saw me as her fearless, adventurous eighteen-year-old baby girl. She believed it was God's answer to her unspoken prayers and a blessing in disguise when Gwen decided to join us on moving day. Tiny said she always felt safe in numbers and felt more peaceful whenever another one of "her girls" was with me.

Although I was now a young adult, Tiny's protective mother nature had never wavered. She still hoped that I would never feel lonely or be alone. As usual, Tiny's words stemmed from love, experience, and wisdom. I silently thought of some of the never-told truths about Gwen and me. While we were blindly exploring the party scene in California, there was more than one occasion when we found ourselves in an unsavory atmosphere. One outing that stuck out in my mind was attending a 1978 summer barbeque with Roslyn shortly after being hired by AA. Roslyn was expecting her first child, my Goddaughter, Lakenya, who would be born later that year. Gwen and I befriended some guys at the party. Shortly afterward, I crossed paths with one of the guys in our apartment building. He was visiting his friends Richard and Belinda, who happened to live on the third floor with their two daughters. These guys had been friends since elementary school, and soon, Belinda and I became friends. The four of us developed a friendship of frequent gatherings, and a double-dating relationship ensued.

In 1982, our family moved to the new property. Tiny and Al were in their house, and I had the furthest unit in the back, my very first apartment. Even before we moved in, God's rain of favor kept coming. Our real estate agent, Annette, knew the property had two additional empty units. She asked my parents if they would rent one to her parents and the other to her elderly widowed aunt. Without hesitation, Al and Tiny agreed. By allowing Annette's family to move in, they would not have to undergo the screening process of strangers. It was a comfortable way of easing them into being first-time landlords. Tiny and Al formed solid friendships with Annette and her husband while these lovely senior citizens lived on the property for the rest of their lives. Within weeks, God's favor returned. Al's Chicago friend, Uncle Charlie, an extended family member of ours, had a niece who was relocating to Los Angeles. So, Annette agreed to rent Deborah and her family an apartment in one of her buildings.

As time passed, Ed and Pansy passed away, leaving "Aunt" Connie as the last living member of her entire family. Having shared Connie's company for many years, Tiny decided that our family would not abandon this elderly woman. Once again, the door was opened, and Tiny saw a sincere need to continue their relationship. In addition to holidays and birthdays, Connie became an extension of our family. This relationship led Tiny to talk with me about friendship, using Connie's alone status as her example for my life. The first thing she said was that our extended family is small. She said this woman alone with no siblings, spouse, or children could someday be me. Tiny repeated something she had said to me on many occasions; "to have a friend, you must show yourself as a friend. Always be kind to people because Al and I are not guaranteed to be with you forever. You never know who you might need." These words resonated with me.

For many years, Connie became a full-fledged member of our family. Tiny and Al ensured that Connie was properly cared for, and providing transportation to doctor's appointments, shopping, and anything else. As she grew weaker, Tiny became her unofficial caretaker. Eventually, confusion and dementia found a permanent home in Connie's mind. The diagnosis was a sad reality that we all had to face because the effects of the disease on Connie's mind progressed very rapidly. It truly broke Tiny's heart when it became apparent that Connie no longer recognized her.

"And I will provide a place for my people Israel and will plant them so that they can have a home of their own and no longer be disturbed. Wicked people will not oppress them anymore, as they did at the beginning."

2 Samuel 7:10-11

8

STAND BY ME

Shortly after the first year of moving into my apartment, I got engaged to Donald. He and I had been dating for a few years. Though Al and Tiny knew that I had been dating him, they were still taken aback by my marriage plans, stating they detected a lack of drive in my prospective husband. Their primary observations and objections were that they saw our potential desires for progression in the future as being very different. Since this was something that I could not see, I believed they were making harsh misjudgments.

Although he was much more worldly than me, when Donald was not at work, he lived each day as a cavalier, fun-loving, party guy. My personality was much more conservative, yet I have never discriminated against the company I keep. If I like a person, being with me is no judgment zone. Although I was twenty-six years old, Al and Tiny found my openness to people concerning. Tiny would say, "Pick your people, Tracie, and stop letting people pick you." Al and Tiny always wanted me to live my days surrounded by positive, Godly people. They told me they did not think this man had the necessary character for a stable marriage. We were not equally yoked in their minds, and he did not seem to be a compatible match for their daughter.

Tiny and Al had been the major influence on my values for my entire life. I never had a problem listening to their opinions, but I chose not to consider their wisdom this time. Instead, my stubborn, rebellious mind took over. Without looking toward the future, I focused on the momentary good times we shared. Rather than heeding the advice of Al and Tiny regarding their obvious observations, I became more determined to continue with my plans. Reflecting, I realize that much of my young adult life was on the naive, obstinate edge.

Regarding relationship matters of my heart, I did what I wanted to do. It confirms the truth of the saying that love can be blind! Honestly, I knew that my potential husband did not echo the model of Al or any of the other good men I had grown up with. Instead, I considered everyone an individual, so I would not use anyone else as a measuring stick.

Once Al and Tiny realized my plans were moving forward, their love for me outweighed their instinctive disapproval. They have always loved me enough to stand by me, no matter what. I can still hear my dad say, "Nobody can tell someone who to love." Ultimately, they put their personal feelings aside because they both believe in doing everything decently and in order. The first thing the two of them discussed with me was how much money they were willing to contribute toward the payment of the wedding. I was stunned by their turnaround level of support. The amount they offered to pay was substantially more than I ever expected. They followed this financial offer by suggesting that my fiancé and I could also consider having a much simpler wedding and use the money toward our future. Either way, the amount will still be the same. I knew they had put a lot of thought into this offer when the conversation continued with Al and Tiny using their own wedding day as an example. They reminded me that while they had not had any of the fanfare that goes with a traditional wedding, they were just as married as anyone else.

While I listened to every word they said, their honesty did not deter my already made-up mind. I advised them that I wanted to have a formal wedding. Even if my parents didn't always agree with me, they were always there for me. My parent's disappointment never stripped me of their love. From that day forward, Al and Tiny graciously proceeded in the traditional parental role of helping me plan a beautiful wedding. I did not have close, local friends then, so I opted to have a very small wedding party. Our flower girls were Roslyn's daughter, Lakenya, and Richard and Belinda's daughter, Colette. Joining them were my AA friend Marcita, the maid of honor, and my husband's neighbors Natalie and Yvonne, the bridesmaids. These ladies had lovingly welcomed me into their community by sharing lunches, fashion shows, church, trips, and anything else ladies gather for. Yvonne was a very talented hairdresser who had taken on both Tiny and me as clients. The groomsmen consisted of his friends and a cousin from Las Vegas.

We mailed the invitations, yielding far more confirmations of attendance than I expected. In October 1983, Al walked me down the aisle in front of a host of family, coworkers, neighbors, and friends. As I scanned the crowd, I realized that my side of the chapel was filled with people who loved me enough to come from near and far to share in the occasion. Tiny's cousin Alan (Cousin Ed's son) was very accomplished in photography. He flew in from St. Louis to take the wedding pictures as our gift. Of course, my family members from Portland and Chicago were in attendance. As a result of this day, my aunt Evelyn and coworker Martha reunited in their estranged cousin relationship. I was thankful to have my airline employee benefits. At very little expense, we could take a flight the following day, destined for a honeymoon in Paris. My fairytale wedding seemed to be off to a great start.

Less than six months from my wedding date, Tiny's airline friend Vernetta invited us to her church. Maranatha Community Church was a fresh, new congregation in the making. I recognized two additional familiar faces. Pat and Faye were both members of my church. What a small world! The topic of young Pastor Bill G. Ingram's sermon was "being equally yoked in marriage." I sat silently from the moment he spoke, clinging to his every word. It was as if this sermon was tailor-made for me. I cried in my heart with a wish I had heard this sermon before my marriage. There was a great possibility that this sermon would have led me to make a different decision. When the sermon was over, Tiny and I smiled at each other. We stood in response to the call to join the church without saying a word.

Following that Sunday, I began to evaluate my marriage more seriously. It became vividly apparent that my husband and I were from two vastly different lifestyles. He had been raised as an only child by an elderly uncle and aunt. I never knew his aunt because she passed away shortly before our meeting. Due to his uncle's heavy drinking, he and my husband did not share an ideal relationship. I soon realized that a person's "back story" makes a difference. As a result of the lifestyle that he was raised in, my husband did not appreciate the value of having a close relationship with parents.

That is when I became more aware of the struggling relationship between my husband and my parents. Al and Tiny have always been highly open-hearted, welcoming people. They consistently made above-and-beyond attempts to welcome my husband as a family member on what often seemed to be a one-way street. Given the chance, the two of them are easy to love! No matter how hard they tried, there were occasions when he continued to behave like an outsider. I soon saw some truth in saying that "actions speak louder than words." Being the family girl I am, this indifferent attitude of distance and division was very difficult for me to understand or accept.

During the 1984 California Olympics, I was suddenly hospitalized due to female complications. The timing was poor, as I would be a member of Yvonne's wedding that weekend. After extensive surgery, the doctors advised that I suffered from infertility. The cause was fibroid tumors that had caused scar tissue to block my fallopian tubes. As a result, my body would not bless me with the ability to have biological children. At twenty-seven years old, this news was totally devastating. Talk about shattering my dreams and bursting my bubble! Receiving such unexpected news was a sad, harsh reality for me. As I lay in the hospital bed in prayer, I found strength and comfort in the scripture that says,

"Father, if you are willing, take this cup from me; yet not my will, but yours be done."

Luke 22:42

Once I overcame the initial shock, I realized I had no control over this situation. Instead of having a pity party, I refused to feel like a victim or let myself become bitter. My only choice was to accept God's plans for my life.

Of course, Tiny was right by my side at the hospital. Due to her history of female complications, she fully understood how I felt. As always, Tiny showered me with words of comfort and encouragement, and it is evident that she shared my disappointment. It was a loss for her as well. Tiny never said it, but I realized the opportunity to be a loving grandmother would not happen for her. Together, we prayed the Serenity Prayer, which reads,

"God grant me the Serenity to accept the things I cannot change, Courage to change the things I can, and Wisdom to know the difference."

Afterward, we sat and talked about all the childless women in our lives. It is something that you would not usually think about. When we finally stopped counting, the number of names on the list was daunting. As disappointed as I was about my physical limitations, I continued to trust God. In no time, I became increasingly calm about the diagnosis. I had to accept what I had no control over and believe God still had a promising plan for me.

The year continued with several unexpected changes to Al and Tiny's open-door home. My cousin Willie was a Marine stationed in the San Diego area when an auto accident on the base left him with a devastating, crippling injury. His mother, Marilyn, traveled from Chicago to be by his side. My aunt has always been solidly grounded in God's word, always full of just the right prayers for encouragement in all situations. Due to the severity of Willie's injuries, Marilyn transferred her job with the United States Postal Service to California. Just as Al and Tiny had lived with her in Chicago, she lived with Al and Tiny until she could get established in her home. Marilyn's daughter, Debra, also relocated from Chicago to California once Marilyn settled in her new home.

Crossing into 1985 led to Mother and Daddy's lives being overwhelmed by one life-changing situation after another. The first change was that Mother's sister, Jessie, became increasingly forgetful. As time went on, her memory loss became increasingly more pronounced. After undergoing a series of tests, her diagnosis was Alzheimer's. It was something that no one in our family was familiar with. Suddenly, Mother and Daddy were once again living their lives as caretakers.

Less than a year later, cancer reared its ugly head in our family. Daddy was diagnosed with inoperable throat cancer. The tumor was in a position that eventually limited his ability to swallow. The effects were so severe that a tracheal tube was placed in his throat for breathing, and nutrition was limited to a feeding tube in his stomach. Mother suddenly took on the role of caretaker for two people. Tiny desperately wanted to take some of this load off of her mother. The only way to do this was by extending her days off to fly back and forth to Portland as often as possible. I would travel with her or alternate our trips when my work schedule permitted.

We were blessed when our caretaker support group became a team of four. Tiny's dear sister-friend, Nancy, was unemployed at the time. Nancy had been to Portland on many occasions, loving Mother as family. Once she became aware of the need, she wasted no time flying from Chicago to Portland. Nancy extended her stay for several weeks to help fill the care taking gaps. Her presence in Portland was a load lifter for Tiny and me. For the next four years, I traveled to Portland as often as possible to assist Mother as we helplessly watched Daddy continue to suffer with this horrific medical condition. Upon his passing in 1991, our entire family traveled to Montgomery City, where he was laid to rest.

Following the 1986 celebration of Tiny's forty-sixth birthday, our family was shaken by disappointing health news. While showering, Tiny discovered a lump in her left breast. Of course, she immediately scheduled herself for a mammogram. The results of her exam were that she had Breast Cancer! Once again, this quiet invasion of cancer had found a way to penetrate our family. Although Tiny already had a long list of medical conditions, hearing the words breast cancer came with a different kind of sting. None of us had ever known anyone personally with this dreaded disease.

The diagnosis caused a sudden wave of fear to come over me. I had seen the devastating effects that going through cancer treatments had on Daddy. My prayers led to my negative feelings being short-lived. Knowing this day was coming, God had already sent us a prayer warrior. When the call came in from the doctor, my Aunt Marilyn was already present in the house. Marilyn started by boldly quoting the scripture,

"God has not given us a spirit of fear."

2 Timothy 1:7

We all joined in, repeatedly reciting that prayer and others. By the end of the day, everyone was smiling and praising God. Fear had gone, and faith had taken over. God prepared Tiny and the rest of us for battle!

Her treatment began the following month. The process consisted of a lumpectomy followed by months of radiation therapy. Tiny was physically and emotionally shaken, but you would never have known it. Throughout her entire treatment, my mother remained graceful and composed. Tiny had enough faith to stand on the word of the Lord in all circumstances. Her motto has always been to Celebrate Life! Once she completed the radiation treatment, the doctors told Tiny the survival statistics. They said that if there were no recurrence within five to seven years, she would be classified as a cancer-free survivor. From that day forward, Tiny faithfully continued having her annual mammograms. As the years continued to come and go, we all felt more confident each time we thanked God that she was, in fact, cancer-free.

As if my family did not already have enough to deal with, my marriage began to dissolve. The problems came as furiously as a sudden freight train derailment. To my shock and dismay, I learned that my husband was, unbeknownst to me, using drugs that went beyond marijuana. Suddenly, trust, communication, and everything else it takes to have a successful marriage were gone. This unbelievable problem was a mess that I had insisted on walking into. The repercussions were something that I felt I had to deal with on my own. Although I knew there was no way that God was happy with this lifestyle, I still prayed for a change. For some strange reason, I was reluctant to throw in the towel.

Al, Tiny, and I had always prided ourselves on open communication. As close as we were, I could not bring myself to tell Al and Tiny about this drug abuse situation. Instead, I made the decision that I would weather this storm alone. I later realized that I should have been more open. Trying to carry the entire load on my own was causing me to become stressed beyond my wildest imagination. Over the next two years, my body began to take on one illness after another. These illnesses were combined with extreme emotional fatigue and exhaustion. I stopped at Tiny and Al's house one afternoon for a short after-work visit. Tiny looked at me with a concern that only a mother has. When she told me I looked tired, I told her I did not feel well. Tiny said, "Do not play with your health," adding that she was flattered by the fact that I wanted to be just like her, but not in this way!

In 1988, I went to work on what seemed like a normal day. I was driving home when, without any advance warning, I suddenly went completely blind in my left eye. Rather than continue driving home, I went to the nearest hospital emergency room and transferred to UCLA Jules Stein Eye Clinic. Al, Tiny, and my husband rushed to meet me at the hospital. After an extensive examination, we sat together patiently waiting to hear what the doctors determined was the cause. The initial diagnosis was swelling in the nerves behind my eye. The technical term was Optic Neuritis.

Ironically, the doctor said stress usually causes this condition, and there was no medical treatment. The only cure was to rest and eliminate the stress. He went on to say that if my job was the source of my stress, I needed to change careers. He directed his following comment to Al and Tiny. He said if she has children, you must take them for a while to let her have a break. Finally, he turned to my husband. This doctor bluntly said, "Husband, if you are the source of the stress, you must stop doing whatever you are doing." Donald and I looked at each other without saying a word.

Al asked if the condition might be caused by eight hours of daily computer use at my job. As I listened to this question, my mind was racing. In my heart, I knew my condition was in no way work-related. Still, I sat quietly without telling Al and Tiny anything different. We left UCLA, and I was on medical leave from my job. I was restricted from driving because I had no peripheral vision. In addition, the concern was that there was no way of knowing if I would lose sight of the other eye. In addition, they wanted me to get as much rest as possible. That day, my husband vowed to stop using drugs. In the immediate days and weeks to come, he kept this promise.

After nine weeks of blindness, my 20/20 vision returned just as abruptly as it had left. Unfortunately, my husband's promise of sobriety was short-lived. Within four months, his substance abuse reared its ugly head again. When I became aware of his backsliding, I went blind again! This time, the loss of vision was in my right eye. I decided to go alone to the eye doctor. Once again, he told me I needed to determine my source of stress. For the first time, I admitted the traumatic, personal truth. The doctor showed an overwhelming level of empathy towards me. I will never forget his explanation regarding my condition. He said that when someone says, "You are getting on my nerves, or you are giving me a headache, these words can literally be true." This doctor went on to say that we all have weak nerves or areas of our body that succumb to stress and tension in one way or another. Unfortunately, the chronic stress-induced attacks that I was having were targeting the weak nerve sensor area in my face and primarily behind my eyes. He added that prolonged stress can affect the immune system and cause hormonal imbalances. This explanation of my condition left me feeling totally horrified! At that moment, I decided that I would not allow myself to continue compromising my health by being content to live in this ungodly lifestyle.

All I wanted was to hear a familiar voice of wisdom and reason. Al and Tiny were on a cruise, so I called Mother in Portland. I have always trusted her godly counsel. Whenever we talked, she would deliver food for thought with a kindness that sweetened even the darkest moments. As I poured every detail of my trauma out to her, she quietly listened. I told her that I realized if I continued thinking that my marriage could be saved, I was being delusional. Apologetically, I sadly said that it looked like I would be the first person in our family to get a divorce.

Mother offered a few words of truth at that point, starting with, "Do not base your marriage on the rest of the family. Some of us probably should have gotten a divorce; we just did not have the nerve to do it." She added, "Hard times do not last forever. You must develop a hard shell like a turtle; tuck your head in when things get too rough, but never stop moving forward." This analogy caused me to smile! Then she reminded me that she had been a widow at a very young age and proudly declared herself as living proof that no one ever died from a broken heart.

"The Lord is close to the brokenhearted and saves those who are crushed in spirit."

Psalm 34:18

Mother told me never to let my heart become so hardened that love cannot penetrate it. Her final statement was that based on what I had told her, this sounded like my husband was going to "live fast, die young, and make a pretty corpse." As always, she was a wealth of much-needed support and encouragement with a lighthearted twist. We ended the conversation by praying for God's guidance.

That night, I remembered Al and Tiny's words when they said you will get better results when you "think before you speak." I spent that entire night praying as I pondered how to approach my husband and what I would say. I found myself at a place of peace, admitting that by allowing myself to remain in this relationship, I had become co-dependent. That was something I refused to continue to be. I knew that I was not equipped to help my husband, believing his drug addiction had progressed to a point that required professional assistance. Suddenly, God spoke to my heart, telling me that I was made for more!

The following morning, I decided to take full responsibility. I honestly felt no anger towards Donald regarding my failing health. Blaming him for being himself seemed pointless because I had insisted on entering this relationship of my own free will. Self-preservation was at the forefront of my mind. I was convinced that to live a healthy life, I had to remove myself from our lifestyle. My strong desire to restore my health helped me stand firm in my decision.

> *"Then you will know the truth, and the truth will set you free."*
> John 8:32

I calmly told Donald that we should immediately end our marriage. With an initial amount of surprise, he stated that I was overreacting. I assured him that due to my health, I just could not continue watching him do what, in my opinion, was destroying his life and mine. Although my husband seemed resistant to ending our marriage, that day, we officially separated. Feeling as if a load had been lifted, I was finally free of this toxic relationship.

When Al and Tiny returned from their vacation, I finally opened myself to share the horror of the life I had been living. Without overreacting, they quietly sat as I poured my heart out. Since the two of them had no idea what I was going through, these disturbing details led to a mixture of emotions. First and foremost, they were both appalled! Once they got over the initial shock, Tiny and Al told me they were proud of me for putting my health first, standing my ground, and having the strength to make my own decisions. They felt that recognizing my mistakes and moving forward was even more admirable. Al calmly stated something I had often heard him say: "You do not know someone until you know them." As always, they were full of compassion for me, offering to provide any assistance that I needed. Never once did they say, "We tried to tell you." Instead, they remained true to form by being supportive and encouraging. Once again, my ever-present parents were standing by my side, ready to protect and defend me as if they were my fire extinguishers.

From my early childhood days, Al and Tiny told me to think before I act, cautioning that "thoughts determine actions and choices come with consequences." They also told me to weigh my decisions' possible "what if" outcomes before acting. Tiny's emphasis was that I should always pray for discernment. You know, I had heard all of this before, but admittedly, I did not regularly follow this advice. It took this marital mistake and suffering very drastic consequences to put me back on track. These days, I actively stop and look before I leap. So many disciplines Al and Tiny taught me have become much more valuable.

The experiences of this dysfunctional marriage were not all in vain. Living through a lifestyle of adversity was a reality check for me. Throughout the trials and temptations, one thing I never did was compromise my morals or my values. I thank God for giving me parents who raised me to know the difference between right and wrong. This extremely adverse chapter in my life truly took me through a period of lessons, maturity, and growth. Thanks to the goodness and mercy of God, my story did not end there. This separation and eventual divorce restructured my life aspirations.

"In all this you greatly rejoice, though now for a little while you may have had to suffer grief in all kinds of trials.

Peter 1:6-8

I finally came to myself, realizing that it was time to rise above this misguided life. I vowed to never again settle for what I know is less.

Now, it was time to start thinking about receiving what God had already designed for my life. Praise the Lord for not allowing me to be devoured by my careless decision. Instead, His mercy saved me! While praying the negative away, I focused on reviving my relationship with God. I knew it was more important to live like a Christian than just to say I was. Although much of my young adult life was lived on the naive, stubborn, obstinate edge, I always maintained my personal standards.

"Do not conform to the pattern of this world but be transformed by the renewing of your mind."

Romans 12:2

Despite my failures, our merciful Lord fought my battles for me. The transition began once I took constructive action to pick up my pieces.

My priority was to make some positive changes in my health care. I did not comprehend how broken down and frail my nervous system had become. In addition to my current state of blindness, during the coming weeks, I appeared to have had a stroke. A careful examination by the doctors indicated that my diagnosis was Bell's Palsy. To my dismay, this facial paralysis caused my face to become twisted and my speech slurred. Though the symptoms gradually subsided, the attack left my face with a slight, permanent disfiguration. One eye remains slightly smaller than the other, and my smile has a minimal twist. Six weeks after the episode, I regained 20/20 vision. Ultimately, the doctors concluded that each of these physical exacerbations was stress-related. Of course, that did not surprise me. Since my divorce, the sudden neurological attacks on my facial nerves have never happened again. In addition, I continue to see with almost perfect vision.

January 1989 was the start of another year to remember. In the follow-up treatments of my vision loss, a CAT scan showed evidence of plaque on my brain. After going through a series of tests, I was diagnosed with relapsing-remitting multiple sclerosis (MS). I was stunned and shaken to the core. At the time, the neurologist told me that I had probably had this all my life. He stated that some trauma or stress probably triggered the manifestation of this disease. The prognosis was that there was no cure for this disease. One of the most essential treatment recommendations was to do everything possible to keep my overall health under control. It includes healthy eating, getting lots of rest, and avoiding stress! The doctor explained all the symptoms of MS to me. Our conversation ended with him telling me to listen to my body. That day, I left the doctor's office with a new way of thinking. I vowed to myself to follow every lifestyle instruction he gave me. It included never again letting any situation push me to the point of taking on other people's stressful situations.

> *"It was good for me to be afflicted so that I might learn your decrees."*
>
> Psalm 119:71

Through minimal effort of my own, I survived the 80's. During the coming months, adverse health issues continued to run rampant in our family. For some unexplained reason, Tiny started to experience severe pain and muscle weakness. It was becoming increasingly difficult for her to perform even the most basic tasks. Following a series of extensive medical tests, she was diagnosed with Thoracic Outlet Syndrome. In addition, her other neurological illnesses were all flared up, and three years had come and gone since her cancer treatment. It was as if her immune system was completely shutting down. All the symptoms from every disease she was living with started to manifest themselves with a frenzy. Her doctors were doing everything possible to alleviate her pain. Tiny endured several months of pain and suffering. After continuing to lose time from the job, she realized that the required duties of working at the airport were far too strenuous for her physical limitations. Because of the various number of debilitating illnesses Tiny was battling, her doctors deemed her totally disabled. After taking a long-term sick leave, she still was not feeling well enough to return to work. At age forty-nine, Tiny conceded that she could no longer work. That is when she officially took an unplanned early retirement from Continental Airlines.

The timing could not have been better for Tiny to retire. She was about to experience her first true breast cancer mentoring session. Unfortunately, she would be walking her mother through the details of being a breast cancer patient. I was in Portland with her when Mother got the diagnosis. As we listened to the doctor, I thought, *here we go again.* Since Mother was twenty-two years older than Tiny, we never imagined that she would also be stricken with Breast Cancer. For some strange reason, we all believed that at seventy-one years old, Mother was beyond the age of being at risk. Mother's cancer required her to undergo a radical left breast mastectomy. As traumatic as this treatment was, it became another learning experience for all of us.

The three of us realized that the silent onset of cancer does not discriminate. We all took steps toward becoming more educated on the various stages as well as the different types of Breast Cancer. Everyone agreed that it would be better to know than not to know. Once again, God gave our family peace and strength as we weathered another medical storm together. Mother having breast cancer was now an indication of a possible genetic history. Based on medical recommendations, that is the year that at age thirty-two I had my first mammogram. As the years went on, Tiny continued to find herself in encounters with more and more women with Breast Cancer. It was obvious that her talking about her journey through the disease just seemed to come naturally. Tiny truly had a desire to help and encourage others in any way possible. Her welcoming smile and positive attitude led her to become an unofficial advocate to any other cancer patient that crossed her path. Rather than live her life in despair, Tiny continued to remain hopeful.

"She is clothed with strength and dignity; she can laugh at the days to come."

Proverbs 31:25

Whenever Tiny spoke about her cancer, she always smiled as she said, "I'm still here." Tiny said that battling cancer taught her how to really Celebrate Life.

During this time of testing and trial for Tiny, her long-time Chicago friend Velma (V.K.) decided to take a winter break. She came to California for one month which added much needed daily support and companionship for Tiny. With a few short getaways to northern California and Las Vegas, the trip proved to be rewarding for V.K. as well. We had such a good time together that an annual monthly gathering began for many years to come. Having a personality that loves being around people, as Tiny began to feel better, she started to become restless at home. She learned that there were part-time clerical openings in the warehouse district not far from her house. Tiny was hired with Danza Wine Freight Forwarding Company. It was great for her to get out of the house and mingle with people. Her supervisor was a lady named Nellie, who was in California working on a temporary assignment from France. She was closer to my age, but that was not a barrier for the two of them. Immediately, they bonded, becoming friends both on and off the job. When Tiny learned that Nellie had no relatives in California, she invited her to our house. Eventually Nellie became so comfortable in their relationship that she opened herself to discuss her personal life with Tiny. Their relationship grew to a level as if Tiny were her surrogate mother.

Tiny and Nellie worked together for the next few years until a promotion caused Nellie to move back to France. Tiny decided to leave the company and return to retirement. Prior to departing, Nellie left our entire family an open invitation to visit her. The distance between the two did not end their relationship as they continued to communicate on a regular basis by mail, email and phone. To this day, whenever business brings Nellie to the United States, she arranges her schedule so that she can spend a few days of seclusion at my parent's home.

> *"I will lift my eyes to the mountains -where does my help come from? My help comes from the Lord, the maker of heaven and earth."*
>
> Psalms 121:1-2

Threads
of Love

Celebrating a Life Well Lived

Tiny & AL – Wedding Picture

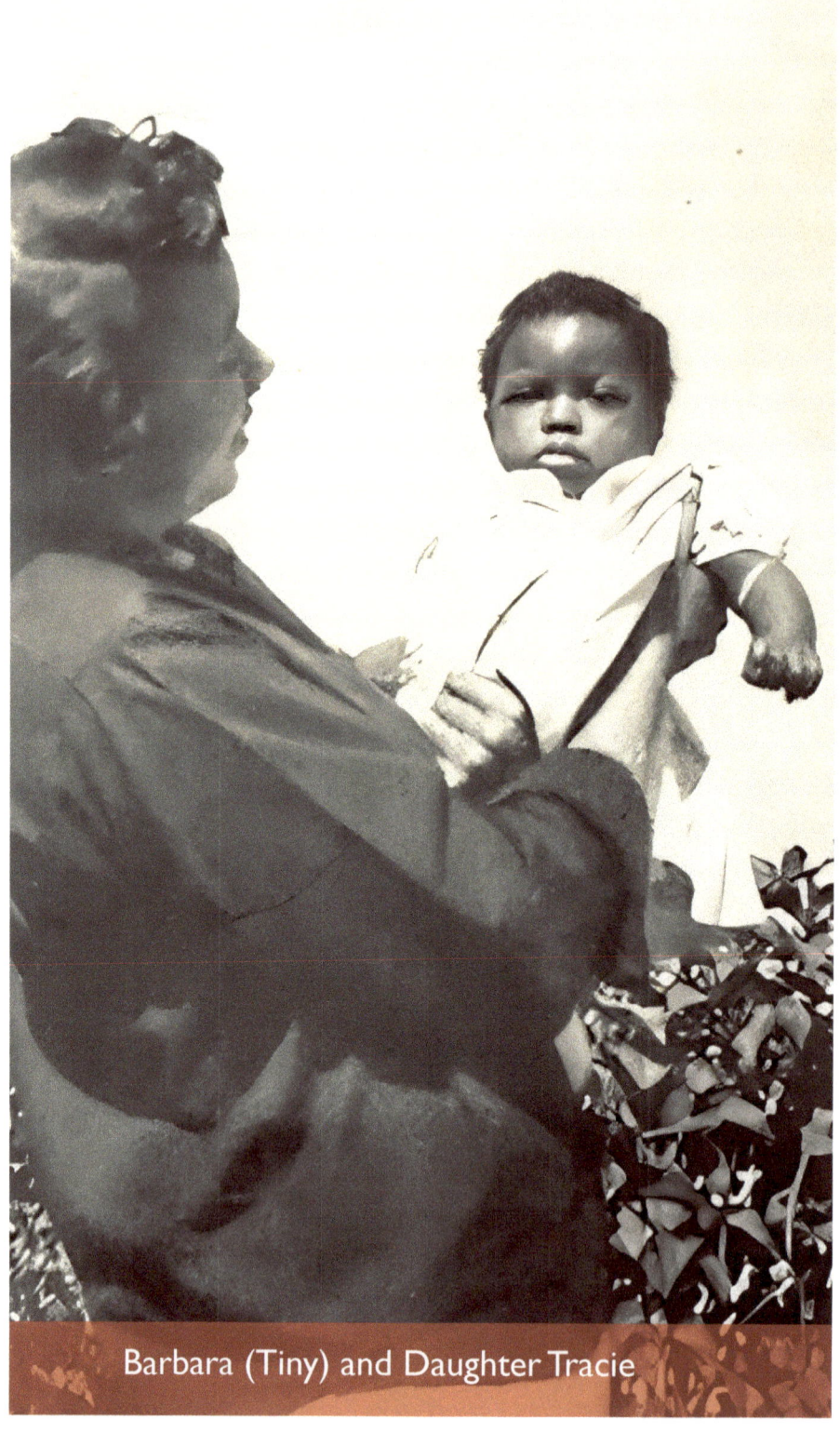

Barbara (Tiny) and Daughter Tracie

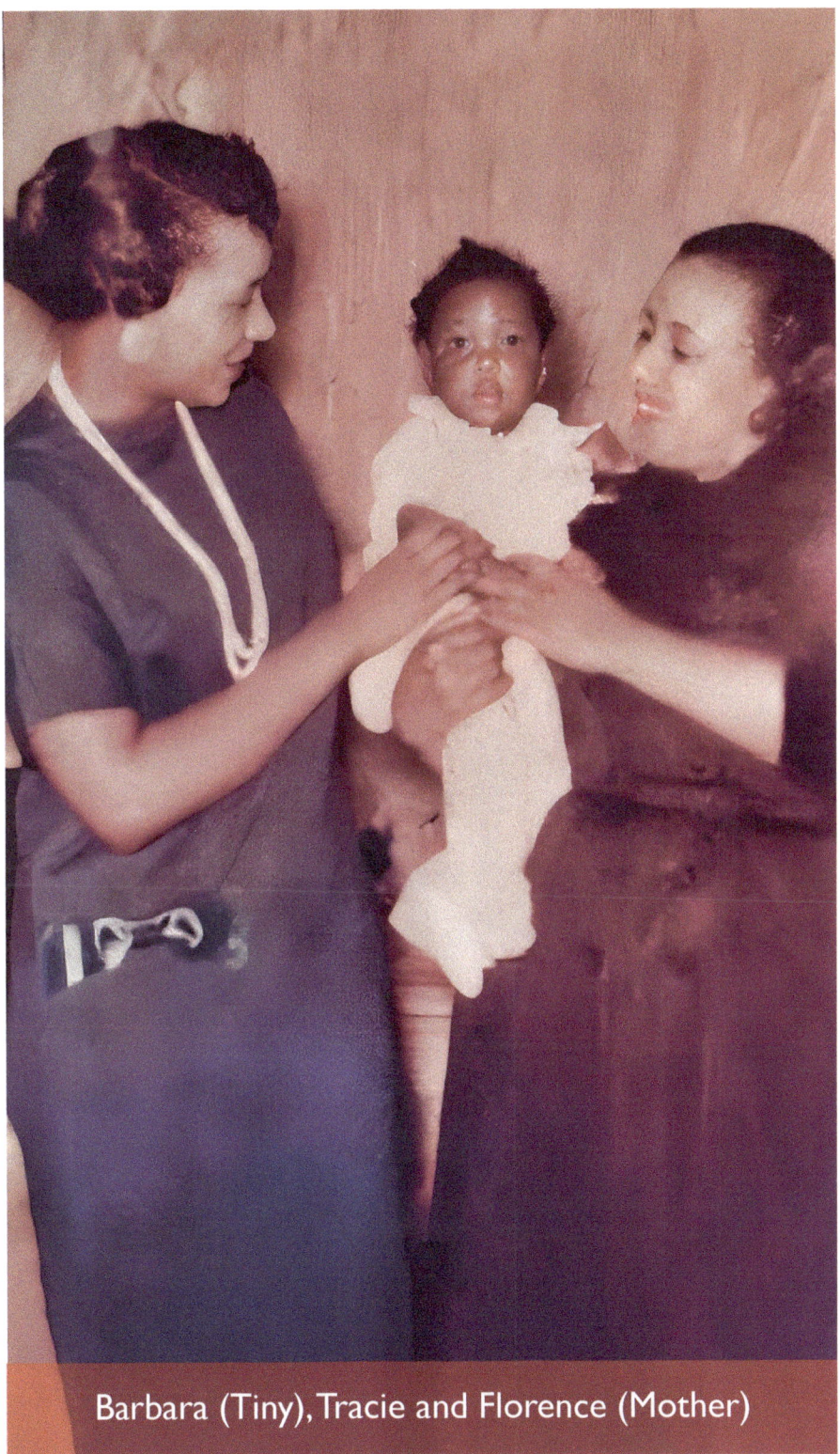

Barbara (Tiny), Tracie and Florence (Mother)

Creston (Daddy) and Tracie

Toddler Tracie

AL, Tracie, and Tiny

William (Grandpa) and Amelia (Grandma) Rosser

AL & Tiny – Chicago Days

Tiny & AL in Chicago

Tiny & Tracie – Chicago Days

Tracie - Portland, Oregon - John Adam's
High School 1974 - Rose Festival Princess

Tracie, Mother, and Tiny

Tracie, AL, and Tiny

others and Daughters

ey're best friends and closest confid

A three strand cord that cannot be broken

Tiny and AL – Can't take my eyes off of you!

New Love! First New Years 1990

Tracie & Kevin – Wedding day

We are one! June 5, 1993

Tracie, Sasha, Kevin Jr. & Kevin in Las Vegas

We are Family! Tiny, AL, Tracie, and Kevin

Kevin Jr., Mother, and Sasha

Tiny & Tracie

Tiny & AL – On the Move

Tiny & AL – Still Getting Their Grove On!

Tiny and AL Living California Life Like it's Golden!

AL – Our Forever California Grill Master

AL & Tiny at Sasha's Graduation

Sasha graduates Cal State with her BA followed a few years later by her Masters Degree in Special Education

Kevin Jr. earns Black Belt

Rookie Firefighter, Kevin Jr., Awarded a Purple Heart
for saving lives in a freeway crash while off duty

Tiny & AL after Tiny's hair loss

After several years of chemotherapy,
Tiny's first day of hair loss

Tracie's 50th Birthday

Kevin and Tracie's Holy Land Jordan River Baptism

Kevin's Children – Victoria (Tori) – Maxwell (Maxi) and Benjamin (Benji)

Sasha's Son – Levi

Tiny

The Star of the Story!

9

LET'S GET IT ON

After eleven years of employment with AA, the company announced that they were closing the Los Angeles west coast reservation office that I worked in. As a result of the high cost of operation in California, the office was being relocated to Tucson, Arizona. When this revelation was presented, I had absolutely no intention of moving to another state. There were two reasons that I would not take the transfer. First of all, my parents were my covering, and they lived in California; but more than this, with all my mother's medical issues, living out of reach would have caused me nothing but stress.

When I discussed my job status with Al and Tiny, their response was not only unexpected, but unbelievable. They both said, "Tracie, we know that you enjoy your job, and you are comfortable working in this company. We see no reason for you to consider giving up your job. Arizona has a warm climate that is suitable for health requirements. If you decide to transfer to another city, we will relocate too! With you gone, we will not have anything holding us to California." This relocation conversation flowed out of my parents' mouths as if we were talking about moving from one room to the next. I was totally stunned by their willingness to uproot themselves for me, once again. This possibility was the most far-fetched thing in my mind.

Once again, Tiny and Al showed that we are one! Their level of love for me is limitless and has no boundaries!

After several weeks, the company advised all the reservation employees that there were a limited number of vacancies available at Los Angeles International Airport. Unfortunately, they did not have enough vacant positions for everyone in our office. Since I wanted to remain in Los Angeles, I immediately applied for one of the Ticket Agent positions. Within the week, I was scheduled to participate in a very competitive group interview which included a test. When I was notified that I had been selected, all I could say was thank you Lord for your Favor. I had no idea what to expect at this new position, but without a doubt, things were changing! The transfer interview had been conducted less than one week before Thanksgiving. Prior to my initial airport reporting date I was given a few uniform pieces. The uniform sizes come in one length that requires tailoring based on your height. Because this was a holiday week, I was unable to find an available tailor to hem my raw edge pants or shorten the dress. This forced me to wear the dress at the longer length. In addition, the LAX administration office was closed so I was unable to get a pass to enter the employee parking lot.

My first day at LAX was November 24, 1989, the day after Thanksgiving. For holiday air travel, that Friday is traditionally referred to as one of the heaviest travel days of the year. My father also had to work that day. Since I did not have access to the employee parking lot, he volunteered to drop me at the front door of the terminal. I had been instructed to find a lead agent in a red coat when I arrived. As I entered the terminal, I recognized a former reservation agent friend named Joanne. She had transferred to the airport earlier and was now a Red Coat Lead Agent. Joanne introduced me to another Lead named Juanita and two supervisors named Eloise and Moe.

After a brief conversation I was given an assignment as a Passenger Service Representative. This was a temporary introductory position that would be my assignment through the holiday season. The basic duties of a PSR are to maintain crowd control in the lobby. In January, I was scheduled for a three-week Ticket Agent training class at the Dallas learning center.

Although I had dealt with the same passengers over the phone, I was amazed by the level of anxiety they presented as they hustled around the terminal. While I mixed in with the crowd of hundreds of passengers, I was approached by a fellow employee. With a big dimple smile, he introduced himself as Skycap Kevin Green. As the morning progressed, Kevin would pause to say something to me each time he entered the lobby. When I took my first break, he showed up in the break room and sat with me. Kevin was full of questions beginning with "was I a new employee or a transfer?" As the conversation continued, he casually made a matter-of-fact statement. "I can tell that you are a young woman. The ladies do not wear their dresses that long around here. It makes you look homely." Surprisingly, I was not offended. Instead, I found myself explaining my tailor situation to this man. Our fifteen-minute break was over, and we went back to our duties.

My scheduled lunch break was two hours later. Within minutes, Kevin walked into the break room and once again sat with me. By this time he had become even bolder with his curious line of questioning. He innocently asked if I was married, and I said no. Then he asked if I was involved with anyone and again, I said no. Of course, I returned the same questions to him. The conversation seemed to be flowing in a normal manner as our getting acquainted questions progressed to the subject of children. That is when I learned that Kevin was the divorced father of a five-year-old daughter and a three-year-old son. His next question was "If you are not involved with anyone, who was that man that you kissed when he dropped you off?"

Suddenly, I felt my defensive energy level rise. I thought to myself, *this grueling line of questioning is becoming very brazen*! I composed myself enough to tell him I needed to make a phone call to check on my mom. As I exited the table, I decided to comply with an answer to his question, stating that the man in the car was my father. During the phone call I told Tiny about the events of the morning. With her usual motherly wit, Tiny chuckled as she said I had been out of the dating game too long. She told me to "put my defenses aside and enjoy the moment, adding that I was much too young to have forgotten what it is like to have a guy hit on me."

By now Kevin and I had determined that we had the same shift—6 a.m. to 2:30 p.m. He just happened to be there early that morning. During the last break of the day, Kevin asked where I lived. When I told him, he said "Since I pass there on my way home, do not have your dad fight this airport traffic again. I parked in the lot right across the street. Please let me drop you off." Initially I was hesitant to accept this offer. As I looked out of the lobby window, all I could see was a sea of stand-still, bumper-to-bumper traffic. My concern heightened when I thought of Al coming from his own long workday to this cluster of roadway chaos. I mentioned Kevin's offer to Juanita, and she said "Kevin is a good guy. Take the ride; I promise you he is harmless." I trusted her judgment, so I accepted his offer as well as his offer to pick me up the next morning. Suddenly, I made a new friend, a break buddy and carpool partner. Though I eventually received a parking pass for the employee lot, I rarely used it.

Within a week Kevin invited me out for our first official date. He took me to Panchos Mexican Restaurant in Manhattan Beach. Once we were seated the waiter smiled as he and Kevin greeted each other by name. This made me aware that he was a regular patron of this establishment. The waiter started by taking our drink orders, to which I said iced tea. He then asked

Kevin if he wanted his usual. At that point, Kevin hesitated, telling me to feel free to have any drink I wanted. My answer was that I did not drink alcohol, but I had no problem with him having a drink. Kevin turned to the waiter and said, "I will have the same thing the lady is drinking." As we ate, the topic of our conversation involved our histories with alcohol. I openly shared my deterrent stemming from my mother's near-death pancreatitis experience. Without any encouragement from me, Kevin said, "I am with you. If you don't drink, neither will I." He proved to be a man of his word and has not had an alcoholic drink since. That day I felt like my emotional relationship setback was a setup for a step up.

Kevin and I continued getting to know each other better during our riding to and from work together. In addition, we shared lots of phone time after work. From our very first meeting, the two of us became inseparable. Although I had never worked at the airport, during my eleven years with the company I had traveled in and out of there quite often. By the time we met, Kevin had been working at the airport for sixteen years. The two of us found it amazing that we had never crossed paths before. Following the breakup of my marriage I vowed that I would take my time before entering another dating relationship. I had matured enough to know that having fun was not my first priority. I really wanted to get to know a person's faith and family values. Eventually, Kevin and I agreed that the timing of our meeting was all a part of Gods plan and destiny for our lives.

The lobby stockroom was located behind the ticket counter escalator. On New Year's Day 1990, Kevin and I found ourselves in this room alone as we collected stock for our departments. Out of the blue, I opened my heart! As if this were a scripted fairy tale, we secretly smiled and flirted before sharing our first kiss. Within days, I flew to Dallas for my three weeks of ticket agent training. The learning center was filled with people from around the globe. Every night after dinner I would call Kevin from a corner phone booth. We would talk for hours until it was time for me to go to bed. When I returned to Los Angeles, I exited the plane to find Kevin waiting at the door. This man was rapidly gaining my admiration. Fortunately I learned that I would be able to maintain my original work schedule. Each day our newly found romance continued to blossom.

Shortly after Valentine's day Kevin asked if I was ready for him to introduce me to his children. I agreed to come to his house later that afternoon. When I arrived, I was greeted by two adorable little tikes standing on the porch. As I got out of the car, they greeted me with a "Hi Tracie." The change of pace that afternoon proved to be so welcoming! I was immediately wrapped in the pleasurable ease of their innocence. They were not at all shy, which I loved. By the time we reached the restaurant they were reaching out to hold my hand and debating as to who would sit next to me. When I saw the smile on Kevin's face, I knew that he was delighted with the way this outing had panned out. This was the first of many get to know you days that I spent with Sasha and Kevin Jr. Our outings would extend to the zoo, Disneyland, Sea World, and other child attractions.

As time went on, I wanted Kevin to meet my parents. Al and Tiny were hosting a barbeque for the 4th of July. Several friends and family members were going to be there. Realizing that Kevin did not know these people, I decided to invite his childhood best friend, Ricky, and a few coworkers to join us. The holiday turned into more than we expected. Kevin's birthday is July 5th. Without telling me, Tiny had ordered a birthday cake for the dessert. We were totally surprised! My mother knew how to open the door and make a positive impact. The day was filled with laughter, smiles and a feeling of togetherness.

Later that summer, I found myself suffering from what I thought was a severe sinus condition. At that time I did not have a primary care physician. I contacted Dr. Omar Stratton who had been referred by Tiny's coworker Vernetta. He had been both my and my mother's OB/GYN since shortly after our arrival in California. Dr. Stratton told me to come in for some lab work. This trip to the doctor's office proved my self-diagnosis to be very wrong. After all of the reproductive negatives that I had been told six years before, I was astonished to learn that I was pregnant! Having performed my nineteen eighty-four myomectomy surgery, which gave him full knowledge of the condition of my reproductive organs, Dr. Stratton was equally stunned. One of his first comments was that this is an extremely high-risk pregnancy. That day he ordered me to be on immediate light duty at work.

In no way did I want Kevin to feel that my pregnancy was an intentional attempt to trap him. The first thing I did was to ask him to sit with me for a very important conversation. When I opened my emotions to bear my female history to Kevin. I told him this pregnancy was my only opportunity to have a child, adding that I would completely understand if he would rather not be involved. He smiled and adamantly said "I am not going anywhere! He went on to say that he was not staying because of the baby." With a hug he added "I love you and we are in this together." Of course, the news of this pregnancy came as quite a shock to Al and Tiny. They too had given up hope of ever becoming biological grandparents. As always, they immediately rose to the occasion showing their full support of me.

Day after day, I found myself on an emotional high like I had never been on before. Kevin seemed to be equally excited, sharing the news with his family and friends. He was exceptionally proud that he had fathered this baby, accomplishing something that the medical profession had declared impossible. As the days went on, Kevin was adamantly devoted to catering to my every whim. The next two months were filled with pizza cravings, weight gain and frequent visits to the doctor. By the third month Dr. Stratton sent me to see a specialist located at Glendale Memorial Hospital. Since I felt perfectly fine, I saw no need to have someone take time off from work to accompany me. Instead, I made the decision to drive to the appointment alone. The examination turned into a grueling day of pushing, probing and ultrasounds. Repeatedly there was the constant question of "are you in pain" and "does this hurt?" By the time the exam was over, the doctors told me that my pregnancy was ectopic. They added that the baby was growing inside the fallopian tube on the verge of rupturing. Because I lived so far away, they did not feel I would make it driving home. I was horrified as I listened to these words in total disbelief.

As if that were not enough, the doctor stated he would have to perform surgery right now! I really could not believe that something this emotionally and physically traumatic was happening to me. This was my first visit to this hospital, and I was suddenly under the care of a doctor and his associates that were total strangers to me. My first phone call was to my trusted Dr. Stratton. As we talked, he told me that my most recent lab work was what prompted him to send me to this doctor. Unfortunately the numbers had stopped climbing at the normal rate. He stated that he totally agreed with their findings, and it would be safer for me to allow him to do the surgery right now. I could not believe my ears! My next call was to Al and Tiny who told me to ask the doctors not to begin the surgery until they arrived. Finally, I called Kevin at work. Without hesitation he said that he was on his way! I was placed in a room waiting until my family arrived. Heartbroken, I turned my thoughts to God. Not in anger, I cried out WHY? Wanting not to add any more stress to my loved ones, I realized that I had to compose myself in prayer to accept once again what I could not change.

"For the time will come when you say, Blessed are the childless women, the wombs that never bore and the breasts that never nursed!"

Luke 23:29

When everyone arrived, we shared a time of prayers, hugs, tears and disappointment, before I was taken into surgery.

When I woke up, the three of them were waiting together. I learned that the procedure had taken much longer than they were initially told, with the doctors adding "we almost lost her." By this time I was completely exhausted. It had been a very long day. Once everyone saw that I was settled in my room, they all left. The goodbyes were sealed with "see your tomorrow." I fell asleep and the next time I opened my eyes Kevin was sitting in the chair. Early the next morning, Tiny called to check on me. When I told her I was talking to Kevin she said, "he's there this early!" to which I responded, he never left. Tiny said that the three of them had walked to the parking lot, got in their cars and exited the lot together. I asked Kevin what time he came back to the hospital. He said when they all left, he drove a few exits, but just could not leave me that far away alone, so he turned around and came back. He had been there all night!

Kevin sat with me until Al and Tiny arrived while I continued to nod. I assured him that I was fine. We could talk on the phone, but it was not necessary for him to keep missing work. I finally convinced him not to come back that day. The next morning I woke up facing the window. As I stared outside, I could hear lots of conversation in the hallway. They were saying things like "oh wow," "I have never seen anything like this" and "who is she?" I finally turned toward the door. To my surprise, there was a beautiful, huge bouquet of one hundred long stem red roses in my room! I realized these flowers from Kevin were what was causing all of the chatter. That afternoon when Kevin came to visit, he told me he chose that bouquet because it had ten roses for each of the ten months since we first met.

During my hospital stay, Dr. Stratton was in constant phone communication with me. He was a very well-respected gentleman, with a comforting bedside manner. Knowing how traumatic this entire event was for me; he went out of his way to be supportive. Dr. Stratton told me that without a doubt I had experienced all that pregnancy has to offer. With a tone of professionalism combined with empathy he went on to say "My dear, it is better to have loved and lost, than never to have loved at all." While this was extremely hard to accept, I knew that God had not given me more than I could handle. His blessings had always outweighed my hardships.

Kevin and I continued dating and getting to know one another better each day. On our one-year Thanksgiving weekend anniversary we went out to Panchos after work. That day he presented me with a beautiful engagement ring. I accepted the ring as a major declaration of our eventual intent to be married. Still, we agreed that we would not rush into marriage. The fact that we both had already been through unsuccessful marriages was a major contributor to our hesitation. I am sure that you have heard the old saying, "Haste makes waste!" Neither of us wanted to see a repeat of our short-lived failed marriages. Although we decided to take our time, we both understood that God is a God of a second chance! In all honesty, I had another major consideration. Kevin was a handsome divorcee that came complete with shared custody of two very young children. I wondered how this marriage would affect the children's acceptance of me. By now I had been through so much heartache which is why I felt the need to proceed with caution.

Of course, I sat down for a very honest, heart to heart "mom talk" conversation. Tiny has never been a person to say something just because it is what you want to hear. If you are bold enough to ask her opinion, you must be prepared that she is bold enough to give it. I knew that I needed her honest wisdom regarding such a major life altering decision. Our conversation started with my being completely transparent to her about all my reservations, doubts, and fears. This was by no means a short conversation. Instead it turned out to be thoughtful, lengthy and very intense conversation. After Tiny heard the direction of my thoughts, she started giving me encouragement. She told me that as my mother she always knew that I had never been a self-indulgent person. She felt that I had all of the qualities necessary to become a good mother by simply being my open, honest, loving self!

Since Tiny had spent time with Sasha and Kevin, she had observed that the three of us seemed to be very comfortable with one another. Tiny believed that they were young enough for us to make a loving bond. As we continued to talk, my mother changed the tone of the conversation. Tiny is a person that does not look at life through rose colored glasses. She has always been very good at putting herself into the other person's shoes, so she presented a scenario to me. Tiny told me that if she and Al had divorced when I was a child, she would have found it hard to submit to my development being influenced by another woman's input. She went on to say that should I decide to get married, I must always stay mindful that my presence is possibly uncomfortable for the children's mother, adding that within reason, I must respect their mother's parental boundaries, even if there are times that we do not agree. As my graceful leader, she told me to do all possible to always stay at peace with everyone. I had already met the children's mother Natashia. To this point, our relationship had been quite cordial.

Tiny's advice did not end with her telling me how to treat everyone else. She also added how she felt I should care for myself as the adult in the relationship. Tiny said that I should never be insecure, intimidated or shortchange myself for not being a biological mother. She told me to be devoted to whatever I was called to do, adding that as a parental figure I should always walk in authority, patience, and compromise. She read a scripture that said,

"To the best of your ability with the help of the Lord, make every effort to confirm your calling and election. For if you do these things, you will never stumble."

2 Peter 1:10

The conversation ended with her telling me that you love the people you invest in, and experience would be my best teacher.

This conversation with Tiny was just the boost of confidence that I needed. It left me with a lot of soul searching, knowing that I had to be true to myself. Obviously, everyone should have dreams for their lives. Still, we must realize that dreams are not etched in stone. Not having children of my own and becoming a stepmother had not been part of my fairytale. By now, I had been through enough heartache to realize that fairytales do not always come true. Often you find yourself making God appointed choices that you never planned or imagined. That is exactly what happened to me.

Kevin and I remained engaged for over two years before setting a wedding date. To some, that probably seems like a long time for two adults over the age of thirty-five to date but neither of us saw it that way. As I fell more in love with Kevin, Sasha and Kevin Jr., God prepared me for a decision that would change my entire life. On Christmas day 1992, Kevin and I announced our plan to spend the next few months preparing for a June wedding. Since it was the second marriage for both of us, neither of us had a desire for a formal church wedding. We agreed to have an official ceremony on a small scale in Las Vegas. Al and Tiny were supportive and ready to assist in any way possible.

The planning began with lots of details to handle. Tiny flew to Las Vegas with me to look at the wedding chapels. Once we selected a chapel that fit my style, we went shopping for my dress and accessories. The two of us were engulfed in finding something unique. We were able to find everything for Tiny, myself and the dresses for my bridal party at Neiman Marcus. When we returned from Las Vegas, Tiny and Al insisted on giving Kevin and me a very sizable check. Though we were more than capable of handling our expenses, my parents would not allow it. Their unexpected generosity more than paid for all our wedding and honeymoon expenses. At thirty-five years old, I was still their baby girl. Just prior to the wedding, my dear friend Yvonne retired as a hairdresser. Fortunately, Tiny and I were able to become clients of another stylist in the same salon. Linda is a lovely Christian woman who would grow to become a forever family friend. She made sure that Tiny, Mother and I looked our best on my wedding day.

On June 5, 1993, God blessed me with the desires of my heart. With Sasha and Kevin Jr. by our side, the four of us were united at the Las Vegas Rivera Hotel Royal Wedding Chapel.

"So they are no longer two, but one flesh. Therefore what God has joined together, let no one separate."

Matthew 19:6 NIV

Sasha and Kevin Jr. had their roles as flower girl and ring bearer. Stephanie flew in from Chicago to be my maid of honor with Kevin's brother, Michael, was our best man. My high school sister LaTanya and her husband Joseph (Joe) were now officially in ministry. She was not only there as my friend, but as a woman of Godly counsel. Already married many years herself, LaTanya arrived filled with words of love, spiritual advice and guidance. As a wedding present, she and Joe gifted us with a beautiful, family bible! Today, it remains one of the precious wedding gifts that we use on a regular basis. My AA sister Marcita had relocated to Philadelphia. She flew in to assist Tiny in making sure everything flowed properly. Juanita surprised us with the addition of heart-shaped candies and a special, scented broom for us to jump.

Our guest list consisted of family, close friends, and co-workers. My co-worker Sandy is a truly talented calligrapher. She agreed to address our invitations as a wedding present. Although we sent out invitations, I did not see the necessity for requesting people to RSVP. Kevin and I did not think there would be very many people willing to travel to Nevada to witness our marriage. How wrong we were! Immediately, upon entering a completely full chapel, I realized that we had underestimated the number of people that would attend. Kevin's grandmother, parents, three siblings and their families were present from Los Angeles. In addition, his lifelong friend Ricky was there. Uncle Dub and Aunt Evelyn were there from Portland along with several other friends and family members from California, Missouri, and across the country. Of course, our special guests included my aunts and cousins from Chicago along with Sherl, Nancy, and Liz. Unfortunately, due to diabetes resulting in the loss of a leg, Grandma was unable to attend the wedding.

There were so many of our AA co-workers, supervisors and managers in attendance that I do not know who was manning LAX that day. Our manager friend Morris (Moe) and his AA wife Linda were there with us. Kevin's skycap friend Illia was there along with his mother Ellen Reese. Having been in and out of her home on many occasions, Ms. Reese was no stranger to Kevin and me. Along with the rest of her children, we would all grow to become dear surrogate family friends. Other coworkers included our former Sun Garden apartment neighbor Carol that had been instrumental in my getting the airline job. In addition to working for the airline, Gail was now an accomplished photographer. She took our photos as a wedding present. In my estimation, this turned out to be a beautiful day where everyone was able to meet and mingle at the reception.

Being an airline employee comes with the benefit of reduced rate travel. We could easily have selected to spend our honeymoon anywhere in the world. Since Kevin had never met my Grandma, I asked if we could postpone a formal honeymoon so that I could visit her. Without hesitation he said that he would love to meet my grandmother and since he had never been to Chicago, that would be a perfect honeymoon for him. We arrived, making the hospital visit to Grandma our first stop. For the rest of the week we enjoyed a wonderful time touring the entire city and visiting with as many family members and friends as possible. By the time the week was over, Kevin thanked me for bringing him to Chicago. He felt that seeing my background helped him to know me better, adding that just like Al and Tiny, everyone made him feel like they had known him forever. Hearing this was a delight to my heart! This would be the first of many trips to Chicago.

Our next trip to Chicago came sooner than expected. Just one month after our marriage, Kevin and I joined Al and Tiny on our first family trip together. After suffering years of diabetes, Grandma passed away. Even under such sad circumstances, Kevin fit perfectly with our family. The four of us were together in Chicago for an entire week. By the time we returned to Los Angeles, I knew that Kevin and my parents were developing a loving bond. We could not wait to introduce the kids to my family history as well as the museums, parks, and other friendly attractions Chicago has to offer. We took future short trips during the winter months so that Sasha and Kevin could experience the snow.

Kevin owned a home prior to our marriage where he had developed his own bachelor style of living. During our engagement, we devoted time towards making upgrades inside and out, so the environment became more suitable for a family. By our wedding date, the only thing I had to do was move myself and my clothes in. I soon made friends with the neighbors directly across the street. Mr. and Mrs. Bush were an older couple. Both teachers and owners of a catering business. They were good, Christian people which opened the door for us to share many prayers and conversations about the Lord. In addition, whenever they were hosting events, (which was often), they were kind enough to make sure our family had a complimentary dinner. I was also able to make a connection with our next-door neighbors. James and Mary Abbey were equally welcoming. Mary and I spent many days talking across the back fence while watering our flowers.

Marriage changed so many things in my life. Suddenly, I not only had a husband, but a daughter and a son.

> "He settles the childless woman in her home as a happy mother of children. Praise the Lord."
>
> Psalms 113:9

Though Al, Tiny, and I did not receive these children in the natural way, they came to us as special blessings from God. My entire family had absolutely no problem adopting Sasha and Kevin Jr. into their hearts. The two of them are all that was needed to fill the empty love wells in the Rosser family. Our hearts and mutual love for one another is confirmation that they are my children and Al and Tiny's grandchildren! Apparently, God had a plan B for all of us. Al always says that "Everything happens for a reason." It was so refreshing for me to see Kevin, Al and Tiny becoming closer to each other. My feelings were confirmed one day as Kevin, and I were riding home from work. During our conversation, Kevin started to tell me about some plans Tiny had. When I asked how he knew, he said "she told me when I called her today." This was puzzling to me. I wondered why he had called my mother. When I asked Tiny about their conversation, she said Kevin calls me often, just to say hi. I had absolutely no idea that the two of them had become this close. This unknown relationship between the two of them truly spoke volumes to me.

In addition to building a comfortable bond with Al and Tiny, Kevin, and my Uncle Dub also developed a special relationship. The two of them discovered that they share a mutual enjoyment for raising dogs. Uncle Dub is a member of a hunting club in Portland. Every October the group travels to eastern Oregon where they hunt elk for two to three weeks. He wasted no time in inviting Kevin to join them. Since Kevin had never been hunting, he decided to fly to Portland and try his hand. The trip was more fun than he imagined. Kevin made quick friends with the other club members, and they were successful in shooting an elk. He had the time of his life, making this an annual guy trip for him!

Before our second anniversary, I found myself pregnant again. After all that my body had been through, I could not understand how this happened. My doctors had assured me that the previous ectopic pregnancy should never have been able to happen. Adding that the use of birth control was not necessary. Kevin and I excitedly welcomed the news. Unfortunately, I miscarried in the third month. This started us on a flurry of discussions with my doctors. After several tests and examinations, they agreed that I was a candidate for Invitro Fertilization. Although this was a very costly procedure, Kevin and I agreed to try. As a potential dad, he was fully involved with administering my shots and ensuring that I rested. Blood tests confirmed that the procedure was successful! Based on my history I was deemed high risk. We opted not to shout about the news until I was further along.

As time went on, an ultrasound confirmed twins. This was amazing! Eventually, my HCG numbers ceased to increase. I miscarried one embryo and weeks later I lost the second one. This was a time that I had to stay calm during the crisis. This was truly an emotionally draining time for me. I found myself in a negative mental state of asking God "why." My family rallied around for support, as did the few friends I had shared the pregnancy with. My Italian co-worker friend Elaine and her husband had transferred to Raleigh. They were the proud parents of three boys. Elaine and I had been friends since before being hired with American and still shared a close relationship. When she learned what happened, without hesitation she said, "I don't mind being pregnant. If you can afford to do another procedure, I'll be a surrogate and carry the baby for you." I was stunned by her selflessness. Had she been local, I probably would have accepted her offer. I invited God into my decision making. The Bible has a word for every situation.

"Each of you should use whatever gift you have received to serve others, as faithful stewards of God's grace in its various forms."

1 Peter4:10

After lots of prayer, I was convinced that maybe the steps I was taking were out of God's will. He had already given me two children. I thanked God for His plan over my life, accepting that it was not my will but His! In our blended family, I was already enjoying all that comes with raising children.

Many of our friends and coworkers have been kind enough to verbally complement Kevin and I regarding our marriage. Some have honestly stated that they do not understand our ability to spend so much of our time together. As I look at other relationships, I realize that not everyone wants to be with their spouse twenty-four hours a day. That has never been a problem for the two of us. It is probably easy because we are best friends who not only love each other but like each other. We have shared many open conversations about the unexpected curves of relationships so neither of us entered into this marriage expecting perfection. Even so, Kevin has proven to be perfect for me.

Having faith in God and devotion to one another continues to help us enjoy our marriage. Although I come from a small family, I grew up observing Al and Tiny's daily interactions with one another. The example of honesty, compassion and understanding that I witnessed is exactly what I always envisioned myself having in a relationship. Kevin has a similarly small family with the same type of stable background with parents whose marriage continues to stand the test of time.

"But those who hope in the Lord will renew their strength. They will soar on wings like eagles; they will run and not grow weary; they will walk and not be faint."

Isaiah 40:31

10

QUIET STORM

Once things started to settle down, Tiny decided to have some of her new friends over to lunch. The ladies had such a wonderful time together that she suggested we form a birthday club. The idea was that we would come together whenever someone had a birthday, celebrating at a restaurant of their choosing. It turned into a successful outing to include Juanita, Marian, Martha, Geneva, and Eloise. Loreda was Eloise's sister living in Buffalo. She would fly in to join us, as well as Eloise's best friend Sharon from Seattle. Sharon invited her cousin Michelle to join the group. She lived here in the Los Angeles area. Michelle and I are the youngest two in the group. Our birthday girl lunches grew to include some events with the guys. We all enjoyed years of holidays and card parties at one another's homes. We added mystery night events and trips to Las Vegas and Laughlin. Through this birthday club, everyone built lasting friendships.

Still, life was not always the way Al and Tiny initially dreamed it would be. Tiny said life happens, while you are making plans. Due to her many afflictions, she often suffers with fatigue and weakness. Because of my own physical limitations, I am able to offer very little help. Having lost Daddy in

1991, Mother would travel from Portland to spend months at a time. Ironically, she was more physically fit than Tiny or me.

"Though one may be overpowered, two can defend themselves. A cord of three strands is not quickly broken."

Ecclesiastes 4:12

Al realized there were some days that Tiny simply could not do even minor things. He also saw the importance of the two of them sharing more quality time together, so my father decided to take an early retirement. Al and Tiny's plans had always been to spend their retirement traveling.

Awareness of breast cancer was becoming a hot topic. In 1994 the Revlon Run/Walk for breast cancer was founded. When I learned about the event, I excitedly wanted to be a part. Due to my debilitating physical illnesses, my stamina was very low. Because I was unable to participate in the walk, I signed up to be a volunteer along with my mother-in-law Mary, sister-in-law Diane and coworker Juanita. The event started at the University of Southern California campus where we manned the tables for signup, tee shirt and water distribution and medals. I truly felt a rewarding sense of contribution, so I continued to volunteer at this event for years to come.

In April 1995 Al officially retired from Federal Express. Since that time, his ongoing commitment has been to ensure the wellbeing of his family. Al's retirement lifestyle is not that of the average man. He actually took on a new job! Grocery shopping, banking, cooking, cleaning, and anything else you can think of. My father does it all, (very well I might add) and never complains once. Along with his unending devotion to my mom, Al is a dedicated father to me and a loving son-in-law to Mother. He will tell anyone that the three of us are his primary focus. Always ready, willing and available, Al is the solid rock in our entire family! He refers to us as "his God given assignment." Seeing Al work so tirelessly at our beck and call is sometimes overwhelming. We all look forward to the times he decides to take a moment away from home for himself. This is the time that he can enjoy some of his favorite simple pleasures such as bowling, fishing, and going to the casino! In addition, Tiny and Al were able to occasionally continue their lifestyle of entertaining and traveling. Whenever Tiny was feeling up to a trip, they were gone. Eventually, Kevin and I even started planning to travel with them. The four of us always take at least one yearly vacation together.

During the coming years, in 1997 Alzheimer's took its toll on Mother's sister, Jessie. When we returned from laying her to rest in Missouri, Tiny and Al had a vacancy in their building. It was actually in the same unit that I originally lived in. Tiny saw this as a perfect opportunity to have her mother leave Portland and move to California. Just a few months shy of her seventy-ninth birthday, Mother was living alone, a widow for the second time. While Mother was still healthy and independent, there were some downfalls. Foremost was the fact that she lived in a fairly large home, with a laundry room in the basement. Tiny and I often had visions of her falling on the stairs or becoming ill alone in her home. Her agreement to join us in California would surely ease our minds. For once in her life, Mother would experience the role reversal of having someone available to take care of her. I was really excited about the possibility of her being in California so that the three of us could share her remaining quality years.

The truth is that Mother enjoys our company as much as we do hers. With very little coaxing, she agreed that if her home sold in a timely manner, she would make the move. Tiny immediately called one of her friends in Portland. Earline was a lifelong family friend and a very prominent realtor in the city. She immediately set things in motion. Obviously, God agreed. At the very first open house, Mother received a buyer with a full price offer. None of us could have been happier! When Mother arrived California, she was still very physically active. Without hesitation she was willing to be on the move with Tiny and me. At least once a week, the three of us would go to church and to the shopping malls.

Unfortunately, it was not very long before her physical condition changed. In 1999, Mother had to have surgery for a knee replacement. During her stay in rehabilitation, she shared a room with a fellow patient. Maryann Smith is a single, Christian woman that is young enough to be her daughter. That did not stop the two of them from developing a fast friendship. Each time we visited, we would find the two of them laughing or engrossed in a movie. When Mother was released from the hospital, they exchanged phone numbers. It was not very long before Maryann came to Mother's house for her first visit.

As time went on, our entire family became very fond of Maryann. One day, we were all together when Maryann was visiting Mother. I was there to take Tiny and Al to the airport. At that point, Maryann made a comment to Tiny about our travel patterns. She had noticed that the four of us never traveled together. Tiny advised her that none of us were comfortable leaving Mother alone in California. Because of her age, we preferred that one of us was available at all times. Tiny went on to explain that since we were such a small family, the four of us could not be gone at the same time.

At that moment, Maryann made the most heartening gesture. She told Tiny that, if Mother would agree, she would be honored to come and stay with her at any time. Wow! It happened again. We witnessed another unplanned incident of God sending a beautiful blessing into our lives. Tiny and I smiled at each other as we both said "Favor." When Tiny discussed this possibility with Mother, she was in full agreement. Before long, Tiny took

Maryann up on her offer. She stayed two days with Mother while the four of us went to San Diego. When we returned Mother said that the arrangement was perfect. Moving forward, we had no hesitation about making travel plans. Anytime the four of us wanted to travel together, we knew that Mother was in good hands with Maryann.

Through the years several of Al and Tiny's friends from Chicago, Indiana, Detroit and Portland had relocated to Las Vegas. Since Vegas is a short driving distance from California, my parents found themselves visiting these friends on a regular basis. Many had settled in the new suburb community of Summerlin, Nevada. Bobbi had come from Chicago and her cousin Jean had moved from Chicago to Los Angeles and now to Las Vegas. Because Jean was a realtor, she immediately started trying to entice Al and Tiny to follow her move. Whenever they were in Las Vegas, Jean took them to see available real estate. Al and Tiny found the property to be not only very appealing but more than affordable. Add to that the card parties, music, dancing, and fun they always had with their group of lively friends. Suddenly, the thought of another major move slowly started to become a possibility.

Tiny came to me for a one-on-one discussion about moving. She shared the love that had grown in her heart for Kevin and her admiration of our marriage. As she talked her face lit up with a smile when she said that God had answered her prayers. Tiny told me she had noticed a similarity in Al and Kevin. She laughed about the way they both say the same thing in two different ways. Al always says, "everything happens for a reason" and Kevin always says, "nothing just happens." Tiny went on to say that, in Kevin, she sees a devoted and trustworthy man with many admirable qualities. She actually went as far as to compare some of Kevin's attributes to those of my dad. What a compliment! Tiny and I were having this conversation during the 2000 New Year's holiday season, just a few months before Kevin and I would celebrate our seventh wedding anniversary.

This was not the first time Tiny told me that she believed I had made the right choice with this marriage. What she did not realize is that, even though I made a wrong choice in the past, her marriage has always been my measuring stick. It remains a mystery to me how my first decision took me so far off track. When it comes to relationships, Al and Tiny are the first to say that their marriage has not been perfect. My question was, are any marriages perfect? Tiny and Al both agree that their marriage continues to work because they have mastered the art of give and take. I know my feelings are probably a little bit prejudiced but all anyone has to do is spend a little time with them to realize that they are truly Best Friends!

Of course, no move would be made without the three of us having a "family table discussion." Everyone, including Mother, agreed to Al and Tiny making the move. The plan was to purchase a home large enough for Mother to have mother-in-law quarters in the home with them. Kevin and I had been happily married for seven years so I was completely comfortable with the possibility of them moving. After all, we would be able to drive to each other's house within four hours. The plan was that Al and Tiny would rent their Los Angeles house out and buy a new home in Las Vegas. Should they have a change of heart, they would still have a California home to come back to. Everyone's opinion mattered when it came to Al and Tiny picking a house, so a date was set when we would all drive to Vegas.

The day before we were to leave, I was at work when I suddenly found myself having trouble breathing. It was severe enough that I went to the medical department to get checked by the company doctor. They examined me and decided that my symptoms indicated a possible heart attack. Kevin and I worked the same shift, so he and my friend, Shay were right there with me. The company had me transported by ambulance to the nearest hospital emergency room. My initial thoughts were total denial, believing the company doctor was mistaken. I could not possibly have had a heart attack. After all, I was only forty-two years old!

While we were in the ambulance, Kevin called Tiny so that she and Al could meet us at the emergency room. The hospital doctors put me through an extensive round of tests. Praise God, it was not a heart attack! At the time, there were several wildfires burning in Southern California. The test results determined that I was having a reaction to breathing the soot. The irony of this event is that I had not been anywhere near the actual fire zone. I worked and lived at least 50 miles from where the fires were burning. Still, fierce winds caused the air quality to be poor throughout the entire region. This was a frightening event for my entire family.

Immediately, Al and Tiny brought their plans for moving to Las Vegas to a screeching halt! For days, their conversation was consumed by "what if's." They decided that four hours away was too far to live. More than that, they said that being together as a family was more important than any friends or fun. I did not see the need for them to change their moving plans. This illness was obviously nothing major. I jokingly called the events of that day a "fake" heart attack. No matter how I tried to convince them to continue with their relocation plans, my words were futile. Both Al and Tiny's minds were made up. Any thoughts they had of moving to Las Vegas were definitely off.

Talk about love and selfless sacrifice! Tiny and Al have always lived, every day of my life, believing that God put parents here to nurture and protect their children . . . Forever! Anytime I have, even a hint of a need, I know without a doubt, Tiny and Al will come to the rescue. Obviously, in the parent department, I got the cream of the crop. Tiny and Al's decision was firm that moving to Las Vegas was no longer an option for them. As time went on, the two of them continued making their occasional visits to Las Vegas as well as enjoying other trips. When they were at home, we all enjoyed our happy, California lifestyle . . . together.

A few weeks later, the minister at our mid-week Bible study announced that he would be having a baptismal ceremony for anyone that was interested. Both Tiny and Al believed that they had been baptized as young children. Because neither of them had clear memories of the events, they decided that they wanted to do it again. On Saturday, April 15, 2000, we all went to church where I witnessed my parents being baptized together. They left the church excitedly telling everyone about what they had done. The next two years were pleasantly uneventful.

Since the beginning of her cancer battle, Tiny truly believed there could be nothing more physically or mentally devastating. Unfortunately, that was not to be the case. What none of us knew was that her greatest challenge was yet to come. In April 2002, I accompanied Tiny to a doctors' appointment. She had been experiencing ongoing stomach discomfort, so her doctor scheduled her to have a scan of her abdomen. After the scan was complete, the doctor gave Tiny the results. The diagnosis was more than we ever dreamed or imagined. The scan detected a massive tumor attached to her liver and bile ducts!

Within days a biopsy was performed. The results caused the condition to become even more complicated and devastating. The diagnosis confirmed that the tumor was indeed cancer. However, it was not Liver Cancer. Instead, it was the fourth stage of Metastatic Breast Cancer growing on her liver! How could this be? As a family, we were all completely stunned! To add to our horror, this cancerous mass was positioned in an area that made it completely inoperable. Our initial reaction was that there must be a mistake. For seventeen years Tiny had lived with the notion that she was safe! This sense of security was based on the initial lumpectomy surgeon specifically saying that if Tiny survived more than seven years without a recurrence, she was cancer free!

At this point I had a growing need to learn more about metastatic breast cancer. I started reading every medical book possible. To my dismay, everything I read said that it was incurable and ultimately terminal. Reading this information literally made me physically and emotionally sick. I felt like my lively, vibrant mother was being cheated! Because I did not want to take away any hope Al and Tiny had, I made the sole decision not to repeat certain details of what I read. It seemed pointless to upset Tiny and Al any further. In the coming weeks I was right by Tiny's side as she obtained second opinions about her cancer from several other doctors. Tiny wanted to be completely certain that the diagnosis was accurate. Everywhere we went, the diagnosis and prognosis remained the same. There simply was no way out of this dark wilderness!

Tiny finally decided on being treated by a female Oncologist at the UCLA Medical Center. Al and I accompanied Tiny to her initial consultation with the Oncologist. The three of us listened intently as the doctor explained the treatment plan. She started by saying that Tiny would be treated with some form of Chemotherapy . . . for the rest of her life! My mind raced and my heart sank. I panicked inside! Over and over, I kept hearing the words, "for the rest of her life!" Was this doctor saying that Tiny did not have long to live? This initial visit went on for hours. Tiny's Oncologist was so very pleasant. She had a bedside manner and conversation that was both comforting and convincing.

Ultimately, this doctor was successful in giving us hope for the future. She assured us that the tumor was obviously very slowly growing and non-aggressive. In great detail, she explained that this cancer had been living and growing undetected and untreated in Tiny's body since her initial Breast Cancer. At this time Tiny was sixty-three years old. Her initial Breast Cancer and lumpectomy had been seventeen years earlier. While all the doctors we had seen agreed they could not remove this invasive tumor, there was still a treatment plan. The oncologist felt certain that the growth of the tumor could be stabilized.

> *"God is our refuge and strength, an ever-present help in trouble. Therefore we will not fear."*
>
> Psalms 46:1

The plan was to keep it under control with the use of chemotherapy drugs. The oncologist assured us that as long as the drugs keep the tumor stable, Tiny would be fine. She even went as far as to say that "Barbara's life will continue as normal."

Within days, Tiny's treatment began. Initially, she took chemotherapy daily in a pill form called Femara. When she took the first pill, Al and I both had so much anxiety. We all watched closely with anticipation of what might happen. Days turned into weeks, and with the exception of a little fatigue Tiny suffered no mentionable side effects. As a family, we slowly began to relax. Along with taking the daily chemo pills, the treatment plan included quarterly body scans. These scans consisted of drinking a contrast that would allow clear views of the tumor. They are designed to measure and monitor any growth or even the miracle of possible reduction in the size of the tumor. For the next few years, everyday life seemed somewhat normal. To look at Tiny, you would never think she had cancer. With heightened spirits, she was handling her treatment remarkably well.

Tiny was a few years into chemo treatments when she faced another major health decision. Her trusted Oncologist advised Tiny that she had decided to move her practice out of the UCLA Medical Center. She was going into private practice. This news came as quite a surprise! Without advance notice, Tiny had to make another severe decision regarding her health. Tiny felt that the years of care and comradery they had developed were irreplaceable. The mere thought of having to start treatment with another doctor was frightening. Hence, Tiny made her decision. She would remain under the care of UCLA for all of her medical needs except her cancer treatment. Regarding her chemotherapy, she decided to leave UCLA and follow the Oncologist to her new location.

Admittedly, everyone in the family developed a false sense of comfort. In 2007, five years into chemotherapy, Tiny went in for her quarterly PET scan. Surprisingly, the scan showed activity in Tiny's cancer cells. The tumor was starting to grow! Tiny's Oncologist assured her there was no reason to panic. Immediately, the doctor explained that this was common. She said that cancer cells often become resistant to a drug after a period of time. The doctor attempted to offer reassurance by telling us that there are many different forms of chemotherapy. It was the first time we had heard any of this. It was like taking a mandatory class to enhance our rapidly growing cancer treatment knowledge. From this point on, Tiny's new treatment plan was that anytime the tumor showed evidence of growth or resistance, the doctor would just switch drugs. Over the coming years, that is what continued to happen. While we remained grateful that there is a variety of chemotherapy drugs, there is also a downside. With each new drug, the side effects were different and often significantly harsher.

When we thought nothing else could go wrong, an unexpected tragedy struck! Much to our dismay, in March 2006, Sherl was discovered unresponsive in her New York penthouse. Her sudden death left our entire family devastated! A few months later, Tiny and I flew to New York, where Sherl's sister had organized a beautiful rooftop restaurant memorial for family and friends. Whenever we talk about Sherl or look at photos, it is obvious that Tiny still has not gotten over losing her. The mere mention of her name causes Tiny to have evident sadness!

God did not allow us to stay in a state of grief. Marian's daughter Stephanie invited us to her wedding in Jamaica in April. This getaway could not have come at a better time. By this time, our families had become very close, with Marian's daughters, Stephanie and Leslie, becoming my "little sisters." Tiny, Sasha, and I flew to Jamaica and were joined by Eloise, Sharon (from Seattle), Geneva, Martha, and Ben for a fabulous time. I watched as my mother pushed through her physical and emotional pains. In addition to attending a beautiful wedding, Tiny, Geneva, and Sasha took the daring sightseeing adventure and went Jet Skiing in Dunns River Falls. I was experiencing an MS crisis at the time, so I watched from above. With Sasha and Geneva by her side, Tiny could enjoy making a bucket list memory.

In November of the same year, LaTanya's family gave her a surprise fiftieth birthday party in Maryland. When Tiny saw my reluctance to go, she said, "We're going." Her longtime friend Velma from Chicago had a brother and sister-in-law living in Virginia. The three of us stayed in the home of Mamie and Artist. What a wonderful time we had at the party and for an entire week. Artist was available to tour us all over D.C. When we left, the feeling of family love was mutual. Mamie labeled us her, "God-Sent Sister" and "Sister-Mama." I thank God for all of these good times.

The spring of 2008 bloomed with great things for our family. We all gathered at Cal State Northridge to see Sasha receive her BA. Al and Tiny were so excited to share this accomplishment with their granddaughter.

Kevin Jr. was also celebrated this spring for completing his pre-hospital paramedic studies at UCLA. Not long before, we gathered again to witness Kevin being pinned at his graduation from the Fire Fighter Academy. It was a time in our family that all was well! God blessed me with two good children. I can say that because I know firsthand what temptations teen peer pressure can bring. Sasha is a Special Education Teacher with the Los Angeles Unified School District, and Kevin is a Los Angeles City Paramedic Fire Fighter. Our kids knew what they wanted to do, and they did it, making Kevin and I very proud of them.

There is always calm before a storm. When it comes to genetics, I am truly my mother's seed. The familiar traits go beyond being distinctly similar in appearance. My body has taken on most of Tiny's illnesses, being plagued with debilitating inflammatory and autoimmune diseases such as Fibromyalgia and Sjogren's Syndrome along with MS. As fate would have it, in July 2008, these disabling illnesses started to have their way in my body consistently. Because of my growing physical limitations, my doctors recommended I take a leave of absence from my airline employment. Once again, even in the face of adversity, we found a blessing in disguise. Due to the pain and fatigue that I was experiencing, part of my treatment plan was to get plenty of rest. At the time, Tiny was not feeling her best. From the very beginning of this cancer journey, I arranged my work schedule so that I was always off for office visits. My officially being off from work allowed us to enjoy spending our days resting together. It was a lifestyle that we would continue to share for the next several years.

In August 2009, Tiny and I had doctors' appointments at UCLA Medical Center. When we arrived, we separated, going to our designated treatment areas. Tiny headed to the lab to give blood while I went to the breast center for my yearly mammogram. Due to our family history, I had been getting mammograms for several years. By now, I knew what to expect. This time, things were different. After finishing my exam, the radiologist asked me not to get dressed and to wait in another room until the doctor came to talk with me. At that moment, I started to pray. Because Tiny had openly shared every aspect of her breast cancer, I felt emotionally calm and prepared for whatever blow was about to come my way. Tiny had gone before me 23 years earlier. She paved the way so that I could sidestep the feeling of horror that many women undertake. As I sat waiting for the doctor, I replayed many of my mother's words over and over in my mind. I remember her telling me she always tried not to give in to fear because the battle was God's. She also said that there is a purpose in every problem. Tiny was my biggest source of strength and wisdom in the face of cancer.

It was no surprise to me when the doctor gave me my diagnosis of Breast Cancer. When we finally finished talking, Tiny awaited me in the lobby. She already knew while she sat there watching other ladies come and go! Still, that did not make sharing this news any easier. Of course, the mother in her was heartbroken.

"Do not let your hearts be troubled."

John 14:1

Tiny did not want to see me go through this battle. I am so thankful that she always thinks positively. Whether a situation is good or bad, Tiny is full of hope in both her attitude and her conversation. As we drove home, our first words were to pray. From that moment forward, our heart-to-heart conversation was nothing but positive. Every word she said to me was like a battle cry, inspiring and encouraging. Tiny boldly said, "Be brave, Tracie." She told me not to let the circumstances discourage me but to trust God. I believed every word of hope that Tiny spoke. All Praise to God, Our Comforter, for not allowing me to have a spirit of fear. By the time we got home, we were smiling. Tiny looked at me and said, "Baby Girl, you are taking your desire to be like me just a little too far. You need to do as I say and not as I do." We hugged each other and shared a hearty laugh.

My medical treatment plan was the same as Tiny's: a lumpectomy followed by radiation. And yes, like Tiny and Mother, my lump was also in the left breast. I underwent a lumpectomy and had a six-week waiting period before beginning twelve weeks of daily radiation. I developed a loving relationship with Kevin's cousin, Debra, through the years. At the time, she was employed by Delta Airlines and living in Atlanta. Knowing the situation with Tiny's health, Debra scheduled a one-week vacation. As soon as I had my surgery, she flew to Los Angeles. Debra handled all the cooking and cleaning and helped Al with Tiny and Mother. Having her with me was indeed a way to keep our house running smoothly and my mind off of the trauma.

Al was dedicated to me through this entire radiation treatment process. He never missed a beat in picking me up at my house and driving me to my appointments. Before taking me home, he would stop at his house so that Tiny, Mother, and I could spend time together. The fact that I am the third generation Breast Cancer survivor in our family caused the doctors to want a closer look for a possible link. Mother, Tiny, and I all underwent the genetic testing process. The test results were favorable, indicating that our cancer was not genetic. We happen to be three family members with different forms of Breast Cancer.

The day before I started my radiation treatment, our family was hit with another bump. Kevin Jr. had recently graduated from the training academy as a Paramedic Firefighter with the Los Angeles City Fire Department.

While driving home on this stormy night, he and his date encountered a freeway car accident. They saw injured people outside of the car with no help in sight. When Kevin stopped and got out to assist, another car suddenly rear-ended his truck, crushing him between the two vehicles. As a result of this accident, his leg was shattered. That midnight-hour call caused everything else to come to a standstill. Kevin Sr. rushed to the hospital to be by his side. Shaken, I canceled my very first day of radiation. Everyone in our family and many of our friends gathered at the hospital for days until we knew that he was out of danger.

Kevin would spend the next two months in the hospital, undergoing multiple surgeries as he fought to save his leg.

"But I will restore you to health and heal your wounds,' declares the Lord."

Jeremiah 30:17

With determination, excellent doctors, therapists, and the Lord on his side, Kevin eventually returned to full duty with the fire department after nearly two years. In October 2013, our family was invited to a ceremony in Sacramento to honor his valiant service in saving lives that night. Natashia, Kevin, and I sat proudly with Sasha and others as our son received a Purple Heart Award.

By now, my childhood friend LaTanya was living in Maryland. She and her husband Joseph had both entered the ministry. LaTanya often contacted Tiny and me with prayer and words of encouragement. The three of us shared many prayerful conversations about our history, friendship, and of course, about breast cancer. Little did we know that these conversations served as a preparatory ground for LaTanya. Within two months of my cancer treatment, the tone of our discussion made an abrupt change. LaTanya called to say she had been diagnosed with breast cancer. As a result of our frequent conversations, LaTanya knew what to expect. Tiny and I had already shared the details of this battle. LaTanya's trial proved to be one more victory for God! Being the warrior that she is after completing her treatment, LaTanya wasted no time in supporting the fight against breast cancer. One of her first ventures was joining a breast cancer walk. LaTanya sent me pictures of the sign on her back that said she was walking in support of survivors Virginia, Tiny, and Tracie. It was a genuine gesture of her love for me and the three-generation survivors in my family.

Tiny soon discovered that some of the cancer drugs were harsher and less tolerable than others. That was the case with a pill Tiny's doctor prescribed in October 2010. Immediately, Tiny began having no energy at all. In addition, her breathing became extremely difficult. The chronic fatigue put a damper on my mother's quality of life. Everywhere Tiny went, she would have to find a seat after only a few short minutes. One day, while we were shopping, Tiny suddenly started breathing hard and sweating profusely. Truly frightened, I had her sit on a towel display. While I stood fanning her with a magazine, I opened a bottle of water for her to drink that I had not paid for. The store's security camera shot us, and it was not long before a security guard approached us to offer his assistance. After that day, Tiny became reluctant to go shopping.

This new pill was too harsh for Tiny's system. It was less than a year when Tiny and her Oncologist agreed that she could not continue to take this pill. It robbed Tiny of her quality of life. With all the years of changing chemo drugs, the doctor told us that every chemo pill form option had been exhausted. The next step was IV chemotherapy infusions. The doctor started to explain the side effects of the IV infusions. Honestly, she first said that the IV is stronger and harsher. In explaining the side effects, the doctor added that Tiny should expect to be tired and nauseous for the first three days. The last thing she said was that swelling and blistering of her hands and feet were another possible complication.

By 2011, Tiny took her first IV infusion. It is tough for me to see my mom constantly sick. I sat helplessly in the treatment room with her for the entire time. We were there for about three hours with blood work, hydration, and the actual chemo infusion. We spent the next few days waiting and watching for any change in her health. Praise the Lord, absolutely nothing happened! The following Wednesday morning, we went to our Bible study. After two hours of sitting in prayer and fellowship, Tiny still felt energetic. We left our study group and continued for an afternoon of lunch and shopping at Century Plaza Mall.

On Friday, Tiny started making phone calls to invite a few friends over for Saturday dinner. She cooked a complete meal for the first time in months. Fortunately, my dad is also an excellent cook, so he assisted with the preparation. That afternoon, Tiny single-handedly hosted a prayer and praise dinner party for ten ladies. She gave everyone a personalized thank you letter at the party for their ongoing support. Her letter spoke profoundly and sincerely about the difference between being cured and being healed. Tiny had researched the meaning of these two words to determine that cured was an absence of disease and healed was wholeness, peace, and well-being. She was comfortable telling each of us that although she was not cured, she was healed. Seeing her so accepting of this disease was truly amazing. Everyone enjoyed a wonderful afternoon filled with laughing, talking, and sharing!

Tiny's stamina was strong for the next two weeks, and her emotions remained absolutely wonderful. Now that she had moved to the infusion stage of her treatment, I was off on disability, allowing me to be with her for every treatment. It had to be God's perfect timing. Even though I had my own physical issues, I believe He made it possible for me to be sitting right beside my mother, watching, praying, believing, and praising! At the time, Tiny was on a bi-weekly infusion regimen. Infusion involves two or more large bags of toxic liquids. I learned that chemotherapy is not a one-size-fits-all drug. The ingredients and dosage are individually mixed for each patient. The nurses refer to this drug mixture as Tiny's personal "cocktail." Each treatment takes about four hours, while Tiny is limited to quietly sitting as the drugs flow through her veins.

Being with Tiny is the absolute best investment of my time. By now, I had not worked in over three years, my health had not improved, and my rest restrictions had not changed. I could not have been given a better way to rest than to attend every infusion appointment with Tiny. We can spend these long afternoons together. What an awesome blessing! We spent these hours sitting, laughing, talking, reading, and often napping. Now that the doctors saw me with her for every treatment, they started to refer to me as "Barbara's advocate." To me, that title is a privilege and an honor! As I pondered being called her advocate, I realized that my mom has been my advocate for my entire life. To some degree, because of her ongoing cancer treatments, our caretaker roles had simply reversed.

In 2012, AA offered an early retirement option. It was nothing short of amazing due to my age and years of seniority; I qualified! That October, I officially retired with 34 years of service. Kevin, Tiny, Al, Sasha, Kevin Jr., and Cousin Debra from Atlanta hosted a celebration backyard party. It was so much fun! We had all of Kevin's family, neighbors, our local friends, and many coworkers, some of whom were also taking the retirement option. In addition, Uncle Dub and Evelyn were here from Portland, Tiny and Al's friends Barbara and John from Oakland, and former coworkers Pat from New York and Diane from Atlanta also flew in. Only God would allow me to retire at fifty-five years old. Our future is a mystery to us, but He sees all, knows all, and always has a plan!

A few months later, we were struck with a personal tragedy. In recent years, Tiny's sister friend, Nancy from Chicago had been diagnosed with Alzheimer's. Sadly, she passed away on March 24, 2013. When we received the news, Tiny was in the hospital from a very bad chemotherapy reaction. This health crisis prohibited us from traveling to Chicago to attend Nancy's funeral services. Losing Nancy was a tough blow to all of us! Tiny and I spent many hours talking on the phone in the coming days with Nancy's daughters, Gwen and Dorothy (Dot). Without a doubt, the loss of her life-long sister friend weighed heavily on Tiny's mind and in her heart!

Throughout the years, Tiny's cancer ordeal has turned out to be another Open Door for many. After so many years as a patient, She became quite popular with the cancer center staff members. In response, she is extremely fond of them, knowing her doctor, the nurses, aides, receptionists, book-keepers, and everyone else by name! Greetings go beyond a hello and smile to include hugs. During their lunch breaks, some staff members sit with Tiny. They laugh, talk, and share stories about their lives, including kids' pictures, discussing marriages, and anything else you would typically discuss with personal friends. The bonding of these relationships even progressed to the level of exchanging birthday and Christmas presents. Who ever heard of someone looking forward to their chemo treatments? Most cancer pa-tients complete their chemotherapy treatment within several months. It has been years since Tiny took that first Femara chemotherapy pill. During these years, my mom has been on at least eight different, stronger forms of chemotherapy.

My fears and concerns started to cause me to watch Tiny more carefully. I am always looking for anything I can do to ease her burden. Whenever Tiny is in the company of people who do not see her often, I constantly hear them comment about how good she looks. The standard line is that they would not believe she was sick if they did not already know her condition. So goes the saying that you cannot judge a book by its cover. While receiving her treatments, Tiny loves sitting with her earphones on and listening to gospel music. She always starts with her favorite song, "I Won't Complain" by Rev. Paul Jones. The song is about having good days and bad days. When I listen to the lyrics, it is almost as if Tiny wrote them herself. They are words that seem appropriate for how she handles every aspect of the things she has been through. Her next song is "Open My Heart" by Yolanda Adams. When that song plays, I take a tearful walk to the bathroom. I never see Tiny cry about cancer, so I surely do not want to upset her by letting her see me cry. Without a doubt, Tiny is truly a Phenomenal Woman!

I thank God for blessing me with a praying mother.

"I can do all this through him who gives me strength."

Philippians 4:13

11

THINGS ARE CHANGING

By June 2013, once again, a scan indicated that Tiny's tumor markers had gone up. As a result of this tumor growth, she started treatment with a more potent drug. Tiny's infusion treatments took her through waves of up-and-down effects. For as long as I can remember, Tiny always said, "If you look better, you feel better." She decided to color her hair the week before her next scheduled chemotherapy. As a result of the ongoing fatigue caused by chemotherapy, Tiny's arms tire quickly. As usual, Al was helping her rinse the dye from her hair. Suddenly, Al saw Tiny's hair coming out. Through all the years of chemotherapy, she had never experienced hair loss. Imagine their horror! Al and Tiny stood and helplessly watched as most of her hair washed down the drain.

Later that day, the two of them got over their initial shock. Tiny called me to tell me what happened. I immediately asked her if she would like to go somewhere to purchase a wig. She replied, "Not yet," followed by, "I am just looking a little patchy, so I need a barber to give me a complete shave." That same day, Kevin asked his long-time barber, "Tee," to come to our home. It was a beautiful California day. Sasha and Kevin joined us, and the family gathered in the backyard. None of us knew what Tiny's emotional demeanor would be. Everyone felt the need to be present so we could support her in any way possible. We all knew we would follow her emotional lead without even discussing it.

Tiny sat with her usual calm and composure. She took a firm stand in the face of this adversity. I watched as my mother refused to become sad or have a pity party! I took pictures of the entire haircut so that Tiny could witness the whole process. Ironically, the day ended with smiles and picture-taking. Everyone started pulling out different caps and hats for her to choose from. We were concerned that she may develop a cold without discussing it, so we wanted her to keep her head warm! Tiny humored us and modeled our hat selections. She finally decided on a few baseball caps. The irony of her losing her hair is what quickly became apparent to all of us. We were much more concerned about the day's events than she was. With her usual grace, Tiny shook off the day's events and continued to press forward.

I took her to a wig salon a few days after the haircut. We were in the store for quite a while, trying on styles and colors. It was a first for both of us. Tiny had never worn a wig before. Eventually, she selected one. Everyone in the store agreed it looked adorable, so Tiny wore the wig home. When we walked into the house, Al was surprised—his first reaction was that he liked it! Tiny continued to wear the wig for the rest of the day. She said it felt hot and uncomfortable when she took it off that night. Tiny never wore the wig again. As fate would have it, our cousin Bunny was also battling breast cancer. She, too, had recently experienced hair loss as she was going through the chemo process. A few weeks after the wig purchase, Bunny came to Tiny's house for a visit. As the three of us sat talking, Bunny told us she was invited to a function she wanted to attend but due to her baldness, she was uncomfortable about going out to this fancy, public affair. Tiny immediately told me to go and get the wig. As soon as Bunny tried on the wig, we all agreed that it looked perfectly natural. All of her hesitation was gone. Tiny told Bunny to take the wig, wear it, and keep it!

One week after losing her hair, Tiny and I went to the cancer center for her regular chemo session. Al does not always go to the treatments with us, but ironically, he joined us on this day. It would be the first time any staff members or other patients saw my mother bald. When we arrived, Fox News was setting up to interview the Beverly Hills Cancer Center Nutritionist, Carolyn Katz. The topics were diet, health issues, and overall concerns for cancer patients. The reporter said he would like to interview a patient. The nutritionist approached Tiny and asked her to join the taping as if Fox News had preplanned or placed it strategically. Unashamedly bald, Tiny agreed to do the interview. My dad and I sat together, bursting with pride and admiration as we watched this live televised taping of Tiny publicly showing herself to the world as a true champion. Her dignity, along with her overflowing, positive attitude regarding this ongoing cancer battle, was seen by all. That day, not only did Tiny stand up, but she also stood out! In no way was she in bondage to her circumstances. This interview is now on YouTube. Of course, we have a copy of this treasured video to watch as often as we like. Here's an opportunity for you to watch as well.

https://bit.ly/3VajEeX

Having cancer and going through chemotherapy treatments are such a heavy burden. Often, the atmosphere seems uninviting, and some people appear weaker or sadder than others. Tiny never complains about how she feels. She always fights hard to overcome the signs of weakness that come along with this disease. Looking around at other patients affirmed that my mother was extraordinary in how she fought her battle. Yes, extraordinary is what some would call Tiny—a real people person. Her positive "bright light" about life always shines. Just a few minutes spent with her, and there seems to be a shift in the atmosphere. She takes every opportunity to open the door to her heart. Tiny starts by greeting everyone with her infectious smile, which always leads to a conversation. Her willingness to engage and befriend strangers inspires me. She has no problem sharing her knowledge, listening, counseling, and supporting others. Not only on the subject of Breast Cancer but any need they may have. Simply put, Tiny is a true humanitarian.

On one occasion, a female patient confirmed what I always knew regarding the impact and importance of Tiny's outgoing personality. This lady was being treated when we walked in. Tiny smiled, entered the cubicle, and introduced herself to the lady. A big smile came over the woman's face. She said, "I have seen you here before and hoped you would be here today." She added, "You are the first person here that I have seen smiling instead of filled with gloom and doom." The lady said she had watched us on several occasions, curious as to why we were always laughing! That was the conversation springboard! The two of them spent the next few hours getting acquainted. I read my book and did cafeteria runs as they sat, sharing. By the end of the day, they were checking their appointment schedules to see when they would meet again.

At the next session, I left the treatment area to get lunch. When I returned, an African American lady was sitting in the cubicle with Tiny. Their conversation was flowing as if they already knew one another. When we left, Tiny told me she felt she knew this lady from somewhere. By the next visit, the two remembered that we had all met at a mutual friend's birthday party. What a small world! Bonita and Tiny continued to get better acquainted with one another at their treatments. Eventually, the relationship grew and became a friendship that included lunches, home visits, and Al meeting her husband, Tom.

Another memorable treatment session was the day Tiny sat with a woman who barely spoke English. We had only to look at this woman to realize she was devastated. Her daughter started to talk with us, explaining some of her mother's side effects. The chemo had taken her mother's hair out, and she had lost her appetite. Tiny shared her battle and struggles with losing appetite and taste through the daughter's translation. She made every attempt to convince this lady that eating is important. While being both compassionate and sensitive, Tiny shared a picture of herself, adding that baldness is temporary. Eventually, the lady was moved from the treatment area to an exam room. Not long afterwards, a male doctor walked into the treatment area, looking for Tiny. He wanted to personally thank her for whatever it was that she had said to his patient because her attitude improved more that day than it had ever been. Now, when we cross paths with this other patient, she is obviously much more at ease. She greets both Tiny and me with a smile and a hug. Her daughter told Tiny that thanks to her words of encouragement, her mom started eating again. She added that for them, Tiny was an image of victory.

The encounter with this woman and her doctor was a game changer. As we were riding home, Tiny told me that this day had given her a revelation. For the first time, Tiny said that she felt that all of the challenges of her cancer were not about her at all. Instead, she now believed that God had placed her on this cancer journey for a reason, sustaining her so that she could be used as a vehicle to motivate others. Tiny continued by saying, "Let's just watch and see. I know that I am right." She went on to tell me that she would do her best to stay the course. At every opportunity, she desired to be God's servant. She wanted to share her lessons and experiences with others truthfully. Tiny has always been transparent when talking about her battle against cancer. I recalled the countless times she had already been a witness to so many. I actually had coworkers call Tiny when a family member had cancer, just for reassurance. Tiny would say, "Give them my phone number, and I'll answer any questions I can."

Tiny ended this conversation by telling me that when God comes for me, I want Him to say,

"Well done, good and faithful servant! You have been faithful with a few things; I will put you in charge of many things. Come and share your master's happiness!"

Matthew 25:21

While Tiny seemed truly confident and excited about this revelation, my conflicted emotions were trying to comprehend her display of satisfaction and contentment. I simply could not understand how she was able to find any happiness regarding her medical condition.

On almost a daily basis, I began to notice changes in Tiny's physical well-being. When she talks to me, I still hear the peace and positivity of the beautiful Queen she has always been. The fact is that her body is growing older and weaker than when this journey began, and I see the signs of fatigue in her eyes. At the same time, each new chemotherapy drug is stronger, bringing with it much harsher side effects. To name a few complexities, I have watched Tiny endure nausea, chronic fatigue, heart palpitations, hair loss, loss of appetite, diverticulitis, chronic constipation, dehydration, spinal taps, blood transfusions, chemo fog, and lung infections, and as a result of these complications, hospitalized on numerous occasions. One drug caused the pigmentation of Tiny's ears, the soles of her feet, the palms of her hands, and even her tongue to become very dry and eventually turn black, to add insult to injury. The affected areas looked as if they had been burned.

Tiny also developed a diminished ability to breathe comfortably. A chest x-ray showed very unfavorable results. The pulmonary doctor said chemotherapy caused her breathing problems after many years of use. Tiny's lungs were permanently damaged and irreparably destroyed! In describing the damage, the doctor compared the texture of Tiny's lungs to having the appearance of "shattered glass." Eventually, the constant IV Chemo infusions caused Tiny's veins to collapse. In February 2014, a port was implanted in her chest as an alternate avenue in which to administer the chemotherapy. Cancer has taken Tiny on an arduous journey. I feel as if I have had to witness her walking through the valley of the shadow of death. Thank you, God, for your promise of comfort during this time.

"Honor her for all that her hands have done, and let her works bring her praise at the city gate."

Proverbs 31:31

This battle of cancer has brought a multitude of challenges to Tiny's forefront. No matter what the obstacle is, she maintains her composure as she continues to press forward through the adversities of chemo treatments. Her inner strength so inspires me.

Tiny's long-time doctors continue to marvel at her attitude and stamina. No matter how difficult the times are, she continues to tackle the hurdles and remains on her feet. We have shared the same UCLA Primary Care doctor since 1988. For our medical needs, Dr. Friedman is the very best! We make a point of scheduling all of our appointments together. We have shared many personal things through the years of treatment and friendship with this particular doctor. Our relationship has gone beyond the professional doctor/patient level. She knows both of our ins and outs, our good and bad. At one point, she stated that she could not believe our bodies' similarities. Except for our age, the illness pattern is truly remarkable. Our charts are so similar that it was like I was my mother's clone. This observation came as no surprise, and we all started laughing.

After a few minutes, the doctor extended her arms and hugged Tiny. She gently said, "Barbara, you truly are a miracle. Just keep doing what you are doing. By all medical standards and statistics, by now, you should be dead." Wow! Can you imagine hearing this from your most trusted doctor? Without flinching, Tiny looked directly at her with her radiant smile as she calmly replied, "Yes, doctor, I know." My mind was racing as I sat silently listening to the two of them. I thought just how easy it is for some doctors to skim around the harsh truth and sugarcoat the realities of life. As disturbing as this brutally blunt conversation was, there was a place in my heart where I applauded and admired this well-respected doctor. I was genuinely grateful that she took the posture of speaking honestly regarding my mother's condition. She obviously cared enough about the two of us to keep it real!

Through all the challenging years of adversity regarding her health, what helps keep Tiny strong is that we have a solid foundation of faith, prayer, and laughter in the home. Tiny has Biblical scriptures in frames, sitting on tables, and hanging on walls throughout the house. Even if you are not having a problem, reading them will give you a sense of power, comfort, and relief. You can overhear her quoting these and other scriptures at any given time. Tiny lives each day of her life, standing on the promises of God with sincere faith and love for the Lord. She is a devoted Christian servant to the extreme that she is physically capable. For many years, we have been members of Faithful Central Bible Church. Sunday morning service is something my mother always looks forward to. Even on a sick day, missing church is one thing she seldom does.

In addition to Sunday morning service, we attend a mid-week Bible study at a different church. Several years ago, Joy, Tiny's coworker at Continental Airlines, invited her to join a weekly Wednesday Bible study at Crenshaw United Methodist Church. At that time, I was still working with Tuesday and Wednesday off. Had the meetings been any other day of the week, I would not have been able to attend. Once again, I found myself the youngest in the group of approximately fifteen ladies and the pastor. I know this group is part of God's spiritual enrichment plan for our lives. Though Tiny and I did not know the pastor or most of the ladies, they all affectionately embraced us in no time. In addition to the weekly Bible study, we go to lunches and other functions together. Pattye, Josie, and the other ladies remain a constant source of support, fellowship, and friendship in our lives.

Juanita introduced us to her dear friend Barbara Perkins, the founder of Sisters At The Well. This outreach organization is a powerful inspiration for women, providing opportunities to attend luncheons and award ceremonies. These are outings where we dress up and fellowship with positive, motivational women. When Tiny's health permitted, we attended on several occasions. Barbara also invited us to her annual Regalettes events. Tiny will push herself to be involved in such an atmosphere.

Going out for a quick breakfast is also something Tiny enjoys. A heart-warming memory is the two of us joined by my children's Aunt Jacque at the Coffee Company. Having not seen each other in some time, Jacque had no idea how severe Tiny's condition was. She asked Tiny for her contact information and offered to take her to breakfast again. Within days, Jacque sent Tiny an unexpected cancer care package that included toiletries, breast cancer slippers, socks, and a special blanket. Kindness like this is never forgotten!

Each year seems to bring our family to another stunning moment. In early 2014, we faced a physical trial that no one saw coming. Al was diagnosed with Prostate Cancer. I could not believe that both Al and Tiny were being challenged by this dreadful disease that had already left so many scars on our family. After several medical consultations, Al did not seem alarmed by the diagnosis. Unselfishly, Al said he needed this surgery as soon as possible to get back on his feet and care for Tiny and Mother. Al's surgery was performed in April 2014 while Tiny, Kevin, and I waited and prayed together at the hospital.

> *"And the prayer offered in faith will make the sick person well; the Lord will raise them up."*
>
> James 5:15

We were so grateful when the doctor told us that the cancer removal was successful, adding that Al would not need to undergo radiation or chemotherapy.

During Al's time of healing, Kevin and I stepped up, and took care of everything. My dad still felt he needed to be the one to take care of Tiny and my grandmother. With strength and determination, Al was back on his feet in record time. At 95 years old, Mother was still remarkably healthy. She had spent the last sixteen years living (somewhat independently) in her apartment right behind Al and Tiny. Mother does not choose to cook or drive anymore. Her dinners are always eaten with Al and Tiny or at my house and outings. Mother is very alert, wise, welcoming, and pleasant. Without a doubt, Tiny and I continue to gain knowledge, faith, strength, and courage from her!

The previous year, Tiny stopped driving, making her activities utterly dependent on me and Al. Due to her unpredictable physical challenges, committing to social functions became limited. On one of her better days, Tiny decided that a happy atmosphere and being with people could help, so the two of us attended a wedding. As I sat listening to the traditional wedding vows, I focused on some of the words. "To love, honor, and cherish. In sickness and in health, "til death do us part." While it is beautiful that these vows are written with a new husband and wife in mind, I found these particular lines fitting and appropriate for the relationship I share with Al and Tiny. As a child, Tiny was my first friend. Today, Tiny is my Best Friend! No matter how old I am, I know I am still under Tiny's protective eye. I constantly hear words or see deeds and gestures of her forever love for me. These things remind me that I am still "her baby girl." My happiness and well-being are the things that have always delighted Tiny the most.

These words also resonated with Tiny. On our way home from the wedding, Tiny said that she always hoped that someday I would enjoy the closeness of having a child of my own. Instead, she praised God for giving us unconditional love and the wisdom to look at what we do have rather than dwell on what we do not have. As Tiny continued to talk, she spoke of the apparent mutual love shared between Kevin, Sasha, Kevin Jr., and me. She added that witnessing our family unity gives her a true sense of peace, comfort, and relief. This conversation ended with her saying that my life with

Kevin and the children was an answer to her prayers. She knew that when her day came to leave this earthy life, I would not be alone. Having conversations like this only enhances the painful reality that Tiny is thinking about the possibility of succumbing to this dreaded disease. Her brave calmness in discussing her demise never ceases to amaze me. While I respect her devotion to my well-being, I am truly uncomfortable with even the slightest thought of ever living without Tiny. Honestly, I am not sure what bothers me most about her going to be with the Lord. Is it her eternal destiny or my earthly destiny without her?

On the rare occasions when Tiny's health permit, we make time for quick (just the two of us) girl getaways. As long as we are together, it does not matter when or where. Our trip can be as simple as an overnight at a local hotel or as extensive as an island vacation. Wherever we are, we enjoy talking, laughing, reminiscing, planning, and sharing. In August 2014, my Chicago friend, Stephanie, hosted a college-going away party for her youngest daughter, Simone. Stephanie's daughters (Stacie and Simone) are Kevin's and my Goddaughters. When I received the invitation, my first thought was that I probably would not be able to go.

After all, Tiny's health has been precarious lately. I was too uncomfortable to be that far away from home. Anything could happen! When I mentioned the party to Tiny, she asked if I was going. When I voiced my hesitation, she smiled and said, "I want to go too." That day, we started making plans but opted not to tell anyone we were coming. We agreed to wait and see how her health was.

"Therefore we do not lose heart. Though we are wasting away, yet inwardly we are being renewed day by day."

2 Corinthians 4;16

As we approached our departure date, Tiny's strength and stamina seemed to improve daily. She stressed to me that she was ready to go.

The two of us flew into Chicago one day before the party. By the Grace of God, the trip did not take nearly as much out of Tiny as I had expected. I noticed that she was breathing well, and her demeanor was unusually lively and energetic. After we checked into our hotel, Tiny started making phone calls. Even though our visit was unexpected, we instantly had company. Our hotel room started buzzing with an ongoing flow of friends. Liz was the first to arrive to spend the entire day, followed by Geri, Carol, and Vera later that afternoon. Tiny and I continued to have visitors throughout the night and into the following day. Her friend Gladys and her husband drove from Michigan to have dinner with us at the hotel. Friendships like these are truly priceless!

The next day, our family friend, Ernest took us to breakfast. He and his family had left Oakland and moved back to Chicago. Afterward, Tiny and I drove to Stephanie's house for the surprise visit. Talk about joy, hugs, smiles, and tears! I could spend an afternoon with Stacie and Simone for the first time in a few years. My goddaughters have become beautiful young ladies. Tiny enjoyed visiting with everyone, including Stephanie's mom Mattie. The four of us were together, just as we had been some fifty years earlier. When Tiny and I left the party, our next surprise stop was to see Tiny's lifetime friend Terry. In recent years, diabetic complications have caused Terry to lose her vision. On this day, their entire family was together celebrating the eightieth birthday of Terry's husband, James. The house was full of family and friends, including Terry's oldest daughters, Toi and Charla, who are Tiny's Goddaughters. Everyone was as happy to see us as we were to see them. Love was truly in the air!

Once we finally got back to our hotel that night, we absolutely could not stop talking. Tiny and I agreed that the events of this trip were so much more than we expected. Our three-day outing indeed turned into something irreplaceable. While sitting on the flight home, Tiny excitedly told me that seeing so many treasured friends offered a sense of closure for her. To my dismay, Tiny ended the conversation with one of her matter-of-fact comments. She held my hand and smiled, saying, "Thank you for this wonderful trip. I am sure it will be my last!" No matter how much I enjoy talking to Tiny, she is the one person who can say things that leave me speechless.

When we returned home, I had a long phone conversation with Jo. She told me that she has never forgotten the values Tiny instilled in us as young girls. Jo continued by saying that whenever she was with Tiny, she always felt like a "daughter." I have always loved Jo like a sister, and hearing her say that spoke volumes to my heart. As we reminisced, Jo credited Tiny with lots of motherly guidance. She referred to Tiny as always being a true lady and role model. As the conversation continued, Jo praised Tiny for teaching the qualities of feminism. Tiny never wavered when she stressed the importance of always conducting ourselves as respectful ladies.

> *"Then they can urge the younger women to love their husbands and children, to be self-controlled and pure, to be busy at home, to be kind, and to be subject to their husbands so that no one will malign the word of God."*
>
> Titus 2:4-5

Another area Tiny gave us lots of advice on was learning to be financially responsible and independent. She constantly stressed the reality of how bad choices can have lingering consequences. Jo ended our conversation by telling me that she raised her daughter, Asia, with many of the guidelines, principles, and life lessons she gained during her time with Tiny.

This heartfelt phone call brought back so many beautiful memories of my youth. More than that, I was proud to hear another woman pay such accolades to Tiny! Before Jo started kindergarten, her mother had gone to be with the Lord. Tiny's presence in her life had helped to fill a few voids. Tiny had the compassion and ability to encourage anyone and everyone. She always made room in her heart for people. She told me to "never be selfish, Tracie, just lift where you can." Hearing Jo speak these sincere words reminded me of just how many things I take for granted about Tiny. The bottom line is that Tiny is a woman of great character with a loving heart. Jo and her children are God-sent family members who often visit from Chicago.

Thank God, the rest of the year was medically uneventful for our family. Tiny had been off of her chemotherapy treatment for over three months. She continued to get abdominal scans, and all indications were that the tumor was inactive! While off the chemo, Tiny seemed more energetic and happier than she had been in years. In October, Uncle Dub and Evelyn flew in from Portland, and our cousins Alan and Delores came from St. Louis. We had a party with lots of family and friends to help us celebrate my grandmother's ninety-sixty birthday. As always, this was two weeks of great family love and togetherness.

Thanksgiving was a few weeks later. Tiny partnered with Al to cook a fabulous dinner without breaking her stride. Kevin and I drove with Al and Tiny to Las Vegas during the first week of December. We were going to celebrate Jean's eightieth birthday. The celebration was at her home and included the birthdays of four other friends. Unfortunately, the day we got there, Jean had been rushed to the hospital. She was on dialysis, and things were not going well. Although Jean was not released from the hospital in time for the celebration, the party continued. Jean got back on her feet in time to make it home for the Christmas holidays.

December is Tiny's favorite holiday season, so she always makes sure the house is festively decorated. Tiny and Al hosted Christmas dinner in keeping with our usual holiday tradition. They have many years of cooking together, making a good team in the kitchen. Because Kevin and I usually worked holidays, we had never hosted big family dinners. When I take a turn in the kitchen, I am told I am a pretty good cook. In being true to myself, I know that my skills are far from those of my parents. For example, I have never cooked a turkey or greens. This year, Tiny kept telling me how capable I was. She said that if there was a dish I was uncertain about, I should pay close attention because she was getting tired. For the first time, Tiny was adamant that this would be her last year cooking for the holidays, emphasizing that she was "passing the torch." She added that since I had grown up loving and expecting holiday traditions, I should naturally want to provide the same for my family.

Tiny told me that I needed to create what I wanted to see moving forward. That was something that I had never taken into consideration. My family having holiday dinners at Tiny and Al's house was just a given. Even under the circumstances of her failing health, I needed this push to take her seriously. A few days later, I received a FedEx package. The sender was Tiny. Inside, there was a brand-new stainless-steel frying pan. I already had many pots and pans, but none as fancy as this one. When I called to thank her, our conversation ended with the two of us sharing a hearty laugh as she said, "Tracie, you are retired. Start cooking!"

Tiny had taught me to cook at a very young age. For some reason, I had kept my abilities hidden in the shadows. I mainly looked at holiday meals as being someone else's specialty. Suddenly, Tiny officially passed that holiday meal torch to me. I laugh now when someone tastes something I cook and asks, "Who cooked this, you or Al?" When I say I cooked it, several people have said, "This food tastes just like Tiny's." "I didn't think you could cook."

Regarding kitchen matters, knowing and doing things had become totally different for me. That is probably because I have never been opposed to dining out. At that point, I started to cook more often. To this day, that skillet remains in my cabinet, never having been used.

"For it is God who works in you to will and to act in order to fulfill his good purpose."

Philippians 2:13

12

EARTHQUAKE

In January 2015 we got a disturbing phone call. Al and Tiny's Las Vegas friend Jean suddenly passed away. This came as quite a shock! Tiny had just talked to her a few days before. She was at home and said that everything was fine. Ironically, her death was not in any way related to her kidney failure. Jean had fallen in her garage and hit her head. She lived two days, but never regained consciousness. We were all saddened by this unexpected turn of events. Within the week, Tiny and I made our way back to Vegas so that we could attend the funeral.

Shortly after we returned from Las Vegas, Tiny started complaining of constipation, saying she was very uncomfortable. It was not alarming, since it is one of the many side effects of chemotherapy. Tiny had dealt with constipation several times in the past, so there was no panic. After a few days of unsuccessful laxative home remedies, Tiny contacted her doctor. On Wednesday, February 4, Tiny's doctor admitted her to UCLA for a twenty-four-hour bowel cleaning. She was released Thursday afternoon, and we went home believing all was fine. Over the weekend, Tiny continued complaining of fullness and bloat. She contacted her doctor and was told to return for a recheck on Tuesday, February 8. As we headed toward the hospital, the two of us were laughing. Since we knew she would be on a restricted diet for a few days of clean out, we decided to stop for a bowl of soup.

Tiny was admitted to the hospital that afternoon, for what we believed would be a two-to-three-day stay. By Saturday, the doctors were not satisfied with her amount of elimination. They had her spend the entire day having one test after another. Early Sunday morning, Tiny called me. We laughed and talked while I was dressing for church. She told me she had hardly been able to get any sleep. The nurses had been in and out all night, checking her vitals. Tiny said she was going to try napping until the doctors came in for their morning rounds. I told her I would see her as soon as church was over.

Before I could get out of the house, Tiny called again. She was speaking in her normal, calm voice. She proceeded to tell me that a group of doctors had just left her room advising her of the test results. The conclusion was that her blockage was not constipation. Instead, it was a result of the spreading cancer. The best layman description they could offer her was that her solitary tumor had erupted like a volcano. The spread had caused thousands of small tumors to engulf her abdomen. Tiny's cancer had spiraled out of control and the tumors were rapidly growing. This progression began to shut down all of Tiny's organs. Eventually, they would not only prohibit her from eliminating, but from eating or swallowing!

The doctors apologetically told Tiny that there was absolutely nothing more they could do to stop this cancer progression. The final blow was that although they could not give her an exact time limit, their advice to her was that she should get all her personal affairs in order as soon as possible. This horrific conversation ended with them telling Tiny that her eminent demise was inevitable! Maybe three days; maybe three weeks!!! As I listened, tears streamed down my face. Tiny told me that she had already called to relay this news to Al. He was on his way to the hospital and Kevin was on his way home from work. Kevin asked me to please wait and let him drive me. I do not know what describes my emotions at that time best. What I do know is that I was stunned, devastated, and horrified to say the least. As the day went on, I became furious that these doctors had delivered this bombshell news while Tiny was alone!

Of course, the family and a few close friends all rushed to the hospital. Our hearts joined forces, and together we did the only thing we knew to do. We prayed! Late that night, everyone left the hospital except me. The thought of leaving Tiny alone in the hospital never entered my mind. Fortunately, she had a private hospital room. Without any discussion, I moved in! I had lots of mother/daughter questions. That entire day, Tiny appeared to have such a significantly calm peace of mind. She had not shed one tear or spoken with any more emotion than usual. I thought maybe she was in shock, or even in denial. I was mentally trying to prepare myself to be as strong as possible. My instincts told me that I would cry with her and offer all the comfort I could muster up. Once we were alone, I asked Tiny if she was restraining her emotions because she seemed to be holding back. Tiny's response was not at all what I was expecting. She first said, "Let's pray." Together we prayed our own words, followed by The Lord's Prayer and the 23rd Psalm.

When we finally started to talk, Tiny told me that we all had to realize that she had been living with cancer in her body since 1986. "Twenty-nine years Tracie! Who does that?" She went on to say that she had no regrets about the events of the day. The twelve years of chemotherapy had been totally exhausting and debilitating. Tiny finished by reminding me of how bad she was feeling before she stopped taking chemo six months ago. She really believed that if she had continued taking the chemotherapy, she would have died months ago. I thought back to the period leading up to her stopping chemotherapy. Admittedly, at that time Tiny's breathing had become so labored that she could barely stand. Even simple everyday motions such as showering or walking from room to room had become a major chore. Hence, Tiny was in the offices of the heart and lung doctors on a weekly basis. They all agreed that the side effects of the chemotherapy treatment were the cause.

Tiny also reminded me that when she stopped treatments, the doctors had been very honest. They all said that there was a risk if she did not continue taking the chemotherapy. And Tiny's response to them was, "I will take the risk!" Yes, I remembered all of that, but still I never expected this. I thought the frequent abdominal scans and blood tests would have given the doctors some advance warning signs. Tiny saw the events of the day much differently than I did. For her, having been off chemo and able to really enjoy the last six months of her life was worth the risk. As we held each other, Tiny softly whispered to me, "Let's just count it all joy."

This conversation held me in absolute awe. I had always marveled at her level of endurance. Today, I marveled at her level of acceptance! Tiny was facing her death with such an extremely calm countenance.

> *"Do not let your hearts be troubled. You believe in God; believe also in me. My Father's house has many rooms; if that were not so, would I have told you that I am going there to prepare a place for you?"*
>
> John 14:1-2

Tiny told me that no matter how hard these next days may be, she knew God would be with her every step of the way. Tiny's composure about her own death was truly mystifying to me. I always knew she had a heart of gold.

This day, I saw the validation that she had a spine of iron! Truly, she was equipped to tackle anything.

While I pride myself on being able to accept "whatever" the realities of life bring my way, this was one time that I ultimately failed! My tears were totally uncontrollable. I was literally too choked up to speak, so I just sat quietly and listened. Tiny asked me to try not to cry. As I look back, this seems to be such a role reversal, given the circumstances. Her tone became very firm, yet sympathetic. Tiny continued by saying I should cry because I miss her, but never because of "if I could have, would have, or should have." Then Tiny smiled her beautiful smile as she told me that she was thankful and proud of every moment she spent with me. Reassuringly, she added, "Baby girl, you have done it all!"

Still putting me before herself, Tiny told me she had enjoyed every promise God offered her. She said anyone who knew her would agree that she had lived a full and happy life. Because of this, Tiny tried to convince me that I should not be unhappy about her transcending. With all her heart, she knew her destiny was to live eternal life in Heaven! She told me to live in peace, picture her living in paradise, pray like never before, fight back against my feelings of grief, and talk myself out of self-pity. Even now, Tiny could not stop herself from doing what she had done for my entire life. That was to do all she could to cover and shield me from any pain that I may have. Tiny was my mother, and I was hers until the very end.

Tiny continued to talk, and I continued to listen. Suddenly, her tone changed. She apologetically looked at me and said, "I am sorry." I could not imagine why she was telling me that she was sorry. Tiny said she had to pass the baton. She depended on me to carry the load of holding life together for Al and Mother. Tiny felt that it was going to be a big task, adding that she knew that neither of them was going to be alright with her leaving. This change was going to be very difficult for both. She went on to tell me that I would have to be their strength. As I listened to her, my mind was racing. Momentarily, I had what I immediately realized was a very selfish thought. The question came to my mind, *"What about me? I am not alright with this."* Tiny ended the conversation by saying she felt she was leaving me with a big burden, but she knew I was equipped to handle it. She added that I should pray and trust God if I ever feel overwhelmed. She smiled and said, "Remember when you feel like you can't, He can!"

Tiny said you are my mini-me. God would give you the strength, just as He had done for me. All I needed to do was to stay faithful and cast my cares on Him. Admittedly, I was having a problem grasping this reality. Combined with excruciating sorrow, my emotions were in a state of shock and fear. I did not want to disappoint Tiny. She seemed more confident in my strength and abilities than I did. Before I knew it, I thought, *Please help me, Lord.* I honestly did not think I could handle any of this without Him. That night, the two of us barely slept. Instead, we continued talking and praying.

Early Monday morning, the doctors came in for their patient rounds. After they left, Tiny and I chatted lightly for a while. Then, I made my way to the shower. Tiny said she was going to make a few phone calls. I assumed they were with Al or some of her friends. When I returned, Tiny was very alert, ready for business, and in complete authority mode. She once again caught me off guard. Like a boss, she told me that time was of the essence and that every moment was precious. Not missing a beat, she added that we had to do things quickly and in a composed positive way.

I know Tiny was a very mentally strong person, but still, I was in awe at her calm, matter-of-fact demeanor. She had so much discipline over her feelings. Her initial directive involved me to change the names on all the accounts. Instead of being a beneficiary, I was now to be a joint owner of everything along with Al. The same was to be done with Mother's accounts. Hearing these words saddened my heart. It was an action that made things seem so final. I left the hospital to meet Al. Tiny had made a phone call to their credit union. Of course, she and the manager were on a first-name basis through the years of connection with this institution. She told me that manager Jeff was expecting us, so Al and I were very quiet that afternoon as we did everything Tiny had set in motion. When we returned from the bank, Tiny led the conversation for the entire afternoon. She had a check-list, reviewing every financial aspect of their lives with me.

The following day, Tiny had another assignment for me and Al. It was the day she sent the two of us to Inglewood Cemetery Mortuary. She had scheduled an appointment for us to purchase a double burial plot. When we arrived, the representative, who happened to be Juanita's church member, drove us throughout the park, pointing out several available plots. Al and I decided on a plot at the top of a hill called, Grandview Terrace. The plot is located under a tree with a bench nearby. Ironically, when we stood at the grave site, we found ourselves facing the location of Tiny and Al's house. Their house is near the Los Angeles International Airport, directly under the flight path, so we had no problem pinpointing where they lived. Al and I agreed that we had found the perfect spot. I took pictures and showed the plot to Tiny when we got back to the hospital. She was in total agreement. This pattern of Tiny guiding us continued throughout the entire week. By Friday, Tiny told me, "I think we have covered everything." I was entirely in agreement. Tiny had mentally informed and equipped me with every aspect of efficiently running Al's household and Mother's.

As we continued to talk, my mind turned toward God. I realized that I had spent my entire life hearing God's Word. Whenever I heard or read a biblical story, I always found God's miracles to be truly amazing. Sometimes,

I would close my eyes to picture what was going on entirely. Now, I felt like Tiny was living God's promises, and I was a living witness to a miracle.

> *"For God hath not given us the spirit of fear; but of power, and of love, and of sound mind."*
>
> 2 Timothy 1:7

Over those past days, Tiny exuded every single Word of this scripture. The message oozed out of her. All I could do was thank God for his Word. That was the moment that I finally received my revelation. I had no say regarding this situation. No matter what I wanted, God was indeed in control. Tiny seemed so filled with God's peaceful presence.

> *"Be strong and courageous. Do not be afraid or terrified because of them, for the Lord your God goes with you; he will never leave you nor forsake you."*
>
> Deuteronomy 31:6

On more than one occasion, when I briefly left Al to visit without me, I returned to find flowers. Tiny would tell me that one of my friends came by to sit with her for a while, so she told Al to leave and check on Mother. At times, the medication confused her about who the visitors were, but Tiny said their presence made her happy. I can confirm that Kim, Alana, Samantha, Shay, Teri, Shaune, and Jaque were some visitors. I never found out who they all were, but my heart thanks every one of them.

Later, I learned that in her never-ending mother mode, Tiny had asked everyone close to me "not to leave Tracie alone" or "don't forget Tracie." Her request was honored by so many allies. Not one day goes by without

Stephanie, Jo, Gwen, Dot, Juanita, or Shay calling me. In addition, several others call often just to touch base. I trust that each of you knows how thankful I am for your presence in my life.

Tiny spent the next two weeks at UCLA. She was under the watchful eyes and care of several admirable doctors. I witnessed each one of them doing all they could to keep Tiny strong and comfortable. At times, I felt so helpless. All I could do was sit and watch her every move. Thank goodness Tiny had a private hospital room because her room was never empty! Uncle Dub had flown in from Portland. He was seated at the hospital with me and Al every day. After a few days, Liz arrived from Chicago. That visit was a good boost for Tiny. From the moment Liz landed until the day she left, the three of us bunked together at the hospital. Even under these horrific circumstances, we were able to share a very good visit. Our conversations were filled with talking, laughing, and reminiscing.

Then there were the local friends that came from near and far. These were prayer warriors coming to cover my mother with the word and presence of God. The list was endless, including all of my AA co-workers. Samantha and Kim would leave work to come and sit with me on a regular basis. The retired co-workers were in and out constantly including Gail and her daughter Gabrielle, and Alana from Pasadena. The list went on to include our beautician Linda and her husband Columbus, Carolyn from Riverside and her sisters Dorothy and Janice from Long Beach, Bonita and Tom from Long Beach, Jacque from Riverside, Barbara and John from Oakland, and an endless list of others.

Pastor Royce Porter, Pattye McGee, Josie Grant, Joy Henley and other members of Crenshaw United Church Bible study visited on numerous occasions. During Pastor Porters' visits he was a God sent comforter as he prayed with and for Tiny. With Pastor Porter, Tiny was more than just one of many church members. The time spent with him had led to a relaxed feeling of closeness. He also truly observed our family relationship. I will always remember the days that he took the time to come to Tiny's hospital room. His sincere outpouring of prayer and concern cemented my trust in him as an outstanding man of God.

Tiny was also blessed to be treated by an amazing staff at UCLA Medical Center. One morning the team of doctors were doing their basic morning rounds. They asked her if there was anything she would like to have. Her response was surprising! Tiny said her 75th birthday was on February 24th and it would be nice if she could still be here for that. What would normally be a simple request sounded to me like a ticking time bond.

Knowing that celebrating her birthday would bring Tiny even an ounce of happiness in this storm made us determined to make it happen. Al and I seized every second of every day in preparation. My first order of business was to decorate her room. As birthday and get-well cards arrived, I taped them on the closet door of her hospital room. On her birthday, we brought decorations, cake, punch and all of the trimmings. The hospital provided additional chairs for the all-day stream of visitors, which included staff members from doctors and nurses to janitors. That day we broke every hospital rule regarding room capacity. The hospital also provided a harpist to beautifully play a few songs for Tiny, including Amazing Grace. Ultimately, the celebration was a success, depicting her true, full of life personality.

The doctors scheduled her discharge date to be Friday, March 6th. Tiny was coming home on Hospice Care. That day, I truly witnessed just how incredibly popular she was. Each time Tiny had been in the hospital, she was on the same ward, same floor, and had grown accustomed to the staff. This time, the hospital staff knew that she was leaving for the last time. All day, staff members took time to come and say goodbye. There was hugging, picture taking and tears. I watched Tiny as she graciously greeted everyone with calm dignity. As she said goodbyes, she smiled and thanked every member of the hospital staff from doctors to janitors.

While I was at the hospital waiting for the ambulance to transport her home, Al was at the house preparing for her arrival. I walked to the ambulance, watched them load Tiny and called Al to let him know they were on the way. I believed that because I would be in freeway traffic they would arrive before me. As I sat in the bumper to bumper 405 freeway traffic, I called my Al to see if they had arrived yet. He said, "No babe, not yet." I thought that was odd; what could be taking them so long. Surely, the driver could use their sirens and get around the traffic. When I arrived at the house they were still not there. I wondered how I could possibly have beaten them to the house. I found this alarming!

By the time they arrived, I was anxiously pacing on the sidewalk. As they opened the door, I could see that the paramedics and Tiny were laughing. When I asked what took so long, Tiny said they made a detour. She went on to tell me that they had struck up a conversation about her not being a native of California. When she told them what brought her here the paramedics asked what she liked most when she moved here. Tiny told them she and my dad would drive to the beach, park and look out at the ocean. All of this conversation was done with Tiny in a reclined position, so she had no idea what route they were taking. When they finally came to a stop, she thought she was at home. To Tiny's surprise, when the paramedics raised the bed, they had parked in a perfect position for her to have one last look at the beach.

Before the ambulance drivers brought her inside the house, Tiny asked them to pause so she could admire the yard. These gentlemen were so kind and patient. We all just stood outside for a few minutes. While we were enjoying the moment, the hospice nurse arrived. We met LaTonya's supervisor when we made the arrangements but never met her. Ironically, this nurse's name was LaTanya. Not only was she the epitome of professionalism, but she was also an angel of compassion, making her presence all that we could have hoped for. LaTanya demonstrated an extraordinary level of gentle attentiveness. To add to our confidence, she was a Christian woman who not only did her job but asked to join us in our daily prayers!

It was not very long after Tiny came into the house before she went into her (CEO) Chief Encouragement Officer mode. The queen size bed had been removed from the guest bedroom. In its place, the room had been converted to include all the necessary medical and mobile devices, along with a hospital bed. Bonita had been with my mother at the hospital almost every day. She had personally ordered a luxury mattress for the hospital bed, to help Tiny be more comfortable at home. Some friendships are measured by quantity instead of quality. The loyalty that Bonita showed Tiny had nothing to do with how long they had known one another. Their friendship was about walking into each other's lives, saying that "I am here for you" and proving it!

After Tiny got settled, she suddenly told my dad that after she was gone, he should get rid of the king size bed in their master bedroom. Tiny said she felt a smaller bed would give him more floor space to move around. She thought both rooms would be more comfortable with queen-size beds. Their king size mattress was almost new, so Tiny had even preplanned who it would serve best. Our flower gardens were cared for on a weekly basis by a married couple. Nee and Jimmy had been with us for nearly twenty years. Tiny knew their financial struggles, so she suggested that Al give the mattress to them. Al's expression was truly saddened by this conversation. With tears in his eyes, he nodded his head in agreement.

By the second day of Tiny's return home, my parents' house had become a constant flurry of people. Through the coming weeks, this pattern of visitors continued every single day. On the weekend of March 21st and 22nd, the house was busier than ever. People were constantly coming and going with conversations consisting of lots of prayer and echoes of laughter. No one spoke very much about what brought us together. Although my mother was carrying a heavy burden, Tiny never seemed to be pressured or frustrated at all.

> *"Shout for joy, you heavens; rejoice, you earth; burst into song, you mountains! For the Lord comforts his people and will have compassion on his afflicted ones."*
>
> Isaiah 49:13

For the entire weekend, Tiny sat in the living room for hours on end. She seemed to truly be enjoying herself. As if she were hosting a party, Tiny was greeting, smiling, and taking all the conversations in. To the best of her ability, Tiny was carrying on as if she was not sick. The last visitors that day were another married AA couple, Joanne and Vaughn and their teenage daughter. Though they were already acquainted by many years of AA LAX travel hellos, this was their first visit to Tiny and Al's home. We sat for hours reminiscing about the years since Joanne and I first met in the reservation office. Before they left, everyone gathered in a circle for a beautifully spoken powerful prayer led by Vaughn. Immediately, we all knew that the spirit of God had come over the house.

As the days passed, the personal goodbye visitors continued to come to the house. With nearly every visit ending, I overheard many people telling Tiny how glad they were to have spent this time together. Some even said that they thought they were coming to cheer her up. Instead, they thanked her by saying she had been an encourager and an elevator for their spirit. I listened as Tiny thanked each person for coming. Her confident solid response to everyone was that for twenty-nine years God's word had told her to Press On! She added that she wanted to reach the end of the race and receive Gods promise of the victory and the Heavenly prize that was waiting for her. Her words sounded so pleasant as if she was ushering the holy spirit to come!

> *"And the God of all Grace, who called you into his eternal glory in Christ, after you have suffered a little while, will himself restore you and make you strong, firm and steadfast."*
>
> 1 Peter 5:10

On Monday morning, Tiny said she needed to have a serious mother-daughter conversation with me. I heard that soft, familiar, concerned mom's voice I had grown accustomed to for over fifty-six years. During these conversations I have learned to expect to hear words that are unexpected. This one-on-one talk evolved into her gently speaking a series of extremely blunt comments. Tiny's very first words rocked me off guard. She said, "We both know that things are changing. I am the one dying, not you." While hearing her say this made me uncomfortable, it seemed so easy for her to speak of her own demise. I sat quietly, listening as Tiny continued to give me her motherly instructions. It was totally apparent that she really wanted to make her transition as easy on me as possible.

As she continued with her brutally frank comments, I heard one instruction after another. "Do not let my death define you! You are about to enter a new season in your life. God has a promise for you. Look ahead for your purpose and destiny. Do not pitch a tent and stay in the valley of grief.

Instead, she encouraged me to focus on the beauty of life! You must be strong! When the going gets tough, just keep praising God! Pray, trust, believe, have courage, and seek joy. Tracie, you can do it!" It is quite apparent that Tiny had far more confidence in me than I had in myself. In my heart I was unsure of how I would handle life without her. Somehow, I managed to promise her that I would do my best. I wanted her to know that she did not need to worry.

I was fighting my tears and did not want this conversation to continue. Not surprisingly, Tiny was not finished yet. She went on to say that all I needed to do was look around at the big picture. Take note of all these beautiful friends who came to support you. Some are older, but many are women your age. Tiny said that after the conversations she had shared with each of them this weekend, she realized even more how blessed the two of us had been for so many years. She went on to say that of all the visitors over the weekend, I was probably the only one who still has two living parents, and many of them are not blessed to still have even one.

Then she added a bit of humor by making a series of perfectly timed comments geared to convince me not to give up. Her comments were, "You have lots of women who have already been down this road. They are excellent examples to follow. There are no excuses about moving forward. Do not disappoint me. I will always be by your side; watching and cheering you on! Lift your head, pull your shoulders back, and stand tall, Tracie. I did not raise the wimp in the bunch." Tiny ended by seriously acknowledging the fact that I was bound to have some difficult days ahead. It was obvious that this conversation had given both of us a sense of relief. For the rest of the day, we sat together in her bed, talking, crying, hugging, kissing, laughing, and eating popsicles. Unfortunately, in Tiny's last days, this was the only thing she could swallow!

Later that afternoon, Mother arrived from her apartment to join us for a few hours. At this point, Tiny had been home for three weeks. It was their daily afternoon visit. Mother knew that Tiny was sick, but she had no idea that these were her last days. At ninety-six years old, we decided not to tell her the severity of Tiny's condition. We all wanted to spare her the daily anguish of wondering "when." As we had routinely done every other night since Tiny came home, the family gathered at her bedside. I read the scripture from our favorite daily devotional. The reading for March 23rd is taken from Psalm 36. The last sentence says, *"Come to Me with open hands and heart, ready to receive all I have for you."*

After reading the scripture, Mother went home. Shortly after she left, Tiny asked what time it was. It was nine o'clock. Tiny looked at me and said, you are here with me day and night. Since it was Kevin's "work week Friday" and he was probably staying up late, she wanted me to go home. She adamantly said, "I am fine. Go home and spend some time with your husband". She added that Al had a doctor's appointment the next morning, so she asked me to come back early. The plan was that the two of us would enjoy a girl talk together. Nurse LaTanya checked all of Tiny's vitals one more time. With a reassuring smile, she looked at me and said everything was stable! She said she would come by early the next morning before Al left and check her again.

LaTanya and I busied ourselves doing everything to make sure Tiny was comfortably in bed for the night. Tiny was in a very good mood. She started joking with me, telling me not to stop at the gas station or drug store. Tiny said to just go home. Then she added one of her "Mother Hen" comments by stating, "Call me when you get in the house." That was the standard way that she and Al would know I was safely off the street. We all smiled.

"A cheerful heart is good medicine, but a crushed spirit dries up the bones."

Proverbs 17:22

LaTanya and I gathered our purses and left the house together, once again agreeing to return the next morning before Al left at eight o'clock for his doctor's appointment.

After I left that evening, Al was home alone with Tiny. He said that shortly after midnight, the sound of her voice woke him up. He thought Tiny was calling his name to help her to the bathroom. He soon realized that was not the case. As he was walking across the dark hall, he stopped and listened to what she was saying. At the top of her voice, Al heard my mother talking to God. Tiny was declaring her trust in him. Her prayer and petitions were that she did not want to be a burden on her family. He continued to listen as her words went on. Tiny added that, "If this is the best quality of earthly life I have left, please take me Lord. I am ready to go." Al said that he entered the room and the two of them talked and loved one another for the next few hours.

"How lovely is your dwelling place, Lord Almighty! My soul yearns, even faints for the courts of the Lord; my heart and my flesh cry out for the living God."

Psalm 84:1-2

At 4:35 am, my phone rang. I was not asleep, but just laying quietly, thinking and praying. Because it was the darkest hour of the night, my heart immediately started beating rapidly. As I answered the phone on speaker,

Kevin and I both sat straight up in bed. It was Al! My first question was, "Do you need me?" He responded, "Yes Suga, the paramedics just left. She's gone!" I could not believe my ears. My beloved mother was gone!!! A million thoughts were racing through my mind.

"We are confident, I say, and would prefer to be away from the body and at home with the Lord."

2 Corinthians 5:8

Like watching a movie screen, I re-played every word and event of the last twenty-four hours. That evening Tiny had been so insistent that I went home. Immediately, a feeling of regret came over me for leaving her side. Then I started wondering if Tiny somehow knew this was her last earthly night. She had been so adamant about my going home to be with Kevin. Had this been any other morning, Kevin would have been at work, and I would have been home alone. Even though the doctors had told us weeks ago that this day was coming, I still felt cheated. I felt like Tiny was riding a train and got off before her stop. It was as if I had not had any advance notice at all.

I was so devastated and numb that I cannot even remember getting in the car. As we drove to be with Al, I could hear Kevin starting to make phone calls. All the way to the house, I was completely numb and totally speechless. I felt like I could barely breathe. Silently I tried to pray. The only words that would come to my mind were, "Help Me Jesus." When Kevin and I arrived at my parents' house, one look at the intense grief on my dad's face was all it took. I realized that I had to immediately take my mind off of me. The manifestation of a previous conversation between me and Tiny was suddenly a horrible living reality. Over and over, I kept hearing Tiny's soft, sweet voice saying, "I am so sorry baby, but you are going to have to be the strength for Al and Mother." As hard as this reality was to accept, it was obvious that she was right. Suddenly, she was gone, and my time had come!

Within no time, the house was filled with our children, family, and several friends. Tiny has never had a crisis or hospital stay, where our paramedic firefighter son, Kevin, Jr., was not one of the first on the scene. This morning was no exception. Once Kevin called him, he immediately left work and came to my parents' house. Things were happening so fast! It was obvious that Al and I were in no shape for much decision making. I am so grateful that Kevin Jr. is an intelligent and responsible young man. Along with Nurse LaTanya, my son took the family lead. He was in control of the situation as it relates to dealing with the police as well as the coroner. Thanks to his calm, professional training, everything was handled in the smoothest way possible.

Without a doubt, Tuesday, March 24, 2015, was the darkest day of my entire life! Everyone gathered in the living room, joining hands in a circle to pray. My mind was still fixed on my earlier prayer of "help me Jesus." As we stood silently, God gave me direction. My sister Shay gave me my favorite daily devotional. The name of it is *Jesus Calling*. As always, I had read the daily message to Tiny from this book each night before I went home. The book was still lying on the table. Suddenly, I picked it up! Everyone stood silently as I began to read aloud the message for that day (March 24th). "This is a time in your life when you must learn to let go: of loved ones, of possessions, of control. To let go of something that is precious to you, you need to rest in My Presence, where you are complete. Take time to bask in the Light of My Love. As you relax more and more, your grasp gradually opens, releasing your prized possession into My care. You can feel secure, even during cataclysmic changes, through awareness of My continual Presence. The One who never leaves you is the same One who never changes: I am the same yesterday, today, and forever. As you release more and more things into My care, remember that I never let go of your hand. Herein lies your security, which no one and no circumstance can take from you. Referenced Bible Scriptures were: Psalm 89:35; Hebrews 13:8; Isaiah 41:1.

By the time I finished reading, everyone was crying and hugging. All I could say was, "Thank You Lord!" I felt the message for the circumstances of this day could not have been more appropriate. It was as if it had been written and designed specifically for me. Oh, how I needed this Word! As uncomfortable as I was about what happened, God's word helped me to understand why it happened. At that moment I felt a sense of peace. I realized that even the day of Tiny's homegoing was perfectly timed by God. Although the doctors had told us six weeks ago that this day was coming, I still found myself extremely unprepared. Immediately, I had to start making phone calls, and funeral arrangements. If you have never been in this position, let me tell you there is so much to do, and a very short time to get it done. I was like a robot, simply going through the planning motions. Instinctively, Sasha rearranged her days off, staying right by my side all the way. She was a strong beacon of comfort and light in my darkness.

During my lifetime, I have attended many funerals. I instantly realized that having to wear the memorial service planning shoe was a totally different experience! Life can sometimes push us to places we are unprepared to deal with. My mind was racing over the discussions Tiny, and I had shared during the past few weeks. In my opinion, one of the most courageous final conversations we shared was about the details of her funeral. While we did not talk about it in great length, every word Tiny spoke was with conviction. She left this earth very much in control . . . like a boss! Tiny never liked fanfare or overload, so she told me not to go overboard with her funeral. She believed that the service would probably be small, so I should just make it simple and nice. She added a line of words that she had spoken to me on many occasions. "Sometimes less is best!"

For me, this was a truly heartbreaking conversation. Just hearing Tiny speak these words in such a matter-of-fact way, made me uncomfortable. It was one of the rare times that I just sat, quietly listening. Tiny went on to say that her funeral service should not be sad. Instead, it should be a lively celebration. For some strange reason, Tiny did not think she was very popular or that many people would take the time to attend her funeral. Even at such a time as this, Tiny was still very unaware of her own continuing influence and impact on others. Instead, she continued to minimize herself by embracing her usual humble and modest attitude.

No matter how much Tiny had tried to ease the stress of this day for us, Al and I still found ourselves very much unprepared for the task ahead. Among other things, the responsibility of making funeral preparations is emotionally exhausting and mind boggling. When Al and I were starting, we realized that grief had us fumbling our way along. Finally, Al said to me, "Tiny was everyone's open door. This is her last party, so let's try to do things the same welcoming way she would if she were planning this herself." I am so grateful to everyone that calmly stepped in to help. Sasha conducted the selection of the obituary photos. I could not have organized the obituary design and picture selections without her. Gail provided the photos for the funeral stands and the repast. My coworker Joyce was instrumental in setting up the music to include vocals by her sister and one of our coworkers. She also took the responsibility of handling the video that was put together by my brother-in-law Michael's friend, Amber. My coworker Pat directed me to hold the service in the Golden West Galleria and the Marriott Hotel for the repast. I could not have arranged this service without the loving input of these ladies.

Although Tiny had an admirable classic wardrobe, we opted to purchase something new for her special day. Then there was the selection of the floral arrangement. Purple and white were my mother's favorite colors, so that decision was automatic. When the flower order was placed, the florist commented on the meaning of these two colors, saying purple indicated royalty and white was associated with honesty and goodness. Hearing these words really made my heart smile because these colors are so appropriate for Tiny. No wonder, they were her favorites! This prompted me to take the color scheme a little further by asking each family member to wear a purple hint. Together, Al and I put our hearts and heads together in total agreement. Our primary goal was to organize a homegoing celebration and repast that we believed Tiny would have approved of. In honor and respect for Tiny's final wishes, we were able to accomplish what we thought was required.

As the days passed, my God-sent sisters started to arrive. Pastor LaTanya was the first to help with the funeral preparations. I was so choked up, that conversation was in no way flowing. Thank God we shared so many years of personal history that she was able to pull it together on her own. Jo and her daughter, Asia arrived next, followed by Stephanie. In the days leading up to the funeral, these ladies were constantly right by my side. Compassionate support is what I needed, and that is exactly what they provided! Al was covered at his house with the presence of Uncle W.R., Evelyn, Uncle Harold, Aunt Ivy, and my cousins Sharon and Beverly. In addition, Ernest was there from Chicago, Shane and Alice from Louisville, Kenneth from Northern California, and Earline from Portland. We had a viewing the day before the funeral. Because Mother was too heartbroken to attend the funeral, she and Maryann viewed early with the family and went home. All of my AA sisters came to support me. Most of them stayed the entire day, until the last people left. In addition, nurses, doctors, church members, coworkers, neighbors, local families, and friends came to the mortuary.

When the evening was over, we all left to have dinner and get some rest. As my out-of-town sisters and I sat at my house, Kevin received an alarming phone call. Sasha and her roommate had been involved in an auto accident. Kevin Jr. said he would go to the hospital and let us know the severity. The next call was even more shocking. A car had run a stop sign and hit them as they were walking across the street. Yes, this accident was a pedestrian against auto! Kevin assured us that Sasha was being released and would be at the funeral the next morning. This proved to be a very restless night for me and Kevin. We didn't see Sasha until the next day when she pushed herself to join us at the funeral. Shockingly, she was walking with the aid of crutches. I was so full of mixed emotions. My mind remembered Kevin Jr.'s alarming leg injury a few years earlier. I was so proud of Sasha and the discipline she showed to make it through the day. This accident was followed by multiple surgeries and extensive rehabilitation therapy. We were so grateful that God had spared their lives!

Obviously, Tiny had underestimated herself as well as the level of impact she had on others. From Dr. Friedman to Roslyn and her mother Lorena, Ellen and her daughter Jamila Reese, and so many more, the chapel pews were full! I can never thank Pastor Royce Porter enough. His initial call to me was, "We are here for you. Just let me know what you need." Without a doubt, he did a wonderful job officiating the funeral. Of course, Tiny's eulogy was delivered by my friend Pastor LaTanya. Because of LaTanya's long, personal connection to our family, she was the perfect person to deliver a very uplifting eulogy. The designated speakers at the funeral service were our Bible study friend Josie Grant from Crenshaw United Methodist Church, and our cousin Benita (Bunny) Council. In addition, our daughter Sasha (bruised and on a cane) and son Kevin Jr., Gail's daughter, Gabrielle, also spoke about "Aunt Tiny." also spoke about "Aunt Tiny."

Knowing that these young adults were sharing their sincere reflections of their relationships with Tiny was beautiful.

The service ended by opening the podium for impromptu speaking from any other friends and family that wanted to say something. My uncle Harold was the first to the podium, speaking about our yesterdays, just as I remembered them. Stephanie spoke next, of shared memories that spanned our entire lives. Both Al and I were pleased and forever grateful for their presence and willingness to openly share their outpouring of love for Tiny! Seeing our son join the ranks of pallbearers was breathtaking! Following the service, we proceeded to the Marriott Hotel for the repast. Nearly everyone in attendance told us that it was a beautiful homegoing service. Some intimate friends even asked us if she had planned it herself because everything was, "so like Tiny."

Our Inglewood Cemetery funeral arranger, Antoinette (Toni), called me a few days following the service. After asking how we were doing, she said she usually takes a quick peek at the services she arranges to make sure that the families are ok and everything is going as planned. Toni said that once she stepped into the chapel, Tiny's service was something that she could not leave. I will never forget her extremely kind words to me and my dad. "You two did a really good job. I am so glad I stayed for the service. I did not know Tiny before the funeral, but I feel like I know her now." Hearing this was music to my ears. I was so glad that Al and I successfully gave Tiny a homegoing celebration that truly reflected her personality. Just as she would have done, we opened her life to all!

And if I go and prepare a place for you, I will come back and take you to be with me so that you also may be where I am. 4You know the way to the place where I am going."

John 14:3-4

13

DRIFTING ON A MEMORY

The Bible says that to be absent from the body is to be present with the Lord. I miss Tiny's physical presence more than words can begin to describe. The feelings that I live with are absolute confirmation to me that true love creates memories that are both precious and priceless! They are the only thing that no one can take away from me. I advise everyone to spend as much time as possible with the people you love. Your memories are the only thing that will last a lifetime. Someday, memories may be all you have!

In my eyes, Tiny was outstanding. She was a woman above average in so many ways. Her perspective of everyone was always optimistic. Tiny never kept anyone at a distance. Instead, she invited people into her life with wide open arms. This characteristic made Tiny a loyal and outstanding friend to so many people. During her trials, Tiny always displayed insurmountable faith and courage. Like a warrior, she never gave up! Instead, Tiny boldly suffered through all life's hardships, setbacks, and disappointments while she bravely endured the pain. Even after receiving her final terminal diagnosis, Tiny never displayed a victim mentality. It was obvious that Tiny was comforted during these devastating circumstances by her trust in God.

I will always be amazed that during the last six weeks of her life, Tiny never shed a tear in anguish. Instead, as she faced the end of her earthly life, I was blessed to witness Tiny continue to smile as she thanked and praised God. Until the very last moment, I knew Tiny continued celebrating life. I also know that God kept her in perfect peace until she took her last breath! It was my first experience witnessing the last days of someone heading for Heaven. God gave me six weeks of a bitter-sweet, life-changing revelation. I felt like I was witnessing,

"The Lord gives strength to his people; the Lord blesses his people with peace."

Psalm 29:11

I will never forget it was truly an eye-opening experience in God's Word.

While Tiny is no longer physically with me, without a shadow of a doubt, I know that my mother was promoted. Instead of losing a battle, Tiny won her race as a victorious champion! I accept that she has received her coveted prize of eternal life in the glorious place where there is no more pain and suffering. Tiny is in Heaven, embracing God's promise of Everlasting Life! I can only imagine how wonderful it must be to be safely seated at the throne in the presence of the Lord. Al and Tiny always taught me that God never makes mistakes. Everything he does is with a perfect plan and purpose. Hallelujah!

I am a living representative of Tiny and God, trying hard to overcome my selfish feelings. No matter what I saw Tiny going through, how sick she had become, or how many times she told me that she was tired, I still did not want to let her go. Whenever I think about our earthly life, I miss her like crazy! Daily, I find myself trying to make sense of Tiny's death, repeatedly telling myself that she was sick and did not want to suffer or be what she deemed a burden to others. Most assuredly, she told me she was unafraid of her destiny. She felt her assignment was complete! Still, without Tiny's presence, I often feel lost. I have always had her soft voice of reasoning. Tiny was the cheerleader and secret keeper who loved me right or wrong—anyway, I presented myself. The seed of Tiny's love and encouragement is forever buried in the soil of my heart.

Through it all, God continued to bless us. He did not leave us in the desert. That year, we welcomed the birth of our granddaughter Victoria, Kevin's first child. Her presence was a light in the darkness. Being a grandmother was something that I instantly loved. Every moment I spend with this innocent child gives me a reason to smile! It delights my heart to see her next to Al or my Grandmother. I hear a whisper in my soul that says God always has a way to give you what you thought you would never have.

Within a few weeks of this new addition, our family received another reason to celebrate. Al, Kevin, Kevin Jr., and I, along with Natashia and her family, gathered at Cal State LA. We stood together, proudly cheering as Sasha received her master's degree. It was as if the heavens were shouting, "Life goes on."

Tiny was well-associated with several members of the church. She conversed with everyone from the parking lot attendants to the greeters at the door and the ushers as she headed to her seat. Because they had all witnessed her physical struggles and transformation, they helped when needed. Of course, Tiny had her section of comrades in her preferred seat section. On the rare occasions that I went without her because she did not feel up to attending service, I was repeatedly hit with the question, "Is your mom okay?" Initially, it was difficult for me to utter the words that she had passed. I was shying away from people and did not immediately return to church.

One day, Tiny's church friend, Ms. Lillie, called me. She told me Tiny had mentioned that I did not live far from her and wanted to know if I could pick her up for church the following day. By this time, Tiny had been gone for ten weeks. I picked her up the following morning for my return to church services. Ms. Lillie is very pleasant to talk to, so I continued to pick her up, just as I had always done with Tiny. She happens to be from Chicago, so we share stories of our pasts. We were leaving church several months later, and Ms. Lilly introduced me to her daughter in the parking lot. While I knew she had daughters, I did not know that they attended our church. Perhaps her phone call to me had been God's way of pulling me out of my Sunday depression. To this day, Ms. Lillie and I have never stopped just the two of us carpooling.

That same year, our family was hit with a flood of nitty-gritty situations. Two months after Tiny's homegoing, her Uncle Billy's daughter, Tracy, passed unexpectedly in Missouri. By the end of the year, Al's sister, Marilyn, passed in South Carolina, and my friend Shay lost her mom, Mary.

The first Mother's Day without Tiny proved very difficult for me! Having strong sister friends who had previously walked the walk of losing their mothers was a blessing—with the love of true friendship, Juanita, her daughter, Nichelle, and Barbara flatly refused to let me stay at home. I joined them after church for brunch with several other friends and members of their families. I remembered Tiny's instruction about not being the wimp in the bunch. Year after year, their Mother's Day tradition includes invitations for Sasha and me.

In the days and weeks to come, I rarely had a day alone. In addition to the care and concern of my cousin Bunny and local friends, I had a stream of out-of-town visitors. Tiny's former boss, Nellie, flew in from Paris. She spent a few days with Al and me, saying she needed closure. We visited Tiny's grave site together, sitting on a blanket so engrossed in memories that time got away from us. A security guard came to tell us they were locking the gates, and we had to leave. Following this visit, Maime flew in from Virginia. After having lunch together, we also spent an afternoon at the cemetery. It was not long before LaTanya and Joe came in from Maryland, Stephanie from Chicago, and Debra from Atlanta. On the first anniversary of Tiny's passing, Stephanie flew in from Chicago for a week. I am so grateful to have these sisters-in-love. After a lifetime of friendship, these visits were not isolated to me; each spent lots of time with Al and Mother. Without hesitation, they never left us lonely!

These days, more than ever before, I think about all of Tiny's motherly advice. Her words are still the first place I turn to when I need guidance and encouragement. Tiny and I were genuinely like-minded, sharing an unspoken language of the heart. The two of us were able to communicate with each other without ever saying a word. Oh, how I long for her looks, smile, and touch. Some days, I feel myself drowning in emotions about how much I miss her. There is no denying it; I selfishly want her back! I admit there are moments when I still cry without any advance notice. I am still in an emotional healing process, struggling to let the beautiful memories overshadow the loss of flesh. I know that I may be a little slow on this healing journey; probably not yet where I should be, and surely not where Tiny ever wanted me to be. Somehow, after these heart conversations, I always seem to feel better. I exhale and try to focus on the future.

Throughout her cancer battle, Tiny constantly talked about my life after she was gone. She said that while it would be normal to miss her, I still had the God-given gift of life. In her motherly tone, Tiny repeatedly tried to prepare me by emphasizing that I should be brave and love every day of my life, just as she had enjoyed hers. I heard every word she said, but still, I was extremely unprepared. Tiny's homegoing has given me more time with my thoughts and prayers. I miss her tremendously! I mentally talk to her every day, hearing her sweet melody while consciously attempting to keep my life steady. Tiny was always my earthly compass. Today, she is my bright shining light. In all that I do, my heart still feels her love guiding me!

The privilege of having Tiny as my mom was uniquely awesome, a once-in-a-lifetime blessing! There is a magical bond between a mother and daughter that lasts forever! All I think about are the good times we shared together. The sting of death has a potent emotional effect! At some point, most of us will be confronted with the sorrow and pain it brings. Everyone navigates this season of mourning in their own uniquely individual way. My best personal description is the unsteady feeling of riding the waves on a sinking ship. God has the tide-turning power to give me His peace. He is the anchor that continues to calm my raging seas.

Regarding genetics, I am the fruit of Tiny's tree. Though I had lived many years without my body showing the effects of being overly stressed, this proved to be more than I could handle. It was not long before my desire to be "just like my mother" once again became a medical reality. Within three months of the doctor's stunning prognosis regarding Tiny, I lost 25 pounds. Yes, this situation caused a level of emotional and physical stress that I was unprepared for. After a visit with my primary care doctor, I was diagnosed with another of Tiny's medical conditions. Graves Thyroid Disease, for which there is no cure, had reared its ugly head in my body. In addition, both MS and Fibromyalgia were in a major flare. Thankfully, with constant rest, physical therapy, acupuncture, and medication—my symptoms were slowly controlled enough to restore a reasonable amount of health and well-being.

There is only one explanation for our family being where we are today. It is that we have received Favor from God. We have often been down, but through Prayer, Hope, Faith, Trust, and Togetherness, we have always managed to get back up. I also realized that our house was never really an open door. My beloved mother was the open door! Galatians 5:22 speaks of the Fruit of the Spirit, summing up the attributes and virtues of a good Christian life. Tiny lived an admirable life that displayed every one of these qualities. She was truly a woman of excellence! Growing up under the leadership and in the shadows of Tiny's life was another one of my personal gifts from God. Her life was a perfect model for my daily living. She was a guiding sermon for my growth and development. My greatest desire has always been to echo her example, especially her warm, compassionate spirit toward others. In all I say and do, I genuinely hope people see just a little Tiny in me. I want to represent Tiny not only in my physical appearance but also in my words and deeds.

Understandably, both Al and Mother were taking this loss extremely hard. I kept replaying the hospital conversation of Tiny telling me that I would have to take care of them. Though crushed beyond belief, the brokenness the two of them had was more than I had ever imagined. In constant prayer, I displayed an outward level of composure. God strengthened me in a way that I did not think was possible. In reflection, I feel like I lived the "Footprints" poem. "It was then that I carried you." Mother was shattered that at twenty-two years younger, God had taken Tiny before her. Al was able to pull himself together for Mother. He continued to give himself away, looking in on her every morning as soon as he woke up. Not one day passed; they did not visit, watch TV, or have dinner together. Al started having bar-b-ques and other holiday dinners for small groups of family and friends at his house. He said he needed something to do to keep himself busy.

It was 2016 before I could breathe enough to spread my wings and travel. Kevin and I decided to change our scenery with a few trips that fall. We started by celebrating his sixtieth birthday in San Francisco with Sasha and Kevin. A few months later, we went to Maryland for a surprise birthday party to celebrate Pastor LaTanya's sixtieth birthday. This occasional change of scenery seemed helpful, so we continued with just the two of us trips that included Seattle, Hawaii, and New Orleans. In June 2017, Kevin and I celebrated our twenty-fourth wedding anniversary and my sixtieth birthday at Atlantis Paradise Island in Nassau, Bahamas. This week was such a relaxing time for the two of us. I would venture to say this was the honeymoon that we never had! We truly enjoyed the trip as if we did not have a care in the world.

As part of Barbara's sixtieth birthday celebration, she started the Sisters At The Well Monday Morning Prayer group. It is a one-hour call-in prayer line for women from around the globe. This no-judgment zone allows each lady to be transparent about themselves as we pray for one another. When the call is over, we have successfully achieved a jump start for our week. God has blessed this Prayer Line and all participants as we are now in our sixth year. I joined Juanita, Barbara, and the Sisters At The Well in the coming months for a few ladies' retreats that took us to D.C., Atlanta, and The Bahamas. Thanks to Maryann continuing to be with Mother, I also got Al to take a break. I went with him to Louisville, where Shane and his family relocated many years ago. It was a place that our family visited regularly throughout the summers. We are extended family members when we go to Louisville. In the past, Al, Shane, and Ernest were also regular attendees at the Kentucky Derby. As they aged, things slowed down. Al and I also made a few road trips to Las Vegas as the months passed. It was good for him to spend time with his old friends.

My beautician Linda's sister Katherine was the First Lady of Ordered Steps Ministry, and founder of a women's group called, Sister's United. They invited me to their monthly Saturday meeting, where a group of compassionate, godly women warmly surrounded me. That day, I became an official member of this organization, which continues to fill me with support and fellowship. The heartbreak of loss continued as Roslyn's mother, Lorena, transitioned to be with the Lord in 2017, followed by Kevin's uncle, Harry, in February 2018. Kevin and I were blessed to take his dad to attend the service in Atlanta. The funeral was like being at a family reunion. They enjoyed time with Kevin's cousins Debra, Linda, and the rest of Harry's children and grandchildren.

When we returned, I joined Juanita for another Sisters at the Well trip. The destination was Bermuda, which happened to be a place that Tiny and I had always talked about visiting. While I was there, I called Al every morning as usual. On the third morning, when he answered the phone, I could hear voices in the background. He told me that he had found Mother asleep on her living room floor that morning. When he called her name, she was alert and did not appear to be injured. Mother could not explain why she was on the floor, saying she must have fallen asleep in the chair and slid onto the floor. The problem was that he could not lift her because he has balance issues and uses a cane. She also uses a cane and has artificial knees. Calling the paramedics was the only option, which was a blessing. They determined that Mother's vitals were unstable, so the paramedics took her to the hospital. Further medical examination determined that she had suffered a heart attack!

Of course, my first plan of action was to return home immediately. That day, there were severe thunderstorms across the Atlantic, causing flight cancellations for the next few days. I made a few phone calls to Maryann, our hairstylist Linda, and Samantha. Like sisters, I knew I could depend on the three of them. Linda and her husband Columbus went immediately to be with Al. He said having them there really helped to calm him. Samantha joined them as soon as she got off work. Shortly afterward, I received a selfie she took with Mother. As a faithful sister, Samantha assured me that Mother was stable and that I needed to enjoy the trip since I could not get home. When Maryann arrived, she said she would take care of Mother and Al until I got home. God placed these loving, Christian people in our lives to stand in the gap. That day, they were our family of their choosing. After Mother spent three months in the hospital and rehabilitation center, she peacefully passed away. She already had a plot with the rest of our family in Missouri. Uncle Dub, Kevin, Al, and I took a familiar journey to lay another loved one to rest. Within weeks of Mother's passing, we buried Kevin's father, Herbert. My Aunt Evelyn's health had been declining since Tiny's passing. In September, we were in Portland for her funeral.

After all this loss, Kevin and I decided to relieve our stress again with travel. In October 2018, we joined our church (Faithful Central Bible Church) on a trip to The Holy Land. I would say that this was the most memorable trip of my life! Seeing the Biblical things I had read about in the Bible was nothing short of amazing. The highlight for me was when Kevin and I were baptized in the River Jordan. Standing there, I smiled at the recollection of Al and Tiny being baptized together. A few months later, Samantha invited us to join The Footsteps of Paul church group trip. In April 2019, we found ourselves on a tour that would take us to Rome, Greece, Italy, Santorini, and on a cruise. What an awesome time we had! Just like in the movies, Santorini was breathtakingly beautiful.

Many people have said that what is meant for you is meant for you. This saying was confirmed to me in September 2019. I received a phone call that I initially thought was Spam. They stated that I had one day to respond as to whether or not I was available to accept a trip for two that I had won. Stand Up To Cancer and AA partnered to send an inaugural plane full of cancer survivors on a four-day, all-expense paid trip to Orlando. I called Kevin at work, and he said, "Start packing." Imagine flying on a plane specially painted on the outside to include your name! Tiny's name was also on the plane. We left for a fabulous stay at the Hyatt Regency Orlando a few days later. We were showered with a luxury suite, gifts, tours, and lots of food from the moment we landed. During every moment of the trip, we were pampered and treated like royalty! I learned that the recipients of this honor were selected by having their names and stories submitted and selected. Though she never told me, conversations led me to believe my friend Kim submitted our names. I do know that she paid to have Tiny's name added to the outside of the plane. Of course, I am now an avid supporter of Stand Up To Cancer.

By the beginning of 2020, Kevin and I were making a winter trip to Chicago to support Stephanie in the loss of her mother, Mattie. The very next month, Uncle W.R. suffered a heart attack at the bowling alley. His passing was on Valentine's Day, my grandfather Creston's birthday. Al, Kevin, and I flew to Portland to support my cousin Steven, and his son Shalamar through the homegoing celebration. Our long-time gardener Nee also completed her cancer battle and joined the heavenly ranks. The gates of heaven continued to receive those close to my heart, as Terry in Chicago, Gail's mother Marcella, and my hairstylist Linda's mother all joined the ranks. By now, the world was battling COVID, which took the life of Jo's son Ernest. Although the bulk of these losses came with some warning, that did not lessen the heartache.

Unfortunately, since Tiny's passing, I have had a few friends cross over into the cancer battlefield. I am honored that I have found myself on the list of people many of these warriors elect to contact for support. As they share their concerns, the lights of Tiny's path begin to illuminate in my heart. Apparently, these people find some comfort in contacting me because they have seen me share my life experiences. Without hesitation, I am compelled to go into the mode Tiny always modeled for me: aggressively reaching out to join them on the battlefield. I know that the obstacle in front of them is frightening. It requires strength and courage to overcome. My instinctive desire is to comfort and support while sharing hope and encouragement.

During my years as Tiny's, "Patient Advocate," my eyes and ears were wide open. I knew that knowledge about cancer was valuable, so I tried to glean every bit of information available. Whenever I found myself in a situation where free literature was offered, I always took more than one copy. Through the years, I have accumulated a "war room" of cancer literature in my home. When I encounter someone in need, I immediately go to my resources to prepare an information packet for them. I also read about the situation to equip myself to share my knowledge better. As time goes on, as I speak to someone about cancer, it is Tiny's voice that I hear. What a revelation this is for me. Without even trying, once again I realize that in so many ways, I naturally am just like Tiny!

> *"But those who hope in the Lord will renew their strength. They will soar on wings like eagles; they will run and not grow weary; they will walk and not faint"*

Isaiah 40:31

14

COUNT IT ALL JOY

God is the giver, and I am so grateful that He continues to favor me!

Meeting Kevin gave me the best and sometimes only friend. My feelings are balanced and confirmed with a marriage that has allowed us to grow together. We were inseparable until illness forced me to leave the workforce in 2008. Suddenly, when Kevin left for work, I was home alone. It offered me an opportunity to enjoy time with Tiny. After Tiny was promoted to heaven in 2015, I encountered some very lonely days. Five years later, Kevin was furloughed due to the COVID-19 pandemic. After two years of unemployment, Kevin announced his official retirement, having spent 49 years working from the ground up to Skycap Supervisor for AA. Living this 24-hour daily empty nest relationship was a new beginning for us, providing the advantage of getting to know each other again! God has given us a fresh flow with a rhythm that compliments one another. I feel blessed that 35 years after our first meeting, we are still going in the same direction. Standing together through all the highs and lows has made us realize nothing is impossible.

Kevin and I are two of a kind regarding our enthusiasm for our outside acquaintances. Being homebodies, we are learning the difference between what is important and what is trivial. There are times when we must rise above everyday offenses and disappointments. We pray that God will not let our hearts become polluted. Instead, we ask that He give us the power to love others the way He loves us. Like our marriage, we intentionally live with Christ seven days a week. Our communing with the Lord is not limited to Sunday! We invite Him into our life every day. That is when He reveals the specific reasons we should restart, recharge, get up, and keep living.

In January 2022, we had an unusual overnight windstorm. The next day was warm and clear, but the wind had left our front yard full of paper scraps. While Kevin went to feed his mother lunch, I decided to sweep up the litter. By the time he returned, I was almost finished, but I felt slightly lightheaded. I sat on our front porch bench while he finished cleaning up. In the short time it took for him to walk the trash to the backyard trash can and return, I had fainted. While seated on the bench, I fell face forward, hitting my head on the brick porch. When Kevin returned, he sat me up and immediately contacted Kevin Jr. at work via Facetime call. Kevin took one look at me and said I had suffered a Syncope. He immediately sent an ambulance.

The ambulance arrived, took my vitals, and determined that I had to go to the hospital. Due to COVID-19, Sasha arrived but could not ride in the ambulance. She and Kevin picked Al up and met me at the hospital. After a series of tests and questions about my diet, the doctor determined I needed a more nutritious breakfast. Even though they were not allowed inside the hospital, the three of them sat in the car outside of the emergency room for nine hours. Sasha continued to come inside to check my status. Seeing I had an excellent support system, I was released to go home that night. That fall left me with a head injury that resulted in bruising and swelling of my forehead. Although I never had any severe pain or headaches, the fall left a small, permanent dent in the center of my forehead. Once again, my body told me that fatigue and stress are not tolerable. Daily, I began actively focusing on how to self-nurture. It includes learning to pause, pray, and become more intentional with my time.

I am grateful that God has always walked with me through every painful moment of illness, suffering, and despair. I believe in God's infinite restoration power and trust that He will continue to sustain me. When I cry out for help, it is with total confidence that He will answer. I am a very agreeable person who is always willing to help others. Because of lessons learned from Al and Tiny, my heart silently thanks them each time my mouth says yes while my mind thinks something different. I was raised to believe that it is better to give than to receive. As difficult as it is for me, I am slowly becoming more comfortable with saying no. The days of stretching myself to accommodate more than I should are becoming a thing of the past. Admittedly, I am still in progress, learning that self-time is not selfish.

Since our dating days, Kevin and I have been frequent concert goers. Kevin's all-time favorite group is Earth, Wind, and Fire. In 2023, we got tickets to see them in Las Vegas on October 25th. We flew in for a few days of rest and relaxation. The trip was great, but I was feeling unusually tired. Kevin Jr. had not seen us in a few weeks. On his way home from the fire station, he stopped by Saturday morning to say hello. Kevin was out for his usual morning walk, so the two of us were at the house.

When he arrived, I opened the front door, and he stopped in his tracks before even crossing the threshold. Kevin looked at me and asked, "How long have your eyes had been like this?" I told him it was probably from the cigarette smoke in Vegas, and I added that his dad had mentioned that they looked red. Kevin's response was, "Tracie, they are not red. They are yellow, and so is your skin. You have Yellow Jaundice! You need to go to the hospital!" I said I would call my doctor on Monday. He sternly said, "Today . . . Now!" As a parent, you watch your children—good or bad; you know their moods, ups, downs, and expressions. You know their faces! It does not always dawn on you that you are on a two-way street. I thank Kevin Jr. for knowing my face and for saving my life!!! Kevin Jr. could not stay because he committed to pick his children up. He called Kevin to come home immediately.

I texted Dr. Friedman, who said I should come immediately to UCLA Medical Center Urgent Care. When we arrived, they took one look and sent me to the emergency room for admittance. Hospital tests determined that my liver was not functioning, and I had a blockage in my bowels, yellow jaundice, and auto-immune hepatitis. Due to the various issues, I was told I had a team of doctors from different departments. One doctor said, "Thank your son because had you continued to be untreated, this could have become fatal!" After they found no masses, scarring, or cancer in the liver, I was admitted for six days. Upon my release, I was prescribed prednisone. The doctors were perplexed by my symptoms. They said that when this happens, people normally have diarrhea and throw up. Instead, I was constipated. They said most people are doubled up in pain, but even when the liver specialist placed pressure on my stomach, I felt fine!

More than once, my health has been tested and tried. As I listened to these doctors, I realized that my body was under attack. My first thought was to remain positive, knowing this was not the time to buckle or collapse.

"And the peace of God, which transcends all understanding, will guard your hearts and your minds in Christ Jesus."

Philippians 4:7

Even though this presented a danger, just the thought of God, the Great Physician, overrode all of the doctor's speculations. His power to heal sickness and disease entered the room to put my mind at ease. I was determined not to let this sickness defeat me.

Doctors and nurses were in and out of my room every two hours to check my vitals; they determined that when I was asleep, my pressure and sugar dropped to dangerously low levels. Since I have no blood pressure issues, this is very unusual. The doctor asked if I got dizzy in the morning, and my answer was yes. For months, I had been waking up every morning with headaches, dizziness, and low energy. I believed this was because I suffer from sinusitis, vertigo, and constipation. The doctors agreed that I was wrong, and I received consultations from the nutritionist who said if I woke up at three in the morning or later, I should have a piece of candy or a shot of orange juice to jumpstart my sugar. The doctors also emphasized the necessity of breakfast, a meal I usually skip. I was educated that food and the physical benefits of breaking the overnight fast are fuel. The guidelines given to me by the nutritionist were vital in my re-establishing a healthy relationship with food. From the first day they started these practices in the hospital, my dizziness was gone. Of course, I continued to start each morning this way after I came home. Although trying to get sleep and rest while in the hospital was extremely limited, this six-day stay was a blessing in disguise. It equipped me with an abundance of necessary information for my body. God allowed my body to be shaken up to put me back on the right track.

Consider me a living witness that unless you have medical training, please Do Not self-diagnosis, ignore, or delay any signals your body gives. I was way off the mark! Now, I am conscious and appreciative of this precious temple God formed for me to live in. Once again, I was reminded that stress will manifest itself in my body.

"Therefore we do not lose heart. Though outwardly we are wasting away, yet inwardly we are being renewed day by day."

2 Corinthians 4:16

Sometimes, unexpected and beyond-our-control events happen to us. During times such as these, I draw strength from my faith in God and look to the support of those near and dear. Since this test of faith began for me, I have received an abundance of motivational text messages, and the phone rings constantly. I cannot thank my family and friends enough for interceding to pray and pull me through my hospital stay and beyond!

It has been six months since this health ordeal began. If you could see what Jesus brought me through, you would know why I love Him. My diet has drastically changed, and I am happy to report that my lab reports show significant improvement! My faith is in God, the great physician who has never lost a patient. I will wait and watch Him fix this health crisis! His Word has the final say in my body. My medical history proves that God will deliver me from every evil attack. I will praise Him despite any heartache or pain because I know He has a greater plan for my life.

"For the Spirit God gave us does not make us timid, but gives us power, love and self-discipline. So do not be ashamed of the testimony about our Lord."

Timothy 1:7-10

Giving thanks is not just reserved for good times. I give All Praise and Thanks to the Lord our God because Victory is His!

I use my constructive alone moments to learn how to self-nurture. Most importantly, I need to pause, pray, and be more intentional about how I use my time. I am grateful that God has always walked with me through every painful moment of suffering and despair. Because I believe in God's infinite restoration power, I trust He will continue to increase my strength. Thanks to Tiny's example, my personality is beginning to display a subtle, growing sense of self-confidence. One obvious area is that I am shifting and stirring up my faith enough to acknowledge and publicly share some of my hidden strengths with others. Hurdling this transparency accomplishment is more than simply "thinking I can." I have become a believer and not a doubter, speaking out and "saying I can." To God be the Glory for this positive new me! His timing has always shown itself to be perfect in my life.

Every day, God transforms my mind by enlarging my awareness of many things. He is leading me to boldly step into enjoying a new season of my life! I am beginning to have a much more positive outlook about the blessings to come. Slowly, I feel equipped for a future that is inviting and refreshing! Each day offers me abundant possibilities for growth, purpose, and promise. These new strengths and inspiring revelations are gifts from God. Honestly, the blessings bestowed on me are not earned or deserved and are certainly not taken for granted. God is the giver, and I am so grateful that He continues to favor me!

Because God is the author and finisher of my life, I have no reason to fear! I appreciate all He supplies because I have already triumphed much more than I ever imagined. With this upgraded perspective, I have developed purposeful actions followed by positive expectations. Both are necessary for me to reap successful results. While I focus on continuing to enjoy this wonderful new season of my life, I know that God is getting the Glory. It has truly taken me some time to move from grief to acceptance. Praise the Lord for being the God of another chance. I believe that my chains are broken! He has restored the motivational desires inside of me that I thought I had lost forever. My understanding no longer comes from what is behind me. Instead, I am living my life by intently looking forward. As my journey of loving and living an Optimistic Life continues, my broken heart begins to smile again.

"Surely goodness and mercy shall follow me all the days of my life."
Psalm 23:6.

This new me is proof that spring really does follow winter.

"Do you not know that your bodies are temples of the Holy Spirit, who is in you, whom you have received from God? You are not your own; You were bought at a price. Therefore, honor God with your bodies."
1 Corinthians 6:19-20

15

IT'S A NEW SEASON

Just like Al and Tiny, I have always been a talker. While Tiny's conversations are usually poised and calm, Al has a great sense of humor. He can tell a joke at the drop of a hat. I believe I am a valid combination of the two. Whenever I tell Al and Tiny anything, they say I keep them in suspense because I have to tell every detail. Tiny would say, "Come on . . . what happened?" Al says, "Wow, I feel like I was there!" Still, I never intentionally set out to be a storyteller. Perhaps it is a God-given gift I do not see in myself. In addition to hearing it from my family, I have had that same "you are a good storyteller" comment made to me by several other people.

Many years ago, my friend Marcita and I would be having a conversation. Suddenly, she would tell me, "I cannot wait until you write a book."

Pastor LaTanya tells people, "Tracie is an excellent storyteller. One day, she is going to write a book." Ironically, these opinions were independent as these two ladies did not have a relationship with one another. My carpool sister, Shay, and I have shared many ups, downs, victories, failures, and disappointments. Like the sisters that we became, we have always been there to boost and encourage each other. We share times when Shay would say, "Tell me a story, Tracie," adding that no matter how strange it was, she knew if it came from me, it was true. We both break into a hearty laugh, knowing that before our conversation ends, I will have told her something that we have never discussed before.

Everyone knows the hair salon is where a lot of talking goes on. Through the years, someone at the salon occasionally asks me if I have a story. These shared beauty shop conversations culminated when Linda hosted a client appreciation party at her home. We were to bring our spouses for an afternoon of good food, laughs, and comradery. At the party, Linda had a ceremony where she awarded prizes designed for what each lady meant to the success of her business. Of course, I was the recipient of the best storyteller award.

My nicest push to try my hand at writing a book came to me unexpectedly during my daily morning phone conversation with my daughter. Sasha asked what my schedule was for the upcoming week because she wanted to set some time to spend with me. When I asked for a particular reason for the visit, she said, "No reason. She had some free time and just wanted to sit and talk." Then she added, "You can tell me a story. I love to hear your stories." I was caught off guard by her answer. While this statement was unexpected, I realized the timing was perfect! Unbeknownst to Sasha, her words were the encouragement that I needed to proceed with writing this memoir.

In addition, my friend Barbara is an entrepreneur, accomplished author, gifted life coach, and international speaker. In January 2023, Barbara offered a coaching class for new writers. It truly piqued my interest, so I signed up. The first thing Barbara told me was that writing a book requires a lot of quiet time. She suggested that to avoid distractions, questions, and input from others, I should not tell anyone until I finished. Because I love to talk, this was advice that I truly needed. Birthed from my greatest loss, the decision to pursue writing this family memoir was a giant step of faith. My heart desired it, but I believed I lacked the ability to do it. God leveled my mountain. He said,

"Faith without works is dead."

James 2:7

Barbara guided me in how to write a book and how to have it designed, printed, and published. Years earlier, I sat at a dinner table with Barbara's publisher at an awards dinner. That evening, I asked Willa if I ever wrote a book, could I contact her, and she said yes. For years, Willa and I have shared a relationship on Barbara's Monday Morning Prayer Line. Following the coaching class, Barbara formally introduced me to Willa Robinson, the owner of KP Publishing.

When I completed the class, I mentioned a word about this to Kevin. Once I shared the possibility with him, he beamed with excitement! For years, my husband has told me he does not know anyone who can tell a story like I can. Always adding, "You should write a book." That day, as I listened to Kevin's encouragement, I became my own worst critic. I quietly searched my mind and heart to be true to myself. While I know Kevin is biased, in the end, I do believe there was some basis for his encouragement. There have been many times that Kevin teases me by saying there is nothing good on television, so I have to tell him a story. At that moment, I usually start to laugh. I now believe writing this memoir is a part of God's plan for me.

The next thing I had to do was get Al's permission to use our family as the topic. He said, "No problem. I think it will be good for you to occupy your time and mind with something yours alone." Al was agreeable to my being transparent. Even as a youngster, I tried to retain the memories of every interaction. Daddy would say that I listen with my eyes. The authentic, unedited events described were significant factors in molding me and definitely influenced how I cope with life today. Clinging to God's word is breaking my spirit of hesitation. I am stepping out of my comfort zone and moving into tomorrow's blessings.

Before sitting to write the first word of this memoir, I went to God with prayer and thanksgiving! He turned His ear toward me, and the answer was,

"With man this is impossible, but with God all things are possible."
Matthew 19:26

Then, God opened the door and entered to sit with me at each random moment I touched my computer. As I put action behind my faith, He strengthened me, awakened my creativity, and honed my untrained, unskilled abilities. I give all thanks to God for blessing the work of my hands and giving me clarity in my thoughts. Because my life span of memories is so vivid, I did not think that writing them down would be too hard. As soon as I sat down in front of the computer, I felt a sense of passion and enthusiasm. God's perfect love for me turned my dream into a reality. As people read this memoir, I pray His power will shine in my weakness!

I have always had God's appointing over my life; I just had to recognize and desire it for myself. I finally receive that God created me with the gift of supporting others as a friend, confidant, advocate, affirmer, motivator, and intercessor. My heart's desire to motivate others is reflected through my creation of AT&T Daily Affirmations. Yes, the title is from Al, Tiny, and Tracie. I have always used one-liners or short prayers as a quick means of inspiration. Over twenty years ago, I started to share inspirations daily with my family, friends, and coworkers. After my retirement, I continued to share each morning through email and, eventually, text messages. Though these thoughts are not my creations, they are a means of creating happy, hopeful hearts. I want to instill peace, hope, and fulfillment for the best day possible! Tiny emphasized that I should make room for people, even when the situation is unexpected. Angel Touch Today is my way of encouraging all to do the next right thing. I humbly Thank God every day, for all He has given me.

As I think back over my life, I often walked a path of stop and go. Still, Al and Tiny never wavered in their belief that I could do whatever I set my mind to do. All I can remember is the two of them confidently giving me the green light and encouraging me to go! For many years, my true personality existed in a hidden season. God has taken me from a place of stagnant contentment to self-discovery. Writing this memoir has undoubtedly opened my heart to my passions. My ability to see God's appointed promises for my life has become clearer. While my gift was obvious to others, I could not perceive what God had purposed for me. My advice to you is if you want to know what your ministry is, look at what people ask you for. People ask you for what they see as your gift.

During my youth, I dreamed of someday becoming a journalist or opening my own Hallmark store. At that time, I questioned my potential. Al and Tiny ensured I grew up surrounded by a life filled with positive encouragement. Tiny and Al are both very witty. She always said, "You see my glory, but you don't know my story." No matter the circumstances, Al continuously reminds me that "somebody is always watching." What they were saying to me is finally sinking in. I believe that if you do not tell your own story, people will make one up! I have always had a humble nature and could never see myself like others. I believe how you carry yourself and your aura are valuable things that speak for themselves! Modesty is my lifelong, instinctive nature.

Once I realized who I was, the game changed. I enter this new season knowing that God has equipped me to flourish. While writing, I leaned on the word of God. There I discovered that He has a promise for every situation. To honor all He has given me, I plan to live my life to the fullest! The fact is, God has always profusely provided me with things that I did not qualify for. This memoir is a revelation of His unfailing love for me. He has surrounded my life with abundant favor by taking me far beyond my training, abilities, and expectations. I believe completing this memoir is the best personal project I will ever pursue. It was born from my greatest loss and made up of the best and worst moments of my life. Venturing out of my comfort zone to do this new thing nourished my soul. It has given me an unprecedented wave of confidence. No longer am I discounting myself or looking back with a longing to continue living the complacent life of who I was. Instead, I boldly declare that I am growing in self-confidence instead of self-doubt.

Occasionally, I take the time to share a few pages with my father. He repeatedly says, "Baby, you are a great storyteller. In addition, people have always turned to you for advice. Everyone knows that you are a go-to girl. It is something that I really notice when they are going through times of need. Maybe now, you will finally realize what your gift is." Al was so adamantly convincing when he spoke these words. I know he is prejudiced regarding me, but our conversations are always a builder of confidence! The truth is that listening to my parents and grandparents talk about our family history was always interesting to me. I have a desire to measure up to my ancestors. It is why sharing stories about our family life has just begun to flow. Completing this writing has given me a sense of accomplishment, not only for me but for both Al and Tiny.

While writing this memoir, it occurred to me that Tiny had no choice in most of the physical challenges in her life. Had God given Tiny a choice, many of the events of this book would never have happened. No one has a choice when it comes to illnesses, tragedies, and loss.

James 1:2 tells us to,

"Count it all joy!"

Whether good or bad, without these events, I would not be writing this story! God said in His word that,

> *"All things work together for good to them that love God, to them that are called according to His purpose."*
>
> Romans 8:28

If in no other area, I have genuinely grown in understanding the truth of this passage.

The reality is that time waits for no one. The future has already begun, so now is the best time for us to start living. Our marriage proves that things do not have to be perfect to be wonderful. After having lost so many loved ones, we agree that we only have one life to live, so we are trying to live it to the fullest. In our small ways, we want to make each day count! Together, we have concluded that we live our lives better together. When you have been blessed to have that special someone to share your life with, it is great! We know that the struggles of this present life pale in comparison to the Endless, Everlasting Glory that lies ahead! Until that day, it is time for us to Embrace Life.

This year, Kevin began his recharge by committing to a healthier lifestyle. He started by eliminating sugar, red meat, and bread from his diet and walking eight to ten miles every day. The results of his efforts are apparent. He has successfully lost thirty pounds, and his blood test results are youthful. While I can no longer keep up with his rigorous walking, I work with a stationary bike in my home. In addition, I continue to adhere to my medically advised healthy diet. Although we can see further than we can reach, I do not doubt that God wants our marriage to be abundantly fruitful as we grow old together.

I traveled to South Africa in September with the International Black Women's Public Policy Institute (IBWPPI). My desire to take this trip was fostered by a lifetime of stories from my Godmother, Sherl, regarding her many trips to Africa. Visiting Johannesburg and Cape Town was an eye-opening experience that changed my perspective of Africa. One surprise was that in addition to their native languages, everyone spoke English. I viewed this as a tribute to their respect for education. In America, we have access to various avenues to further our education, yet many of us, including myself, take these opportunities for granted. Being introduced to several Black women in government leadership positions was most impressive. It was further confirmation that women can do anything. We were also privy to dinner invitations in two private homes. The firsthand experience of South African hospitality was excellent. While touring the countryside, I was intrigued by the vibrant culture and breathtaking landscapes. Granted, they had their share of poverty, but so do we. The warmth of the people made me understand why Africa is called "The Motherland." Being there felt like a welcome homecoming.

Alone moments are perfect times of escape for me to commune with the Lord intimately. It is when I believe that my spiritual muscles are growing. I diligently seek God's Word, where I find a promise for every problem. My daily prayers include special thanksgiving for His filling my life with many wonderful people. I am eternally thankful for every person, place, and event mentioned in this memoir. When God created man, He gave us the ability to express compassion, sympathy, and empathy for a reason. Unbeknownst to you, in one way or another, your loving support, prayers, and presence in my life significantly contributed to the stories told in this book. Thank you for joining me on this journey through Optimistic Life. My Grandma once said that our lives are like books, and we should share our stories. No matter how slow my walk was, I did not miss my calling. To God be the Glory, I am an Author on this day!

There is always a story within a story. My story began at home. I thank God for blessing me beyond measure with Al and Tiny. They are two wonderful parents who have always supported and believed in me. Living without either is a harsh reality I never imagined until I had to. The continued blessing of Al's physical presence brings me so much joy. We constantly encourage each other to push forward in our new normal through shared reflections, tears, and smiles. Like applying salve to an open wound, revisiting the memories shared in this book has given me much-needed relief.

Tiny has forever influenced my existence. No words can ever describe how honored and eternally grateful I am to have had her as my mother!

"Honor her for all that her hands have done, and let her works bring her praise at the city gate."

Proverbs 31:31

In my heart, Tiny will forever be the Star of our Story! As I close my eyes, I imagine my "Precious" mother in Heaven. Tiny smiles radiantly as she says to every angel crossing her path, "Look at Tracie, my baby girl. She just finished writing a memoir about our family!" And so, it is! ❤️

"If you can?" said Jesus. Everything is possible for one who believes."

Mark 9:23

Tiny's Reflections of Life 2015

ACKNOWLEDGMENTS

My Dear Dad (Elbert William—Al)

In every way that truly matters, you are a man who not only talks the talk as the head of our family but also walks the walk. No matter what the challenge or cost, you have always given your all to me and Tiny. You taught me the true meaning of "family first." My heart is overjoyed that when God created our family, He chose you as our solid rock! When it comes to the three of us, there is never a question. Your actions regarding our lives are always intentional and purposeful. Tiny and I are undeniably sheltered in the cocoon of your love. I genuinely believe that the way you unconditionally protect and serve the two of us gives God glory!

Countlessly, you have always encouraged, supported, and empowered me in more ways than anyone can begin to imagine. This is the catalyst that made me know who I am and who someone loved! As I look into the rear-view mirror of my life's aspirations, I have always valued your opinion. Being a truly interested father and listener, you consistently give me your undivided attention and honest responses. With your usual "what's going on" followed by a minimal number of positive questions and suggestions, your response has usually been, "Yes, you can" to anything that I ever passionately aspire to do. Throughout my life, every piece of sound advice, gentle push, and heart-to-heart conversation we have shared has taught me to try and believe. Your love is the gift that continues to bless me in more ways than I can begin to count.

When we "sat at the table" last year, I laid this memoir-writing idea out for you. Once again, you smiled at me and simply said, "You can." My being completely transparent with details would never have happened without your agreement and approval. I am beyond grateful for your lifetime of shared wisdom and the times that we continue to enjoy together. I pray there is never a day that you do not feel abundantly showered by my love, thanks, adoration, affection, and respect.

All my love!
Suga

> *"Anyone who does not provide for their relatives, especially for their household, has denied the faith and is worse than an unbeliever"*
> 1 Timothy 6:8

Acknowledgments

Darling Mother (Florence Virginia—Maternal Grandmother)

Our love for one another has been effortless and unlimited since day one! Curling up next to you in bed with a chocolate candy bar and a mystery book or watching a cowboy movie (Shoot 'EM Up) are among my most cherished childhood memories. At an early age, you fostered my level of love for reading. As I grew older, I remember anticipating you would separate "my" section of the newspaper. While other children would have preferred to read the comic section, Dear Abby, Anne Landers, and the crosswords were my favorite sections reserved for me.

My formative years with you were when I learned to appreciate the true meaning of home. Once the doors closed, you lived a comfortable life that displayed the epitome of peace and contentment. Thank you for every positive seed sown into my life. The sacrifices you made as you opened your arms to pour out countless examples of kindness and love for family and friends were always above and beyond! I have had many friends who were not blessed to have a loving grandmother through the years. I felt at ease to share you with them, knowing you would never turn anyone away. As a result, you became "granny" to many. My heart is delighted when someone tells me how much they look forward to simply hearing your infamous greeting of, "Hi, Darling." You indeed demonstrated a selfless, Godly example in my life. Today, many of my actions and decisions are led by the mere thought, "What would Mother do."

I love and miss you with my whole heart!
Peach

"Well known for her good deeds, such as bringing up children, showing hospitality,washing the feet of the Lord's people, helping those in trouble and devoting herself to all kinds of good deeds"

1 Timothy 5:10

Acknowledgments

My Awesome Husband (Kevin Matthew—Kev)

I wholeheartedly believe that there are no coincidences in life. In my heart, I have no doubt that our coming together was predestined by God. When I was facing an unknown future, His timing was perfect! Something good happened to me the very first day that I met you. Our union totally changed my lifestyle. Time has proven that we are good to and for each other. The evidence radiates with each beat of my heart every day that we share this marriage journey. I have grown accustomed to the fact that we are undeniably walking this walk together.

The years of loving you have become second nature to me. Thank you for filling days with laughter and the incredible sense of security, contentment, and family that my heart always desired. You are a safe place, whether good or bad. I know that there is comfort and shelter. No matter what, you are always there for me. I am completely confident in knowing that God has ordered my steps so that I will spend the rest of my life with you. How blessed I am that I am yours, and you are mine!

You are my love of a lifetime!
Tracie Lynn

"Two are better than one, because they have a good return for their labor"

Ecclesiastes 4:9

Dear Daughter (Sasha Valentin Marie—'Lil One)

I am so thankful that you are My "God-sent" daughter. No, not the one I dreamed of for myself. I realize that my parental vision was not God's design for me. His plan was to bless my life with a daughter who is a much brighter shining light than I ever imagined. I cannot tell you how much I enjoy the fact that our hearts have been blessed to share a relationship of being both mom, daughter, confidant, and friend!

Al has said that it does not matter if it is family or friends; just because a person has a title does not mean they live up to it. You have truly been a daughter to me in both good times and bad times. Being a stepmother did not come with a manual. To the best of my ability, I have prayerfully tried to fulfill my parental role, just as you have as a daughter. I would say that we have both done admirably well!

Your chosen career as a Special Needs teacher is an excellent public expression of your loving character. I pridefully watch you display an abundance of caring, sensitivity, and devotion to your work, a quality that only a chosen few have. The constant tireless level of dedication and joy that I watch you put into your work is the true meaning of Special!

I love you dearly!
Tracie

> *"Surely, Lord, you bless the righteous; you surround them with your favor as with a shield"*
>
> Psalm 5:12

Acknowledgments

Dear Son (Kevin Matthew Jr.—Kev)

Being blessed by God to partner with your father by having the opportunity to share the responsibility of raising a male child has given me a wonderful sense of pride. I have watched you meet your desires, victories, losses, and challenges with total composure, conviction, and confidence. Personally and professionally, you have grown before my eyes to independently and responsibly walk your own walk of manhood. In you, I have no doubts!

During a family visit to Ground Zero in New York, you announced that you would become a firefighter paramedic. You were still in high school, so I thought you were simply caught up in the time. Before this, I never imagined you selecting a physical or hazardous career. Your scholastic achievements always indicated that you had a very bright mind, capable of doing amazing things. I thank God that my doubts and insecurities were short-lived. Seeing your passion and fearless dedication to others as a Firefighter Paramedic is amazingly admirable. There are days that the potential dangers cause me to hold my breath! I am always so grateful to get that call or text from you that says, "Hi, or I'm Okay."

When you decided to have your arm tattooed with a Breast Cancer Ribbon, I was totally surprised! Thank you for committing to such a bold outward statement of representation for Mother, Tiny, and me. I consider this permanent gesture an honor. You are my "Special K," and I thank God for the gift of you!

Ours is truly a love thing!
Tracie

"In him and through faith in him we may approach God with freedom and confidence."

Ephesians 3:12

Darling Grandchildren,
Kevin Jr.—Victoria Luna * (Tori), Benjamin Irie * (Benji), and
Maxwell Matthew * (Maxi)
Sasha—Levi Monte

With the birth of each one of you, God has blessed me to witness the circle of life. You are the future generation of our family. The gift of seeing the world through your innocent curiosity and excitement is such a delight. While your fresh presence in my life gives me the feeling of being young at heart, you have broadened my vision of the good things each day has to offer. Moments spent with you turn my every thought towards happy and positive things. If only for a short while, my heartaches seem to vanish.

I realize that God is moving me into a new season in my life. As you grow, I am learning and growing with you. Together, we focus on the beauty of all that God has created. Prayerfully, I will do my best to fulfill my grandmother's role in a wise, positive manner. I thank God for blessing me to share your lives, trusting that you will always know the depth of my endless love for you.

Big Hugs, Kisses, and Much Love!
Gigi
Tracie

"Children's children are a crown to the aged."

Proverbs 17:6

ABOUT THE AUTHOR

Tracie Lynn Rosser-Green has been an ardent storyteller, with dreams dating back to high school of someday writing a book. *Optimistic Life: Lessons in Love, Loss, and Loyalty* is her groundbreaking memoir. She is the only child of Elbert (Al) and Barbara (Tiny) Rosser, a native of Portland, Oregon, but she spent many of her formative years in Chicago, Illinois. Tracie and her parents relocated to Southern California in 1975.

She retired from American Airlines™ after 34 years in customer service positions. Since her retirement, her mornings begin with a social media outreach where she uses her "Angel Touch Today" ministry to inspire others. Tracie worships with other Christians in church services and small Bible study groups.

Traveling is an occasional treat; however, she has traveled extensively throughout the states and many countries. Tracie is a breast cancer survivor and advocates for other women through her support of Susan G. Komen and Stand Up to Cancer.

She enjoys curling up with a book, watching movies, dining out, attending plays and concerts, storytelling, and writing calligraphy greeting cards. She is a proud daughter, wife, mother of two, and grandmother of four. Tracie lives in the footsteps of her family's legacy, cooking dinner whenever they gather. These joyful days include having an open door for others. It's a lifestyle!

Tracie has studied at Portland State University in Oregon, focusing on journalism, and at The Fashion Institute of Design and Merchandising in Los Angeles.

She and her retired husband, Kevin, and their dog, Cheyenne, reside in Southern California.

www.ingramcontent.com/pod-product-compliance
Lightning Source LLC
Chambersburg PA
CBHW051134120626
46547CB00012B/799